世遗之城：泉州

QUANZHOU: A WORLD HERITAGE CITY

刺桐花开——宋元泉州的制度保障

"Zayton" in Blossom: Institutional Guarantee for Song-Yuan Quanzhou

中共泉州市委宣传部　编

海峡出版发行集团 | 福建人民出版社
THE STRAITS PUBLISHING & DISTRIBUTING GROUP | FUJIAN PEOPLE'S PUBLISHING HOUSE

目 录

Contents

引 言

“岸隔诸番国，江通百粤舟”，泉州西北面山，东南向海，城区坐落在晋江、洛阳江两江夹一湾所形成的冲积平原上。背山面海的地理环境，造就了历史上泉州人向海而生的生产、生活方式。唐代中后期，海外贸易勃兴，泉州抓住这一历史机遇，迎来了宋元时期的发展高峰期，一跃成为宋元中国的世界海洋商贸中心。在这一过程中，政府通过促进市舶司在泉州的设立、推动涉外法律制度的完善、推进大型公共设施的建设、加强沿海军事设施的布防、推动民间信仰的官方化等政令和措施，结合民间规约所形成的制度化保障，因地制宜形成一套行之有效的制度保障体系，使得泉州在宋元时期形成高效法治的营商环境，与近百个国家通商贸易往来，创造了“涨海声中万国商”的繁盛图景。由此所形成并留存至今的文化史迹包括历代泉州政府不断加固修缮的进城第一道安全关卡——德济门遗址、反映泉州成为宋元时期国家最重要的官方贸易口岸的市舶司遗址，以及在通远王祠举行祈风仪式所形成的九日山祈风石刻、向真武大帝举行祭海仪式的真武庙、出海航行祈求平安的天后宫 5 个遗产点。它们共同组成世界文化遗产“泉州：宋元中国的世界海洋商贸中心”中促进海洋贸易管理体系完备的重要制度保障。

五代时，留从效在泉州城内遍植刺桐树，也因此泉州得名“刺桐城”。（傅捷雄 摄）

During the Five Dynasties (907—979), Liu Congxiao planted erythrina trees throughout Quanzhou City, hense Quanzhou was named Zayton (Arabic name, means olive which is similar to erythrina) City. (Photo by Fu Jiexiong)

Introduction

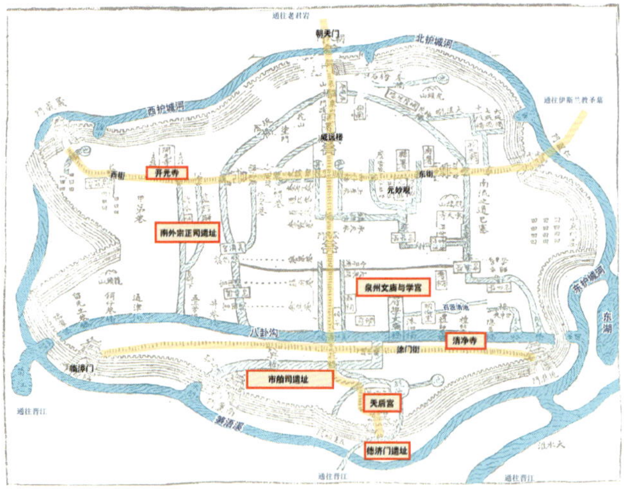

引自（道光）《晋江县志·图考志·城池图》

泉州古代城市结构示意图。（泉州市海上丝绸之路申遗中心 供图）

A schematic diagram of the city structure of Quanzhou in ancient times. (Courtesy of Quanzhou Maritime Silk Road Heritage Application Center)

"Foreign countries are distributed beyond the seas, while their business ships are bustling on the rivers of Quanzhou." Quanzhou faces mountains to the northwest and the sea to the southeast, whose urban area is situated on the alluvial plain formed by two rivers, the Jinjiang River and the Luoyangjiang River. Taking advantage of its geographical adjacence to mountains and facing the sea, Quanzhou people have formed an ocean-oriented production and life style in history. In the middle and late Tang Dynasty (618—907), Quanzhou's overseas trade flourished. Taking this historical opportunity, Quanzhou ushered in the peak development period of the Song and Yuan Dynasties (960—1368), becoming the emporium of the world in Song-Yuan China. During this process, the government formed a set of effective institutional safeguard system according to the local conditions by promoting the establishment of the maritime trade office in Quanzhou, improving the legal system related to foreign affairs, promoting the construction of large-scale public facilities, strengthening the defense of coastal military facilities, promoting the officialization of folk beliefs and other decrees and measures, combined with the institutionalized safeguards formed by the folk statutes. This enabled Quanzhou to form an efficient business environment under the rule of law during the Song and Yuan Dynasties, and to engage in commercial and trade relations with nearly 100 countries, creating a prosperous scene of "merchants from all nations thronged to Quanzhou amidst the sound of rising tides". The five cultural and historical sites that have been formed and preserved to this day include Site of Deji Gate, the first security barrier into the city, which has been continuously reinforced and repaired by successive Quanzhou governments; Site of the Maritime Trade Office, which reflects Quanzhou's status as the country's most important official trading port during the Song and Yuan Dynasties; as well as Jiuri Mountain Wind-Praying Inscriptions formed by the wind praying ceremonies held at King Tongyuan Hall, Zhenwu Temple where sea rituals are held to Zhenwu Celestial Lord, and Tianhou Temple where the safety of sea voyages are prayed. All these combine together to form an important institutional guarantee for the integrity of the maritime trade management system in the world cultural heritage "Quanzhou: Emporium of the World in Song-Yuan China".

山亘水通人和——
泉州地理环境及制度保障

Harmony Between People and Natural Environment: Quanzhou's Geographical Environment and Institutional Guarantee

地理环境

Geographical Environment

制度保障

Institutional Guarantee

地理环境

泉州位于中国东南沿海，西北倚戴云山脉。戴云山脉平均海拔700—1,500 米，主峰戴云山在德化县境内，海拔 1,856 米，是闽中最高山峰，有"闽中屋脊"之称。泉州地势整体为西北向东南呈阶梯状倾斜，由山地、丘陵、台地、沿海平原及广大的海域组成。泉州地貌类型复杂多样，以山地、丘陵为主，山地及丘陵约占总土地面积 79%，平原及台地约占 21%。山地均属戴云山脉及其延伸的支脉、余脉，构成西北及中部的大山带。丘陵分布于山地外侧及河流两岸或河谷盆地的边缘，在沿海一带也有广泛分布，并逼近海岸或伸入海中，组成半岛和岛屿。

Geographical Environment

Quanzhou is located on the southeast coast of China, with the Daiyun Mountain Range in the northwest. The average altitude of the Daiyun Mountain Range is 700m to 1,500m above sea level. Located in Dehua County, the main peak Daiyun Mountain is 1,856m above sea level. It is the highest peak in central Fujian and is known as the "Roof of Central Fujian". The overall terrain of Quanzhou is a terrace-like slope from northwest to southeast, consisting of mountains, hills, terraces, coastal plains and vast sea areas. The geomorphic types of Quanzhou are complex and diverse with mountains and hills accounting for about 79% of the total land area, and plains and platforms about 21%. The mountains are all parts of the Daiyun Mountain Range and its extended branches and remnants, forming the large mountain belt in the northwest and central part of Quanzhou. The hills are distributed on the outside of the mountains and both sides of rivers, or at the edge of the valley basins, and widely along the coast as well, approaching the coast or outreaching into the sea, which forms peninsulas and islands.

泉州地处福建省东南部，依山面海，境内山峦起伏，丘陵、河谷、盆地错落其间。（福建省制图院 供图）

Located in the southeast of Fujian Province, Quanzhou is adjacent to mountains and facing the sea, with terraces, river valleys, and basins scattered among undulating hills. (Courtesy of Fujian Mapping Institute)

泉州域内水系发达，流域面积较大的溪流共有 35 条，其中发源于戴云山麓的晋江是泉州境内最长的河流，全长 302 千米。晋江上游分东溪和西溪，其中东溪经永春县，西溪经安溪县。东溪、西溪在南安丰州汇合，形成了自南朝时期开始对外交通往来的梁安港。双溪汇流后绕泉州城奔流入海，整条晋江的流域面积达 5,629 平方千米。另一条重要河流洛阳江发源于泉州东北部的群山，全长约 39 千米，在后渚港注入泉州湾。而发源于西北部山区的其他河流向东南流经泉州全境，汇入大海，共同联通起泉州的海洋、平原与山区腹地。

The water system in Quanzhou is well-developed, and there are 35 streams with large drainage areas. Among them, the Jinjiang River, which originates from the foot of Daiyun Mountain, is the longest river in Quanzhou, with a total length of 302km. The upper reaches of the Jinjiang River are divided into Dongxi Stream and Xixi Stream, of which Dongxi Stream passes through Yongchun County and Xixi Stream passes through Anxi County. The two streams converge in Fengzhou Town, Nan'an City, forming Liang'an Port which has been open to foreign countries since the Southern Dynasty (420—589), and flowing around Quanzhou City and into the sea. The entire Jinjiang River basin covers an area of 5,629km^2. The Luoyangjiang River, another important river, originates from the mountains in the northeast of Quanzhou and flows into Quanzhou Bay in Houzhu Port, with a total length of about 39km. Other rivers originating from the northwest mountains run through the whole territory of Quanzhou in the southeast direction and flow into the sea, connecting the ocean, plains and mountainous hinterland of Quanzhou.

海拔 1,658 米的九仙山位于德化县西北，属戴云山脉。（陈英杰 摄）
Located in the northwest of Dehua County, Jiuxian Mountain, with an altitude of 1,658m, is an organic part of Daiyun Mountain Range. (Photo by Chen Yingjie)

晋江两岸风景。（陈英杰 摄）
Scenery on both sides of the Jinjiang River. (Photo by Chen Yingjie)

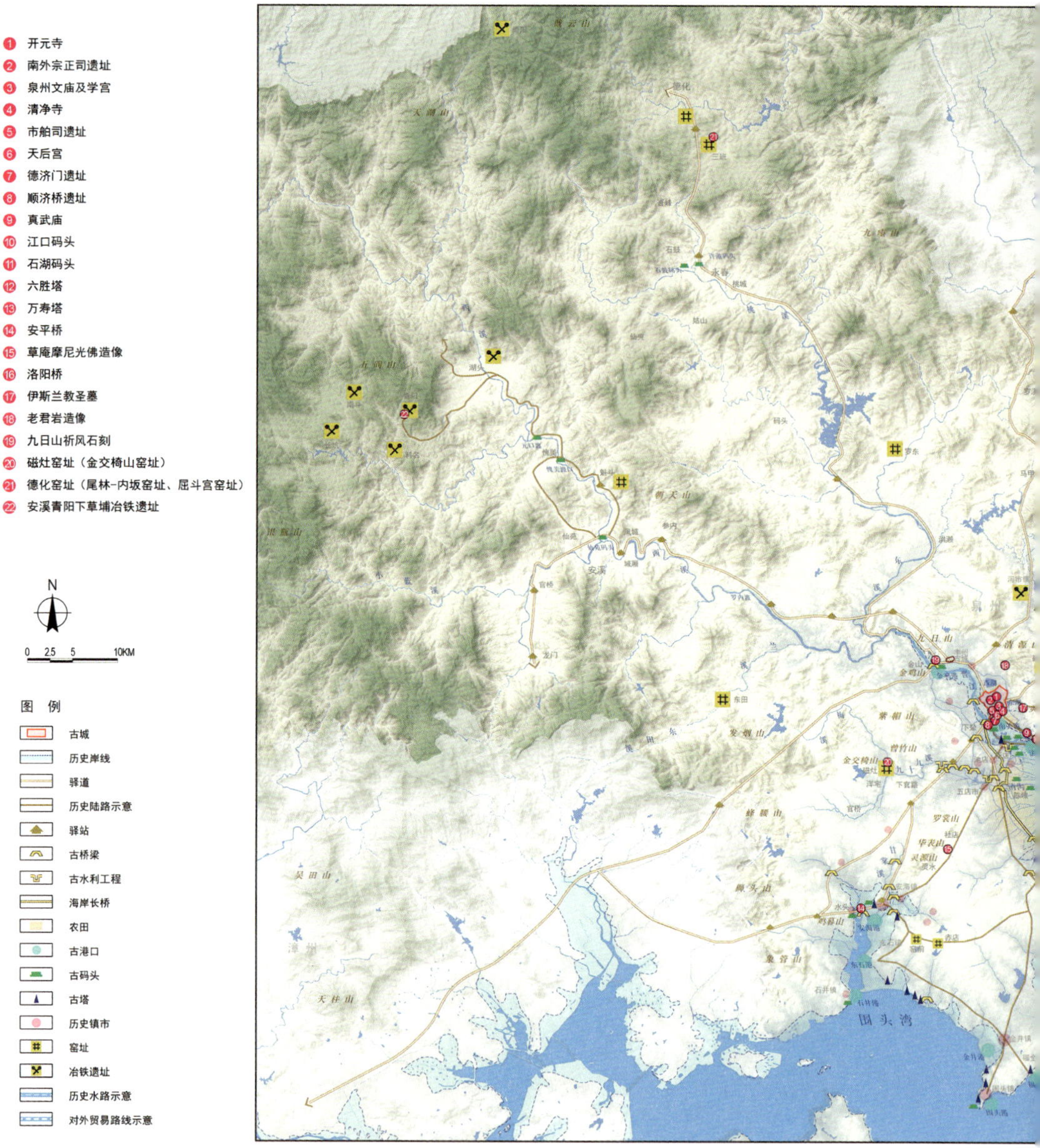

泉州港宋元布局平面示意图。（中国建筑设计研究院 供图）

Layout diagram of Quanzhou Port in the Song and Yuan Dynasties.(Courtesy of China Architecture Design & Research Group)

海港分布

泉州海岸线曲折蜿蜒，大部分为基岩海岸，总长 541 千米。沿海分布有多处天然深水良港，有“三湾十二港”之称，适合建造各类码头以停泊各种类型的海船，具有优越的航运条件。“三湾”自北向南分别为泉州湾、深沪湾、围头湾，其中泉州湾紧邻泉州城。

三湾中每个湾各有四个支港，根据地理位置，可将这些支港分为内港和外港。“三湾十二港”分别为：

泉州湾：该湾北有洛阳江，南有晋江，晋江和洛阳江两江环绕着泉州城，向东南汇入泉州湾，形成“两江夹一湾”的地形。泉州湾港道深，水域宽，离泉州城最近，水陆交通便捷，因此成为宋元时期泉州港海外交通的主港区，是宋元时期外国商人来泉最主要的停泊站和据点，一般意义上的泉州港或刺桐港，就是指泉州湾港区。该港区自北而南分布有洛阳、后渚、法石、蚶江（一说石湖）四个支港。

Harbor distribution

With a total length of 541km, the coastline of Quanzhou is winding, most of which are bedrock coasts. Many natural deep-water ports are distributed along the coast, known as "Three Bays and Twelve Ports". With excellent shipping conditions, they are suitable for building various wharves to berth different kinds of ships. From north to south, the "Three Bays" are Quanzhou Bay, Shenhu Bay and Weitou Bay respectively, among which Quanzhou Bay is adjacent to Quanzhou City.

In each of the three bays, there are four branch ports which can be divided into inner ports and outer ports according to their geographical locations. The "Three Bays and Twelve Ports" are as follows:

Quanzhou Bay: Surrounding Quanzhou City, the Luoyangjiang River in the north and the Jinjiang River in the south flow in the southeastern direction and converge in the bay, forming the terrain of "one bay surrounded by two rivers". Thanks to its deep and wide waters, the water and land transportation of Quanzhou Bay are convenient. Being the closest to Quanzhou City, it became the main port area for overseas transportation during the Song and Yuan Dynasties. Generally speaking, Quanzhou Port or Zayton Port refers to the port area of Quanzhou Bay. It contains four branch ports from north to south: Luoyang Port, Houzhu Port, Fashi Port, and Hanjiang Port (another option, Shihu Port).

洛阳港：位于泉州湾北部，洛阳江的下游，是泉州港的内港。据元代汪大渊的《岛夷志略》记载，元代洛阳江上游吴宅一个地方就有商人带领百余人从洛阳港出发到古里地闷（今帝汶岛）进行贸易。

后渚港：位于泉州湾出海口，也是泉州港最主要的支港，是宋元时期泉州对外经济、军事活动的主要港口。1974 年，后渚港内考古出土的宋代沉船，随船出水有 2,000 多千克从海外运回的香料、药物等，说明当时从海外返回后渚港的商船大量进口东南亚一带的香料等特产。1291 年，意大利旅行家马可 · 波罗奉元世祖忽必烈之命护送阔阔真公主远嫁西亚，也是从此启航，经过两年多的航行，最终顺利抵达波斯。《元史》"爪哇"条记载："爪哇在海外 …… 自泉南登舟海行者，先至占城而后至其国 …… 至元二十九年（1292）二月，下诏福建行省除史弼、亦黑迷失、高兴平章政事，征爪哇 …… 十一月，福建、江西、湖广三省军会泉州。十二月，自后渚启行。"说明后渚港既是宋元时期国家重要的对外经济往来港口，也是重要的军事基地。

法石港：位于晋江下游、江海交汇处的内港，是外国商船来泉的主要停泊点，也是商船进入泉州城的第一道关口。南宋泉州太守真德秀在此设置法石寨，元代蒲寿庚家族在此建高楼瞭望进出港的商舶。

晚霞映照下的石湖港。（苏德辉 摄）
Shihu Port in the sunset glow. (Photo by Su Dehui)

Luoyang Port: Located in the north of Quanzhou Bay and at the lower reaches of the Luoyangjiang River, Luoyang Port is the inner port of Quanzhou Bay. According to *A Brief Account of Island Inhabitants* by Wang Dayuan in the Yuan Dynasty, in Wuzhai Village of the upper reaches of the Luoyangjiang River, there were businessmen who led more than a hundred people from Luoyang Port to Keraeng Timor (Timor Island nowadays) for trade.

Houzhu Port: Located at the mouth of Quanzhou Bay, Houzhu Port is the most important branch port of Quanzhou Port and the main port of Quanzhou's foreign economic and military activities in the Song and Yuan Dynasties. In 1974, the Song Dynasty shipwreck unearthed in Houzhu Port, containing more than 2,000kg of spices and medicines from overseas, indicated that merchant ships returning from overseas to Houzhu Port at that time imported a large number of spices and other specialities from Southeast Asia. In 1291, it was also from here, the Italian traveler Marco Polo escorted Princess Cocochin to Western Asia for marriage at the behest of Kublai Khan, the founder of the Yuan Dynasty, and finally reached Persia successfully after more than two years of sailing. As recorded in "About Java (an ancient country in southeast Asia, now Java Island of Indonesia)" in *The History of Yuan*, "Java is overseas...it can be reached by ship from the south of Quanzhou after arriving in Champa... In lunar February 1292, the imperial court ordered the important officials in Fujian Province to conquer Java... In lunar November, the armies of Fujian, Jiangxi, and Huguang provinces met in Quanzhou and then set off from Houzhu Port in lunar December." It shows that Houzhu Port was important both as a national port for foreign economic communications and as a military base during the Song and Yuan Dynasties.

Fashi Port: As an inner port located at the lower reaches of the Jinjiang River and the junction of river and sea, Fashi Port is both the main berthing place and the first gateway for the coming foreign merchant ships to enter Quanzhou City. Zhen Dexiu, the Prefect of Quanzhou in the Southern Song Dynasty, set up Fashi Military Camp here, and the Pu Shougeng family built tall buildings here to watch the merchant ships come in and go out of the port in the Yuan Dynasty.

蚶江港（一说石湖港）：位于泉州湾南岸，三面临海，正对着岱屿门，控扼泉州湾的门户。唐代时当地有名的海商林銮就已在此有开凿码头，开船通商，是泉州通往勃泥国（今文莱）的重要出发点。南宋吴自牧在《梦粱录》中记载："若欲船泛外国买卖，则是泉州便可出洋……若有出洋，即从泉州港口至岱屿门，便可放洋过海，泛往外国也。"这是宋元以来泉州港重要的外港。

深沪湾：位于泉州湾南部，有祥芝、永宁、深沪、福全四个支港。深沪湾的支港，因位于三湾中间，是泉州港出洋的重要节点，历史上是筑城驻军设防的重要所在地。南宋朝廷设置的永宁寨，就位于深沪湾北侧临海处，可扼守深沪湾，对海外贸易起到重要的保障作用。

围头湾：位于泉州港的最南端，有围头、东石（一说石井）、安海、金井四个支港。自南洋海道入泉州界，在围头港与烈屿岛联合布防可控扼住海道，因此历史上围头港主要作为军事要地而置寨筑城。东石港在唐代就因林銮开发渡口而随之兴起，宋元时期成为泉州湾的辅港，明清时期安海港则是面向东南亚私商贸易最繁盛的港口。

位于泉州港最南端的围头湾。（许兆恺 摄）
Weitou Bay at the southernmost tip of Quanzhou Port. (Photo by Xu Zhaokai)

Hanjiang Port (also named Shihu Port): Located in the south bank of Quanzhou Bay, Hanjiang Port controls the gateway of Quanzhou Bay as it faces the sea on three sides and is right across from Daiyumen main shipping lane. In the Tang Dynasty (618—907), Lin Luan, a well-known local sea merchant, has built a wharf here and sailed for maritime trade. It is a significant departure place from Quanzhou to Burneo Kingdom (Brunei nowadays). As stated in *Record of a Dream of Sorghum* by Wu Zimu of the Southern Song Dynasty, "If you want to trade in foreign countries, you can travel to Quanzhou to go abroad... If you go abroad, you can go across the sea from Quanzhou Port to Daiyumen, then to the outer sea." This is an important outer port of Quanzhou Bay since the Song and Yuan Dynasties.

Shenhu Bay: Located in the south of Quanzhou Bay, there are four branch ports, namely Xiangzhi, Yongning, Shenhu and Fuquan. Located in the middle of the three bays, these branch ports are important parts of Quanzhou Port for going overseas and historically important places to station troops for the defense of the city. The Yongning Military Camp set up by the imperial court of the Southern Song Dynasty, located on the north side of Shenhu Bay near the coast, provides guard for Shenhu Bay and plays an important role in safeguarding overseas trade.

Weitou Bay: Located at the southernmost end of Quanzhou Port, there are four branch ports of Weitou, Dongshi (or Shijing), Anhai and Jinjing in Weitou Bay. The joint defense in Weitou Port and Lieyu Island can control the seaway from Southeast Asia to Quanzhou. Therefore, Weitou Port was a crucial military base setting military camps for defense. Dongshi Port prospered with the ferry development by Lin Luan in the Tang Dynasty, and became the auxiliary port of Quanzhou Bay in the Song and Yuan Dynasties. However, during the Ming and Qing Dynasties, Anhai Port was the most prosperous port for private trade with Southeast Asia.

矿产资源

泉州境内群山连绵，蕴藏较丰富的矿产资源，主要有煤、铁、金、花岗岩、石灰岩、石英石、高岭土等，以砂、石、土为主的非金属矿产资源是泉州具有地方特色的优势矿产。各种侵入岩体遍布泉州各地，大部分裸露地表，有利于露天开采，加之交通便利及开采历史悠久，采石场遍布全市。泉州花岗岩储量丰富，自古以来就是著名的石材产地，位于南安石砻的砻石矿自唐代开始一直开采至今，惠安则出产材质细腻的青斗石。它们被广泛用于塔幢、桥梁、城门、城墙、墓葬，以及建筑的梁柱、墙基、门窗、栏杆、台阶等部位。经过能工巧匠的精雕细琢，石材得到充分利用，且更为美观、耐用。宋元时期用本地石材建造的东西塔、洛阳桥、安平桥等，代表了10—14世纪东亚地区石构建筑的最高水平。

泉州高岭土资源丰富，仅德化一县发现的高岭土矿产地就多达92处、矿点127个，储量达1亿吨以上。此地高岭土呈松软土状，具有良好的可塑性和耐火性，用其烧制出来的陶瓷器，质地优良。德化境内山多，林木资源丰富，可用来烧制陶瓷的燃料充足，水资源丰富，有利于形成丰富的水源动力，用来粉碎、加工瓷土，可大大解放人力，为陶瓷大批量生产提供了良好的

位于开元寺内的东西塔是中国现存最高的一对古石塔。（许师伟 摄）
The East and West Pagodas in Kaiyuan Temple is a pair of the tallest ancient stone pagodas existing in China. (Photo by Xu Shiwei)

自然条件。德化烧制陶瓷器的历史悠久，在距今 3,700 年前的夏商时期，就已生产出原始青瓷，此后不断提升烧制技术和生产规模。宋元时期泉州海外贸易达到鼎盛时期，德化陶瓷生产技术、产品质量和数量也随之发展，德化陶瓷器在海内外陆上和水下沉船考古中均有发现，成为海上贸易最大宗的商品。此外，泉州当地寺庙宫观等建筑中常见的堆剪、堆塑装饰，也是充分利用了瓷器及其烧制原理制作而成的。在开元寺大雄宝殿、天后宫、府文庙等大型建筑中，色泽亮丽的堆剪建筑技术使这些建筑成为当地一道亮丽的风景线。

Mineral Resources

Quanzhou is mountainous and rich in mineral resources, including coal, iron, gold, granite, limestone, quartz sand, kaolin, etc. The non-metallic mineral resources composed mainly of sand, stone and soil are the dominant resources with local features in Quanzhou. Various intrusive rock masses are spread all over Quanzhou, most of which are exposed on the ground, which is conducive to open-pit mining. In addition, due to the convenient transportation and a long history of mining, quarries are distributed throughout Quanzhou. Being rich in granite reserves, Quanzhou has been a famous stone producing area since ancient times. The stone mine in Shilong Village of Nan'an City has been mined since the Tang Dynasty, and Hui'an County produces fine-grained diabase. They are widely used in towers, bridges, city gates, city walls, tombs, and other parts of buildings, such as beams and columns, wall bases, doors and windows, railings, and steps, etc. After meticulously crafted by skilled craftsmen, these local stone materials have been fully utilized and become more beautiful and durable. The East and West Pagodas, Luoyang Bridge, Anping Bridge etc. built during the Song and Yuan Dynasties represent the highest level of stone architecture in East Asia from the 10th to 14th centuries.

Quanzhou is rich in kaolin resources. In Dehua County alone, there are as many as 92 kaolin deposits and 127 ore spots, with kaolin reserves of more than 100 million tons. The kaolin here is in the shape of soft soil, with good plasticity and fire resistance, and the ceramics fired from it have excellent texture. Being mountainous, Dehua is rich in forest resources and water resources. There are sufficient fuel for firing ceramics, and abundant water resources for crushing and processing porcelain clay, which can greatly liberate manpower and provide good natural conditions for mass production of ceramics. Dehua has a long history of firing ceramics. 3,700 years ago, the primitive celadon was produced here. Since then, the firing technology and production scale have been continuously boosted. The technology, quality and quantity of Dehua ceramics production also enhanced accordingly when Quanzhou's overseas trade reached its peak during the Song and Yuan Dynasties. Dehua ceramics became the largest commodity in maritime trade then, which were found in archaeological excavations both on land and in shipwrecks underwater at home and abroad. In addition, the decoration methods of heaping shear and sculpture piling commonly used in buildings such as local temples and palaces in Quanzhou are also based on the principles of porcelain and its firing. In large buildings such as the Mahavira Hall of Kaiyuan Temple, Tianhou Temple, and Confucian Temple, the brightly colored heap-cut construction technology makes these buildings beautiful local landscapes.

承天寺内堆剪建筑技术装饰的建筑。（傅捷雄 摄）
Buildings with heap-cut construction technology in Chengtian Temple. (Photo by Fu Jiexiong)

泉州铁矿资源也是非常丰富，特别是安溪，历史上就是有名的铁矿生产、加工区域，以潘田铁矿及珍地铁矿为代表，铁矿储量达3,000万吨。宋代泉州矿冶技术有较大的发展，朝廷在泉州设置的铁场，北宋盛时有15个，南宋后期仍存5个，其中最有名的，当属安溪青阳铁场。宋人李焘在《续资治通鉴长编》中记载道："庆历五年（1045），青阳铁冶大发，即置铁务于泉州。"泉州冶铁之盛，在《宋史》《元丰九域志》等官方及私人编修的史书中，均有明确的记载。2019—2020年由北京大学考古文博学院主持的安溪青阳下草埔冶铁遗址考古发掘也证实，考古遗址的地理位置和铁矿资源分布均与文献记载相契合。宋元时期，泉州的铁器也有出口到海外，这在明崇祯抄本《留氏族谱》中的"宋太师鄂国公传"有记载："陶器、铜铁泛于番国，取金贝而还，民甚称便。"到元代朝廷则下令"凡金银铜铁男女，并不许私贩入番"。

Quanzhou is also rich in iron ore resources, especially Anxi County. Historically, it is famous for iron ore mining and processing, represented by Pantian Iron Mine and Zhendi Iron Mine, with iron ore reserves reaching 30 million tons. Owing to the great development of mining and metallurgical technology in Quanzhou in the Song Dynasty, the imperial court set up up to 15 iron yards there in its heyday in the Northern Song Dynasty, among which 5 still remained in the late Southern Song Dynasty. The most famous one is Qingyang Ironworks in Anxi. Li Tao of the Song Dynasty wrote in *Extended Continuation to Comprehensive Mirror for Aid in Governance*, "In 1045, the iron yard was set up in Quanzhou since the great development of iron smelting in Qingyang." There are clear records of the prosperity of iron smelting in Quanzhou in official and private history books such as *The History of Song* and *Yuanfeng Treatise of the Nine Regions*. The archaeological excavation of Xiacaopu Iron Smelting Site of Qingyang Village in Anxi from 2019 to 2020, hosted by the School of Archaeology and Museology of Peking University, also confirmed that the geographical location of the archaeological site and the distribution of iron ore resources are in line with the literature records. During the Song and Yuan Dynasties, Quanzhou's ironware was also exported overseas. This is recorded in "Biography of The Grand Preceptor and Duke in the Song Dynasty" in the manuscript *Genealogy of the Liu Family* during Chongzhen's reign (1628—1644) in the Ming Dynasty, "Pottery, copper and iron are widely sold for gold or money in foreign countries, which is beneficial for people." While in the Yuan Dynasty, the imperial court issued an order that "Men and women, gold, silver, copper, iron, etc. are not allowed to be smuggled into foreign countries for business."

安溪青阳下草埔冶铁遗址考古现场。（刘伯怡 摄）

The archaeological site of Xiacaopu Iron Production of Qingyang Village, Anxi County. (Photo by Liu Boyi)

季风气候

泉州作为沿海城市，其气候为典型的亚热带海洋性季风气候。据研究表明，在台湾山脉和武夷山脉夹峙下的台湾海峡具有很强的“狭管效应”。泉州东南面靠近台湾海峡海域，无论是冬季风还是夏季风，在此处风力都有明显增大，风力资源十分丰富。在海洋性季风气候的影响下，泉州夏季盛行西南季风，秋冬季节干燥、少雨，盛行东北季风，适宜风动力帆船航行。作为向海而生的地区，秦汉以前，泉州沿江靠海的土著民俗自成体系。他们傍水而居，善用舟，形成善于掌握季风、造舟航洋的秉性。南北朝时期，泉州就有大舶往来海外，成为当时通往东南亚地区的首选启航之地。

泉州沿海居民世代以海为生，他们“以舟为车，以楫为马”！（陈英杰 摄）
Using their boats as vehicles, Quanzhou coastal residents have been living by the sea for generations. (Photo by Chen Yingjie)

泉州人传承闽越族的造船技能，其造船业十分发达，唐代已能造出身长18丈（约60米）的大船。宋代泉州造船技术日臻成熟完善，泉州湾后渚港出土载满香料的远洋货船证实了当时利用季风进行航海的技术已经相当发达。九日山的祈风石刻就有记载能体现宋代海洋贸易的运行周期与季风密切关联的历史信息，即“冬遣舶，夏回航”，成为珍贵的石刻历史档案。

“泉州人稠山谷瘠，虽欲就耕无地辟；州南有海浩无穷，每岁造舟通异域。”这是北宋泉州人谢履写的《泉南歌》。诗歌形象地概述了宋时泉州人多地瘠的现实状况，并描述了宋时泉州人以刺桐港为依托，掌握季风的秘密，广造舟楫，生产陶瓷器，提升冶铁技术，开拓海上航路与海外通商的盛况。

Monsoon Climate

As a coastal city, Quanzhou features a typical subtropical marine monsoon climate. According to research, there is a strong "narrow pipe effect" in the Taiwan Strait which is between the Taiwan Mountain Range and the Wuyi Mountain Range. Quanzhou is close to the waters of the Taiwan Strait in the southeast, where both the winter wind and the summer wind have significantly increased, so the wind resources are very rich. Under the influence of the oceanic monsoon climate, the southwest monsoon prevails in Quanzhou in summer, and the northeast monsoon dominates in autumn and winter, which is dry and less rainy, making it suitable for wind-powered sailing. As an ocean-oriented area, Quanzhou formed its own distinctive indigenous folk customs of depending on the sea before the Qin (221 B.C.—207 B.C.) and Han (206 B.C.—220) Dynasties. Living by the water, people were good at using boats as vehicles and formed a good habit of mastering the monsoon climate and making boats for sailing. During the Southern and Northern Dynasties (420—589), there were large ships in Quanzhou traveling overseas, making Quanzhou the first choice for setting sail to Southeast Asia at that time.

Quanzhou people inherited the shipbuilding skills from the Minyue people, so their shipbuilding industry was fully developed. In the Tang Dynasty, they were able to build large ships with length of about 60m. In the Song Dynasty, the shipbuilding technology of Quanzhou was more and more mature. The ocean-going cargo ship full of spices unearthed at Houzhu Port in Quanzhou Bay proved that the technology of using monsoons for navigation was quite developed at that time. In the Jiuri Mountain Wind-Praying Inscriptions, there are records of historical information such as the operational cycle reflecting the close connection between the maritime trade and the monsoon in the Song Dynasty, that is, "departing in winter and returning in summer", which has become a precious historical archive of stone inscriptions.

"Quanzhou is densely populated but the valleys are barren. There is nowhere to plow although people want to sow. Seas are endless to the south of the land. Ships are built to connect with foreign lands". This is *Song of Quannan* by Xie Lu, a Quanzhou native of the Northern Song Dynasty. The poem depicted vividly the status quo of large population and barren field of Quanzhou in ancient times, and also described the prosperity of how Quanzhou people, taking advantage of Zayton Port, mastered the secrets of monsoon, built ships, produced ceramics, improved iron smelting technology, and opened up shipping routes for foreign trades in the Song Dynasty.

泉州后渚港古沉船残长 24.2 米，宽 9.15 米，修复后的长度达到 30 米，宽 10.5 米，载重量达 200 吨。（刘宝生 摄）
The shipwreck at Quanzhou Houzhu Port is 24.2m long and 9.15m wide. After repair, it has reached 30m long and 10.5m wide, with a carrying capacity of 200 tons. (Photo by Liu Baosheng)

制度保障

面对"八山一水一分田"、可供耕作田地缺乏的自然地理环境，泉州人自然的应对方式就是"靠海吃海"，从山区腹地走向海洋，向大海讨生活。这个集体本能的选择，在宋元时期，在社会各阶层人士的共同努力下，通过官方自上而下出台的政令措施和民间自下而上形成的规约进行保障及推广，形成了宋元时期维护泉州作为世界海洋商贸中心的制度保障，将海洋贸易推向了发展的高峰。

Institutional Guarantee

Faced with the natural geographical environment of "being mountainous and lack of water and arable land", Quanzhou people naturally took "living off the water when living by the water" as a response, shifting focus from the hinterland of the mountains to the sea, and making a living from the latter. In the Song and Yuan Dynasties, with the joint efforts of people from all walks of life, this collective instinctive choice was guaranteed and promoted through top-down official decrees and measures and bottom-up folk regulations. This provides institutional guarantee for Quanzhou as the emporium of the world in Song-Yuan China, which has pushed its maritime trade to a peak.

泉州拥有丰富的海洋资源，海域面积 11,360 平方千米，大小港湾 14 个，岛屿 270 个，近海渔场面积 50.6 万公顷，海洋生物种类 600 多种。（陈剑 摄）

Quanzhou is rich in marine resources, with a sea area of 11,360km2, 14 ports and 270 islands, 506,000 hectares of coastal fishing grounds, and more than 600 species of marine life. (Photo by Chen Jian)

促进市舶司在泉州的发展

推动市舶司在泉州的设置。泉州以其有利的地理环境、高超的航海和造船技术，北上日本、高丽，南下东南亚诸国交通便利，在设立市舶司前海外贸易往来已十分频繁，引起当时政府官员的重视。北宋熙宁五年（1072），泉州转运使薛向最早向朝廷请求设立市舶司，但未果。元丰三年（1080），朝廷下诏“非广州市舶司，辄发过南番纲舶船，非明州市舶司而发过日本高丽者，以违制论”，来往泉州的商船必须前往广州、明州市舶司进行抽解，给泉州的海外贸易活动带来了极大的不便。两次担任泉州郡守的陈偁为改变泉州商船必须到广州、明州登记、交税的被动局面，多次向朝廷奏请在泉州设立市舶司。经过多方努力，宋哲宗即位后，在负责财政的户部尚书李常再次奏请下，元祐二年（1087）朝廷终于将福建路市舶司设置在泉州。泉州的海外交通贸易得到朝廷的官方认可，正式成为国家对外通商口岸。

给予优惠的外贸政策。据《宋会要辑稿》记载，朝廷于建炎二年（1128）给福建路市舶司二十万贯充市舶本钱。绍兴十四年（1144），出于对番商到泉州贸易的重视，朝廷增拨官钱给福建路市舶司设宴犒劳番商，由市舶司提举和地方长官出面筵请番商，以示朝廷招徕远人之意，鼓励更多的外国商人到泉州经商贸易。乾道三年（1167），朝廷又从福建各州的上供银中拨出二十五万贯，专充抽买乳香等本钱，泉州市舶司的本钱再一次提高。此外，朝廷在泉州还推行优惠的税收政策。据《元史》记载，大司农燕公楠、翰林学士承旨留梦炎言：“杭州、上海、澉浦、温州、庆元、广东、泉州置市舶司凡七所，唯泉州物货三十取一，余皆十五抽一，乞以泉州为定制。”元朝其余六所市舶司“番船货物，十五抽一”“惟泉州三十取一”，这些税收优惠政策的实施，扩大了泉州港在对外贸易竞争中的优势。

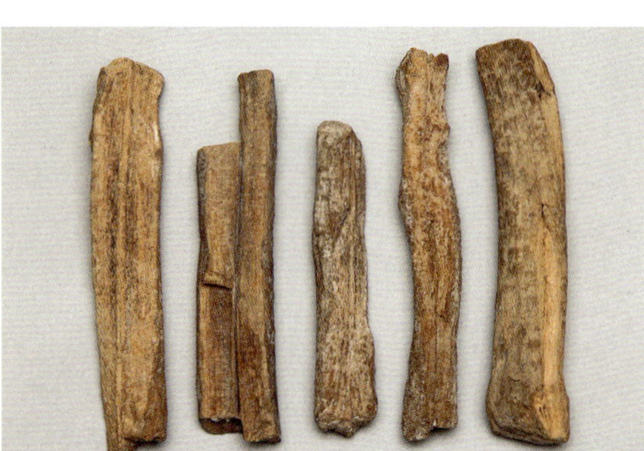

泉州后渚古沉船出土的香料。（成冬冬 摄）
Spices unearthed from the ancient shipwreck in Houzhu Port, Quanzhou. (Photo by Cheng Dongdong)

Accelerating the Development of the Maritime Trade Office in Quanzhou

Promoting the establishment of the Maritime Trade Office in Quanzhou

With its favorable geographical environment, superb navigation and shipbuilding technology, Quanzhou has convenient transportation to Japan and Korea in the north, and Southeast Asian countries in the south. Before the establishment of the Maritime Trade Office, there had been frequent maritime trade and exchanges between Quanzhou and foreign countries, which attracted the attention of the government officials at that time. In 1072 in the Northern Song Dynasty, Xue Xiang, the Transshipment Envoy of Quanzhou, was the first to request the imperial court to set up the Maritime Trade Office, but was futile. In 1080, the imperial court issued an edict that "It will be regarded as violating the rules and regulations for the ships leaving for the areas of Southeast Asia and the Indian Ocean without the approval from Guangzhou Maritime Trade Office, and for the ships going to Japan and Korea without the approval from Mingzhou (Ningbo nowadays) Maritime Trade Office". Merchant ships traveling to and from Quanzhou had to be taxed by Guangzhou and Mingzhou Maritime Trade Offices, which had brought great inconvenience to Quanzhou's maritime trade activities. In order to change the passive situation of applying for registration and being taxed in Guangzhou and Mingzhou, Chen Cheng, who served as the Prefect of Quanzhou twice, repeatedly requested the imperial court to set up a maritime trade office in Quanzhou. With multiple efforts and under the suggestion of Li Chang, the Minister of Finance, the imperial court finally set up Fujian Regional Maritime Trade Office in Quanzhou in 1087 after Emperor Zhezong of the Song Dynasty came to the throne. With the overseas transportation and trade having been officially recognized by the imperial court, Quanzhou has become a national foreign trade port.

Providing preferential foreign trade policies

According to *Song Government Manuscript Compendium,* the imperial court gave 200,000 *guan* copper coins to Fujian Regional Maritime Trade Office as the capital in 1128. In order to show concerns for foreign merchants' trade in Quanzhou, the imperial court allocated additional money to the office in 1141, with which the leading official and the local governor would hold banquets for foreign merchants in order to show the imperial court's hospitality and to encourage more foreign merchants to do business and make trade in Quanzhou. In 1167, the imperial court allocated another 250,000 *guan* copper coins from Fujian taxes to the Maritime Trade Office as the capital especially for buying mastic and so on. Thus, the capital of Quanzhou Maritime Trade Office was increased once again. In addition, the imperial court also implemented preferential tax policies in Quanzhou. In *The History of Yuan,* as stated by Yan Gongnan, Minister of Revenue, and Liu Mengyan, head of Hanlin Academicians,"Of the seven maritime offices in Hangzhou, Shanghai, Ganpu, Wenzhou, Qingyuan, Guangdong, and Quanzhou, only Quanzhou Maritime Office taxes at the rate of 1:30, while the other 1:15. They ask for following the tax rate of Quanzhou Maritime Office." The implementation of these preferential tax policies increased the advantages of Quanzhou Port in foreign trade competition.

重视市舶司官员的任命。宋室南渡之后，经费困乏，一切倚办海舶，因此南宋皇帝对海外贸易的态度与传统大相径庭。宋高宗认识到："市舶之利最厚，若措置合宜，所得动以百万计，岂不胜取之于民？"绍兴二十一年（1151），宋高宗在任命李庄为福建提举的诏令中说："提举市舶司委寄非轻，若用非其人，则措置失当，海商不至矣。"诏令中体现出市舶司给南宋朝廷带来高额收入，所以宋室皇帝对市舶司官员的任命高度重视，并出台加强市舶管理、促进外贸活动的指导方针。市舶司官员不仅按照国家要求开展商贸管理，还积极参与地方事务，包括与地方官员共同举行航海祭祀活动、主持开展地方基础设施建设等。此外，还有特授官职，如据《宋会要辑稿》所载：绍兴六年（1136）在泉州市舶司的一份奏议上，提举福建路市舶司建议授予阿拉伯商人蒲啰辛"承信郎"的官职，并赐公服履笏，以嘉奖他在泉州乳香贸易中给泉州市舶司带来了 30 万贯的收入。

推动相关法律法规的完善。宋元时期，为推动海外贸易的发展，朝廷和泉州地方官员作出许多的努力。地方官员清明廉洁，体恤客商，减免商税。嘉定十年（1217），许多外国商船担心来泉州会受到重税勒索。泉州知州真德秀在全面调查之后，发布法令，放宽税收政策，减免外商税赋，严禁盘剥外商，鼓励外商前来泉州贸易。当时朝廷还以市舶司为主体，注重运用法律手段管理海上对外贸易。宋朝于元丰三年（1080）颁布了世界上第一部专门针对海洋贸易的法规《元丰广州市舶条法》；元朝在此基础上加以完善提升，于至元二十九年（1292）形成《至元市舶则法》，后又于延祐元年（1314）重新修订颁行新的市舶则法二十二条，即《延祐市舶则法》。以《市舶则法》为核心，大量单行敕令为辅助，制定了完整的海外贸易管理体系，实现了从法律层面上规范、保障海外贸易，使得对海外贸易的管理更为制度化和正规化，促进了海外贸易的长远发展。

Attaching importance to the appointment of officials of maritime trade offices

After the members of the royal family migrated south in the Southern Song Dynasty, the government was short of funds and relied heavily on maritime trade. Therefore, the Southern Song Dynasty emperors' attitudes towards overseas trade are totally different from the traditional ones. Emperor Gaozong of the Song Dynasty realized that "Being the most profitable, the maritime trade can bring millions of profit if it is managed properly. Wouldn't it better than taking taxes from people?" In 1151, he said in the edict to appoint Li Zhuang as Supervisor of Fujian Maritime Trade Office, "It is crucial to appoint a qualified leader for a maritime trade office. Otherwise, the maritime merchants will not come because of improper appointment." It can be seen from the edict that the maritime trade offices have brought high income for the imperial court of the Southern Song Dynasty, so the emperor attached great importance to the appointment of officials of the maritime trade offices, and issued guidelines for strengthening the management of the offices and promoting foreign trade activities. Officials of the offices not only carry out business management in accordance with national requirements, but also participate actively in local affairs, including jointly holding maritime sacrificial ceremonies with local officials and hosting local infrastructure construction. What's more, there are also some specifically conferred official positions. For example, according to *Song Government Manuscript Compendium*, "In a proposal to the imperial court from Quanzhou Maritime Trade Office in 1136, the Supervisor of Fujian Regional Maritime Trade Office suggested that the Arabian businessman Pu Luoxin be granted the official position of 'Chengxin Court Gentleman', and the official uniform and shoes be offered, in order to reward him for bringing 300,000 *guan* copper coins of income to the office in the mastic trade of Quanzhou."

Facilitating the improvement of relevant laws and regulations

During the Song and Yuan Dynasties, the imperial courts and local officials in Quanzhou made great efforts to promote the development of maritime trade. Being incorruptible and considerate of foreign merchants, local officials carried out tax relief. In 1217, many foreign merchants worried about being heavily taxed when they came to Quanzhou. After a comprehensive investigation, Zhen Dexiu, Prefect of Quanzhou, issued a decree to relax tax policies, alleviate foreign business taxes, strictly prohibit exploitation of foreign businessmen, and encourage foreign businessmen to come to Quanzhou for trade. At that time, the imperial courts stressed using legal means to manage maritime foreign trade mainly through the maritime trade offices. In 1080 of the Song Dynasty, the world's first book of regulations specific for maritime trade was promulgated, named *Yuanfeng Guangzhou Maritime Trade Regulations*. Based on this, it was improved in the Yuan Dynasty, and *Zhiyuan Maritime Trade Law* was formed in 1292. It was then revised and promulgated as a new law with 22 articles in 1314, namely, *Yanyou Maritime Trade Law*. With *Yanyou Maritime Trade Law* as the core and a large number of separate decrees as the auxiliary, a complete maritime trade management system was formulated to standardize and protect the maritime trade at the legal level, which institutionalized and regularized the management of maritime trade, and promoted the long-term development of maritime trade.

推进大型公共设施的建设

城市设施。泉州子城在唐代营建初期，即在城内开排水沟以纳潮汐，奠定了以后城内排水系统的基础。北宋治平三年（1066）夏大雨，通淮壕沟堵塞，城内雨水无法及时排出，致使淹没损坏民屋数千间。次年，郡守丁竦主持疏浚，郡城诸水皆向东南汇入晋江。北宋在泉州设市舶司，选址于船舶可直通晋江至水口报关的城南水仙门外。南宋绍兴十八年（1148）太守叶廷珪利用潮水涨退冲洗壕沟。淳熙年间太守林枅曾疏浚，后又堵塞。嘉定年间太守真德秀感于"十日不雨，则忧干旱；五日之雨，又虞水患"，亲自主持大修泉州城内水道。南宋绍定三年（1230）太守游九功沿晋江砌筑石头建翼城 438 丈，"沿江以为蔽"，阻止洪水侵蚀，从南关港直通府城。元大德年间宣慰司札剌立丁重浚旧罗城南外壕。至正十二年（1352），监郡偰玉立南拓罗城，建德济门，城南外壕遂为城内壕。宋元时期，泉州地方官员高度重视城内的水道、壕沟的疏浚，联通了城内水系与晋江及笋江、浯溪等溪流，保证城内不受台风、暴雨的侵袭。

泉州古城内河沟渠遍布，组成庞大的水系。（成冬冬 摄）

The ancient city of Quanzhou is dotted with inland rivers and canals, forming a vast water system. (Photo by Cheng Dongdong)

Promoting the Construction of Large-Scale Public Facilities

Urban facilities

The drainage ditch was built to accommodate or drain the tide in the early days of the construction of the ancient Quanzhou Zicheng (minor wall) in the Tang Dynasty, which laid the foundation for the drainage system afterwards. In 1066 of the Northern Song Dynasty, there was heavy rain in summer. Because the Tonghuai Trench was blocked, the rainwater in the city could not be drained in time, resulting in flooding and causing damage of thousands of houses. In the following year, Ding Song, Prefect of Quanzhou, presided over the dredging to make all the water in the city flowed southeast into the Jinjiang River. In the Northern Song Dynasty, the Maritime Trade Office was set up in Quanzhou, and the site was chosen to be outside the Narcissus Gate in the south of the city, where ships could go directly through the Jinjiang River to the river mouth for customs declaration. In 1148 of the Southern Song Dynasty, Prefect Ye Tinggui took advantage of the ebb and flow of the tides to wash the trenches. During the Chunxi Period (1174—1189), Prefect Lin Ji once dredged the trenches but they were blocked again later. During the Jiading Period (1208—1224), Prefect Zhen Dexiu realized that "if there is no rain for ten days, people in Quanzhou worry about drought; but if it rains for five days, they worry about flooding", so he personally presided over the overhaul of the waterways in Quanzhou City. In 1230 of the Southern Song Dynasty, Prefect You Jiugong built Yicheng (affiliated city walls) with stones which was about 1,500m along the Jinjiang River as a shelter from the flood and directly connected to Quanzhou downtown from Nanguan Port. During the Dade Period (1297—1307) of the Yuan Dynasty, Zhala Liding of the Pacification Commission re-dug the south outer moat of the old Luocheng (outer city walls). In 1352, Xie Yuli, Prefect of Quanzhou, extended the south wall of Luocheng and built Deji Gate, so the south outer moat became the inner trench. During the Song and Yuan Dynasties, local officials in Quanzhou attached great importance to the dredging of waterways and trenches in the city, and connected the water system in the city with streams such as the Jinjiang River, the Sunjiang River and the Wuxi River to protect the city from typhoons and rainstorms.

泉州田淮渠。（苏德辉 摄）
Tianhuai Ditch in Quanzhou. (Photo by Su Dehui)

道路桥梁。宋元时期，为便于商民往来港区和货物集散，泉州掀起一股造桥热，陆海桥梁与“三湾十二港”共同构建了海陆联运的交通格局。特别是在10—14世纪数百年时间内，泉州千帆竞发，万国来商，对外贸易获利丰厚，为造桥提供了有力的经济保障，此间造桥多达175座。这些桥梁，多是由官方力量即当地地方长官和社会各界，如地方大族、僧侣、民众等形成合力共同建成的。如号称“海内第一桥”的洛阳桥，是在地方民众尝试建桥未竟，后经郡守蔡襄主持建造而成的；“天下无桥长此桥”的安平桥则先是僧侣和地方大族捐款倡建未能完成，后由泉州郡守赵令衿主持续建而成；“海国冲衢”的顺济桥则是知州邹应龙用外商修建泉州城楼的余资修建。这三座桥梁，极大方便了泉州北上省城乃至更远的内陆地区，南下漳州、潮州及晋江两岸的交通往来。

Roads and bridges

During the Song and Yuan Dynasties, in order to facilitate the traffic of merchants and ordinary people, and the distribution of goods, bridge-building flourished in Quanzhou. The land bridges, cross-sea bridges and "Three Bays and Twelve Ports" jointly built an integrated sea–land transportation system. Especially in the over 400 years from the 10th to the 14th century, maritime trade brought huge profits with thousands of sails departing from Quanzhou and thousands of merchants coming from all over the world, which provided strong economic security for the construction of bridges. There were as many as 175 bridges built at that time, most of which were built on the joint efforts of local governors, representing official forces, and all walks of life such as local clans, monks, and common people. For example, Luoyang Bridge, known as the "No. 1 Bridge in China", was first initiated by the local people for construction but in vain, and later accomplished under the auspices of Cai Xiang, Prefect of Quanzhou. Anping Bridge, with the fame of "no bridge in the world is longer than it", was first donated for construction by monks and local nobles but in vain, and later accomplished under the auspices of Prefect Zhao Lingjin. Shunji Bridge, known as "the transportation hub of the offshore areas", was built by Zou Yinglong, Prefect of Quanzhou, with the surplus funds from foreign merchants to build Quanzhou Gate Tower. These three bridges have greatly facilitated the northbound traffic between Quanzhou and Fuzhou, the provincial capital, and even further inland areas, the southbound traffic between Quanzhou and Zhangzhou, Chaozhou and traffic between both banks of the Jinjiang River.

洛阳桥横跨洛阳江上。（吴云轩 摄）
Luoyang Bridge over the Luoyangjiang River. (Photo by Wu Yunxuan)

加强沿海军事设施的布防

宋元时期，泉州海外贸易之所以兴盛，最重要的基础保障就是当时泉州的地方长官高度重视航道畅通和航运安全。官方在沿海、沿江先后设置了石湖寨、永宁寨、法石寨、宝林寨、围头寨等水寨，配置相应的兵员。水寨官兵的职责主要为定期巡逻、缉拿海盗、驻守边防等。

设水寨、调整驻军。真德秀到任泉州后，选派观察推官李方子、晋江知县徐叔用、同左翼军副将邱全等，遍巡海滨。几人巡视海防设备后，在给枢密院的奏报《申枢密院措置沿海事宜状》中提到：宝林、石湖、永宁三寨归属左翼水军，泉州沿海有四寨，其中紧要的，在晋江是石湖寨，在惠安是小兜寨，虽然对海道已有控扼，但宝林寨位于城南，离城很近，离海较远。而围头到泉州城 120 余里，正瞰大海，是南北洋舟船往来必泊之地，旁有支港可达石井，其地势甚是险要，而此前未尝措置水寨派兵驻防，这里的地理优势没有得到充分的发挥。原先设置"宝林所屯兵 300 人，人数较多；法石有 120 余人，但作为防海冲要之地，其数尚少。永宁的步军之数倍于水军，其布置之未尽得其宜也"。于是真德秀对驻守官兵人数进行调整，从宝林寨水军中抽出 200 人，以 70 人置于法石，以 50 人屯永宁，以 80 人屯围头。腾出宝林寨的营屋，拨给步军居住，以护卫城南。真德秀将防卫重点放在法石寨，申请将其编制增加至 200 人，增设官衙，主将驻扎法石，统一管辖法石、石湖、永宁、围头四个水寨的防务，并有效地布防官兵、修建营房，加以兵备整顿训练，以提高军事防御能力。

具有 600 多年历史的永宁古卫城。（许兆恺 摄）
The ancient Yongning Garrison with an history of over 600 years. (Photo by Xu Zhaokai)

Strengthening the Defense of Coastal Military Facilities

During the Song and Yuan Dynasties, the most important basic guarantee for the prosperity of Quanzhou's maritime trade was that the governors of Quanzhou at that time attached great importance to smooth waterways and navigation safety. The officials successively set up coastal military camps along the coast and the river, such as Shihu Camp, Yongning Camp, Fashi Camp, Baolin Camp, and Weitou Camp, and deployed corresponding soldiers whose main duties were regular patrols, arresting pirates, border defense and so on.

Setting up camps and adjusting the garrisons

After taking office in Quanzhou, Zhen Dexiu sent Li Fangzi, the Official Inspector, Xu Shuyong, the Magistrate of Jinjiang County, and Qiu Quan, the Deputy General of the left-wing legion, to observe all over the coast. After inspecting the coastal defense staffing, in the report "About the Coastal Staffing Affairs" to the Privy Council they mentioned the three camps of Baolin, Shihu, and Yongning under the jurisdiction of the left-wing navy. There were four camps along the coast of Quanzhou, among which the important ones were Shihu Camp in Jinjiang County and Xiaodou Camp in Hui'an County. Although it had control over the sea routes, Baolin Camp, located in the south of the city, was close to the city but far from the sea. Overlooking the sea, Weitou was more than 60km away from Quanzhou City, which was a necessary berth place for ships from both the north and the south, with a branch port connecting to Shijing Town. Its surrounding terrain was of great strategic importance. However, there had never been a camp or garrison before, which had prevented the full utilization of the geographical advantages. The original staffing was that "There is a comparatively large number of 300 soldiers in Baolin Camp but a small number of just over 120 soldiers in Fashi Camp which is an important place for sea defence. Since the number of the infantry in Yongning Camp is several times larger than the navy, the staff allocation is not appropriate enough." So Zhen Dexiu adjusted the number of garrison officers and soldiers by drawing 200 soldiers from the navy in Baolin Camp, among which 70 were added to Fashi Camp, 50 to Yongning Camp, and 80 to Weitou Camp. The barracks of Baolin Camp were vacated and allocated to the infantry to guard the southern part of Quanzhou City. Focusing on the defense of Fashi Camp, Zhen Dexiu applied to increase its garrison to 200 people and add an official agency. With unified jurisdiction over the defense of the four camps, Fashi, Shihu, Yongning, and Weitou, the chief general would be stationed in Fashi Camp, to deploy officers and soldiers, build barracks, and conduct military training in order to improve the military defense capabilities.

备战舸、定期巡逻。宋嘉祐三年（1058），蔡襄奏请：福兴泉漳各有渔船及巡检司船，要求对这些渔船和战船加以修整以备海道巡查。乾道二年（1166），朝廷下令对战船按甲、乙、丙三个番品配搭以备调遣。其后泉州沿海晋江、同安、南安、惠安四县战船分甲、乙、丙三番计 21 艘。淳祐三年（1243），又从沿海诸州的民船中挑选适合船只，重立番次。每座水寨设置战船 3 艘，并安排修理战船的专门预算，以保证战船的性能和战斗能力。同时划定水寨官兵巡逻的分界线，规定水寨官兵根据各自划定的区域，定期出海巡逻一次，执行巡逻任务的官兵姓名、巡逻情况等，真实记录在巡逻日记上，作为考核奖罚的依据。

位于惠安县崇武半岛上的崇武古城。（田米 摄）
Chongwu Ancient Town located on the Chongwu Peninsula in Hui'an County. (Photo by Tian Mi)

Warship preparation and regular patrols

In 1058 of the Song Dynasty, Cai Xiang reported to the imperial court that in Fuzhou, Xinghua (Putian nowadays), Quanzhou and Zhangzhou, there were fishing boats and patrol ships which should be refitted for seaway inspection. In 1166, the imperial court ordered that the warships be deployed according to the three grades of A, B and C. Afterwards, 21 ships in the four counties of Jinjiang, Tong'an, Nan'an, and Hui'an along the coast of Quanzhou were divided into three grades. In 1243, suitable ships were selected from the civilian ships of the coastal prefectures and were entitled with grades again. Each camp was equipped with three warships, and a special budget for repairing the warships was arranged to ensure their performance and combat capabilities. At the same time, the demarcation line of the patrol was defined, based on which the officers and soldiers in the camp should regularly go out to the sea for patrol in their respective designated areas. Names of the officers, soldiers on duty and the patrol records should be truthfully written in the patrol logs as a reference for assessment, reward and punishment.

靖海寇、为兵请赏。南宋时期，海盗在泉州近海作乱，逼近州城。在官军遭受挫败、伤亡惨重的情况下，真德秀祭悼阵亡将士，亲自传授应敌策略，并亲自为有功之人请赏。真德秀专门上《泉州申枢密院乞推海盗赏状》，奏报中提到有海盗侵犯州境，左翼军遣发官兵，并号召晋江、同安管下诸澳的民船与官军会合，前去收捕，如能捕获贼首及其徒党，除优支赏犒外，更专门出证明向朝廷申请补授官资。奏报中还推荐同安县管下烈屿首领方知刚、林枋等人，因其在海盗来犯时，团结丁壮，排布矢石，控扼海岸，使贼不敢来犯；晋江县管下岭兜总首王行已将带人船自备粮食器械，随队左翼军下海会合，擒获贼徒钟宋三等七名，请朝廷加以推赏。真德秀还要求抚恤在缉拿海盗过程中以身殉职的王大寿，并给其长子补授官职，以此激励官兵。泉州沿海一带官兵士气为之大振，不久便肃清了海盗，确保海道畅通。

在地方官员的有效管理下，官兵们上下团结，水寨互为援引，泉州沿海列戍控扼得所、布置得宜，士卒精练、器械整齐、舟楫便利而又熟习风涛，形成较为完善和行之有效的海防防御体系，有效地保障了泉州港的对外航运交通安全。

Putting down pirates and applying for rewards for soldiers

During the Southern Song Dynasty, pirates made troubles off the coast of Quanzhou and approached the city. When the officers and soldiers suffered setbacks and heavy casualties, Zhen Dexiu mourned the fallen soldiers, personally taught the tactics of coping with the enemy, and personally asked for rewards for those who had made meritorious deeds. In his special report "Quanzhou's Apply to the Privy Council for Rewards for Fighting Against Pirates", he mentioned that pirates had invaded the border of the prefecture, so the left-wing legion sent officers and soldiers, and called on the civilian ships from the harbors ruled by Jinjiang and Tong'an to join with them for arresting the pirates. If the head and the gang could be caught, in addition to the rewards, a specific certificate would be issued by the imperial court for supplementary official grant and positions. The report also recommended to reward Fang Zhigang, Lin Fang, and other leaders of Lieyu Island in Tong'an County, because when the pirates came, they called on able-bodied men, arranged arrows and stones to control the coast and prevent the pirates from invasion. Another person worthy of reward was Wang Xing, the headman of Lingdou Village of Jinjiang County, who had led his own boats and fellows with food and weapons to join the left-wing legion in the sea and captured seven pirates, including Zhong Songsan. Zhen Dexiu also asked for compensation for Wang Dashou who died in the process of arresting pirates, and offering his eldest son an official position and compensation in order to motivate other officers and soldiers. The morale of the officers and soldiers along the coast of Quanzhou was greatly boosted, and the pirates were soon eliminated to ensure the smooth sea lanes.

Under the effective management of local officials, these officers and soldiers were united as one, and the camps helped each other. A relatively sound and effective coastal defense system came into being with proper allocation of the coastal garrisons in Quanzhou, well-trained soldiers, well-equipped military weapons and ready ships with experiences, which effectively guaranteed the safety of maritime shipping traffic in Quanzhou Port.

推动民间信仰的官方化

民间规约。恶劣及变化无常的自然环境，让早期泉州先民对自然充满敬畏之心。先民们相信万物有灵，认为在现实世界之外有超自然的力量或实体存在，并认为它们能够影响人们的命运，因而产生敬畏和崇拜的思想感情。泉州向海而生的生产、生活方式，使得当地的海神信仰很是兴盛，民间先后兴起了通远王、真武大帝、妈祖三大海神信仰。为了便于海商、船员往来祭拜，这些海神庙宇一般位于港口附近，如通远王祠（昭惠庙）在梁安港旁，真武庙靠近法石港，天后宫靠近南关港。这三大海神信仰在海商群体中最具代表性，他们为人们所信奉的法力，包括保佑风信如期而至和海上航行平安、救助航海落难人员、惩治不法之徒、见证商业合作行为、助力歼灭海盗等，体现海神对海洋贸易商业行为的约束，并在海商群体中形成强调行为规范和道德约束的民间规约。

通远王是我国东南沿海第一代海神。（陈英杰 摄）
King Tongyuan is the first generation of sea god on the southeastern coast of China. (Photo by Chen Yingjie)

Promoting the Officialization of Folk Beliefs

Folk regulations

The harsh and changeable natural environment made the early ancestors of Quanzhou full of awe of nature. They believed in animism and generated awe and worship because they believed that there were supernatural forces or entities beyond the real world which could affect people's fate. The ocean-oriented mode of production and lifestyle in Quanzhou has made the local sea god belief very prosperous. The folk beliefs of the three sea gods (or goddess), King Tongyuan, Zhenwu Celestial Lord, and Mazu, have risen successively among the people. In order to facilitate the worship of maritime merchants and sailors, the sea god temples are generally located near the ports, such as King Tongyuan Temple (Zhaohui Temple) next to Liang'an Port, Zhenwu Temple near Fashi Port, and Tianhou Temple near Nanguan Port. These are the most representative traditional beliefs among the maritime merchants. They believed in these gods' mana which includes bringing the wind in need, ensuring the safety of maritime navigation, rescuing shipwrecked people, punishing lawbreakers, witnessing business cooperation, and helping annihilate pirates, etc. This embodies the restraints of the sea gods on the commercial conduct of maritime trade, and the folk regulations emphasizing behavior norms and moral constrains among the maritime merchants.

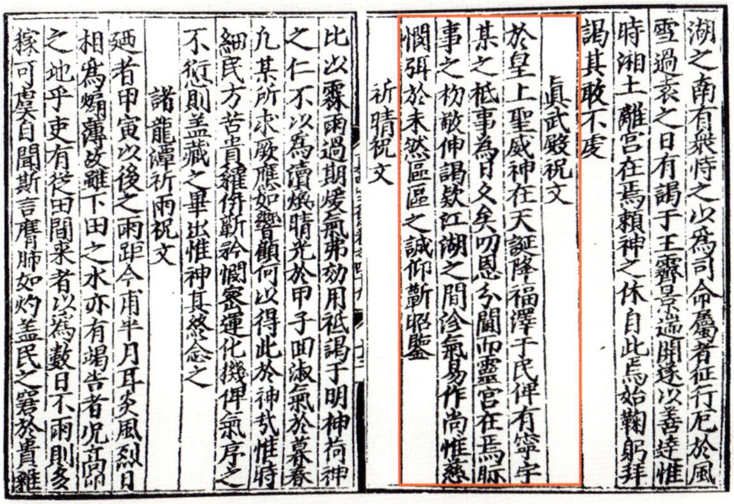
湖之南有衆恃之以爲司命羈者征行厄於風
雪過衰之日有禱于王霽景遄開遂以善歸惟
時湘土離宮在焉賴神之休自此爲始鞠躬拜
謁其敢不虔
眞武殿祝文
於皇上聖威神在天誕降福澤于民俾有寧宇
某之祗事爲日久矣叨恩分閫而靈宮在焉脈
事之初敬伸禱款江湖之間沴氣易作尚惟慈
憫弭於未然區區之誠仰祈昭鑒
祈晴祝文
比以霖雨過期愆氣弗効用祗禱于明神荷神
之仁不以爲瀆焕晴光於甲子回淑氣於暮春
凡某所求感應如響顧何以得此於神哉惟時
細民方苦貴糴仰祈於閽寔運化機俾氣序之
不愆則蓋藏之畢出惟神其終念之
諸龍潭祈雨祝文
迺者甲寅以後之雨距今甫半月耳炎風烈日
相爲煽薄故雖下田之水亦有竭告者況高卬
之地乎吏有從田間來者以爲數日不雨則多
稼可虞自聞斯言膚肺如灼蓋民之窘於貴糴

《真武殿祝文》。（许兆恺 摄）

Prayers to Zhenwu Hall. (Photo by Xu Zhaokai)

官方敕封。这些海神信仰发源于民间，兴盛于官方的册封，绵延发展于官方和民间的联合推动。通远王以其祷雨灵验和能保佑风息涛平，成为当地海洋族群的海上保护神，受到朝廷的敕封，从“崇应公”到“通远王”，后累加敕封“善利广福显济”等封号。因对国家统一和御敌等都有帮助，宋朝历朝皇帝大力提倡敬奉真武大帝，并加封他为“镇天真武灵应佑圣真君”，元代则晋升为“元圣仁威玄天上帝”。南宋对妈祖的敕封达13次之多，封号从“灵惠夫人”到“灵惠显济嘉应善庆妃”；元朝政府出于祈求保护海上漕运的顺利和海上贸易利益的考量，5次对其加以敕封，封号从“护国明著天妃”到“辅国护圣庇民广济福惠明著天妃”。民间信奉的一般信仰就这样通过不断地加封，擢升至朝廷敕封的海神。宋元两朝将海神信仰的祭祀列入国家祭典，由朝廷派员或地方主要行政长官主持或参加祭典。这一民间信仰的官方化过程体现正式的官方市舶制度与非正式的民间信仰的融合，是宋元官方借助海神信仰推动海洋贸易的重要举措。这一举措的核心体现了政府对于泉州海外贸易的重视程度，也是政府有效管理海外贸易的一种表现形式，使得这些海神信仰增添了浓郁的官方色彩。

Official conferments

These sea god beliefs originated from the folk, flourished after the official recognition, and continued to develop in the joint promotion of the government and the local people. King Tongyuan became the sea protector of the local marine community because he was said to be able to pray for rain and bless the mild wind on the sea. He received canonization from the imperial court, and was conferred several honorable titles, such as "Chongying Duke" "King Tongyuan", etc. Zhenwu Celestial Lord, who had helped unify the country and defend the enemy, was greatly advocated by the emperors of the Song Dynasty, and was awarded "Zhenwu Lord" in the Song Dynasty, "Xuantian God" in the Yuan Dynasty. In the Southern Song Dynasty, Mazu was conferred the titles as many as 13 times, such as "Linghui Lady" and "Linghui Princess", just to name a few. The government of the Yuan Dynasty conferred honorable titles on Mazu 5 times out of the consideration of praying for the smooth sea transportation and ensuring the interests of maritime trade, including the title of "Heavenly Princess". Through continuous imperial conferments, the general beliefs held by the people were promoted to the god of the sea by the imperial court. In the Song and Yuan Dynasties, the worship of the sea gods was included in the national ceremonies which were presided over or attended by officials sent by the imperial court or chief executives of the localities. This officialization of folk beliefs reflects the integration of the formal official maritime trade system and informal folk beliefs, and is an important measure for the Song and Yuan authorities to promote maritime trade with the help of the sea god beliefs. The core of this measure reflects the government's emphasis on Quanzhou's maritime trade, and also manifests the government's effective management of maritime trade, adding a strong official color to these sea god beliefs.

撰文宣传。地方官员除了积极参与海神信仰的祭典活动，还亲自撰文为海神信仰鼓与呼。两次担任泉州知州的真德秀，以泉州最高行政长官的身份，多次为这三位海神专门撰写祝文和祭文，在《西山文集》中收录其《祈风祝文》《通远王祝文》《海神祝文》《海神通远王灵著王祝文》《真武殿祝文》《圣妃宫祝文》《圣妃祝文》等文章，主要内容为祈求肃清海盗、海道畅通、出海平安、风信如期等。这些文章上得以跟神明链接，下得以向百姓广为宣传。可见泉州地方行政长官为促进海外贸易的蓬勃发展，将已植入泉州百姓内心深处的海神信仰，不断加以强化和宣传，使之成为当地人尤其是从事与海洋有关职业人员一种日用而不自知的生活方式。用神权来支持政权，并以此推动海外贸易及增加朝廷收入，这是朝廷多次赐封这些民间神仙并对泉州海神多加推崇的重要原因。

Writing articles for publicity

In addition to active participation in the sea god worshiping activities, local officials also personally wrote articles to advocate the worship of the sea gods. As the highest administrative official of Quanzhou, Zhen Dexiu, who served as the Prefect of Quanzhou twice, wrote special blessings and sacrifices for the three sea gods (or goddess) for many times. In his work *Collected Works of Zhen Xishan*, there were articles such as *Prayers for Favorable Winds*, *Prayers to King Tongyuan*, *Prayers to the Sea Gods*, *Prayers to Zhenwu Hall*, *Prayers to Shengfei (Mazu) Palace*, *Prayers to Shengfei*, etc. The main contents of these articles are to pray for elimination of pirates, smooth passage of the sea, safe sailing and seasonal winds as wished. These articles can connect with the holy gods and be publicized to the common people. It can be seen that in order to promote the prosperity and development of maritime trade, the administrative officials of Quanzhou have continuously strengthened and publicized the sea god beliefs which have been embedded in the hearts of the local people, making it a daily and unconscious lifestyle for them, especially for those engaged in ocean-related occupations. Using theocracy to support the regime, so as to promote maritime trade and increase the revenue of the imperial court is the important reason for the imperial court to confer titles on these folk gods many times and to advocate the sea gods in Quanzhou a lot.

作为世界海洋商贸中心，泉州因地制宜形成一套长期使用并行之有效的制度保障体系，这也是其港口运行与发展的关键保障。宋元时期泉州海外贸易的长期繁荣，正是得益于其特有的制度体系——官方制度与民间规约的相互配合与共同保障，全社会共同发力并形成合力。其中泉州海外贸易官方制度的代表是国家推行的市舶制度，并由此产生社会各界为推行市舶制度的发展而做的各项努力；民间规约的代表是海神信仰，体现了国家意志与民间信仰相结合对海洋贸易的共同推动。这两种制度通过官方主持海神祭典的方式得以结合。市舶司遗址、九日山祈风石刻、德济门遗址、天后宫、真武庙等，是泉州共同保障海外贸易顺利运行的官方和民间制度的建筑与场所，在世界文化遗产“泉州：宋元中国的世界海洋商贸中心”22 处系列遗产中，作为制度保障的代表性物证，反映了官方与民间在推动海洋贸易、促进互惠共赢发展上形成高度共识。

As a World Maritime Trade Center, Quanzhou has formed a set of long used and effective institutional guarantee system according to the local conditions, which is also a key guarantee for the operation and development of Quanzhou Port. The long-term prosperity of Quanzhou's maritime trade during the Song and Yuan Dynasties was due to its unique institutional system, that is, the mutual cooperation and the common protection of the official system and folk regulations, which show the joint efforts of the whole society. Among them the official system of maritime trade in Quanzhou is represented by the maritime trade system implemented by the national government, which has led to various efforts made by all walks of life to promote the development of the system. The representative of the folk regulations is the beliefs in sea gods, which reflects the joint promotion of marine trade by the integration of national will and folk beliefs. The two systems are integrated through the official hosting of the sea god ceremonies. Site of Maritime Trade Office, Jiuri Mountain Wind-Praying Inscriptions, Site of Deji Gate, Tianhou Temple, Zhenwu Temple, etc. are the official and civil institutional buildings and sites that jointly guarantee the smooth operation of maritime trade in Quanzhou. Among the 22-item world cultural heritage series of "Quanzhou: Emporium of the World in Song-Yuan China", they are the representative physical evidence of institutional protection, reflecting a high consensus between the officials and the folks on promoting marine trade and facilitating mutual benefits and win-win development.

九日山祈风祭典。（成冬冬 摄）
Wind-praying ceremony on Jiuri Mountain. (Photo by Cheng Dongdong)

从丰州到泉州——
泉州城市营建及德济门遗址

From Fengzhou to Quanzhou: Quanzhou's Urban Construction and Site of Deji Gate

泉州城市营建历史

History of Urban Construction in Quanzhou

泉州城市建设特点

Features of Quanzhou’s Urban Construction

德济门遗址及其价值

Site of Deji Gate and Its Values

俯瞰泉州古城。（吴云轩 摄）
Bird's eye view of the ancient city of Quanzhou. (Photo by Wu Yunxuan)

德济门在天后宫对面，南面临晋江，是泉州古城的南门。德济门由南宋泉州太守游九功始建于绍定三年（1230），元代进行拓建，明代增建瓮城，清代多次重修加固，沿用至 20 世纪中期，历时 700 余年。2001 年德济门经过考古发掘，现以遗址形态进行展示。作为宋元时期泉州城的南门遗址，德济门遗址记录了宋元泉州城市不断沿江向南部拓展的历史，体现了官方对海洋贸易和城市商业发展的行政保障，是"泉州：宋元中国的世界海洋商贸中心"世界遗产中管理保障的代表性遗产。

Opposite to Tianhou Temple and facing the Jinjiang River in the south, Deji Gate is the south gate of ancient Quanzhou City. It was first built in 1230 by You Jiugong, Prefect of Quanzhou in the Southern Song Dynasty, and was expanded in the Yuan Dynasty. In the Ming Dynasty, a barbican was constructed for the gate, and in the Qing Dynasty, the gate underwent repairs and reinforcements. Up until the middle of the 20th century, the gate remained in regular use, with a history of over 700 years. Deji Gate is displayed in the form of remains after the archaeological excavations in 2001. As the south gate site of Quanzhou City in the Song-Yuan Dynasties, the site of Deji Gate records the history of the continuous southward expansion of Quanzhou City along the Jinjiang River in the Song and Yuan Dynasties, reflecting the government's administrative guarantee for maritime trade and the city's commercial development. It is a representative heritage of administrative function in the world heritage of "Quanzhou: Emporium of the World in Song-Yuan China".

位于天后宫对面的德济门。（傅捷雄 摄）
Deji Gate opposite to Tianhou Temple. (Photo by Fu Jiexiong)

德济门遗址考古出土石构件。（成冬冬 摄）
Archaeologically unearthed stone components at the site of Deji Gate. (Photo by Cheng Dongdong)

泉州城市营建历史

泉州作为中古时期举世闻名的"刺桐城"、东方第一大港的所在地，是一个因港而兴、具有浓厚商业特征的城市，其城市建设与发展，与港口的发展、兴盛息息相关。其开发始于商周时期，三国吴永安三年（260），在今晋江中游北岸丰州建立东安县城，为建安郡九县之一。武周久视元年（700），设置了武荣州，州治从南安丰州移至今泉州古城位置，在衙署前开辟南大街为市场，并开始在治地建城，是为唐城。景云二年（711），武荣州改称泉州，泉州建制自此开始。五代至元代是泉州作为州城快速发展的重要时期。泉州城由唐以前的地区性政治中心，逐渐转变为宋元时期全国最大的港口贸易城市。城市性质的转变、城市经济的繁荣，促使城市建设迅速发展，出现几次大规模的城市改建和扩建：

History of Urban Construction in Quanzhou

As the world-famous "Zayton City" and the location of the largest port in the East in the Middle Ages, Quanzhou is a city with strong commercial characteristics, which prospered because of being a port. Its urban construction and development are closely related to the development and prosperity of the port. Its development began in the Shang (about 1600 B.C.—1046 B.C.) and Zhou (1046 B.C.—256 B.C.) Dynasties. In 260 during the Three Kingdoms Period, Dong'an County was established in Fengzhou, which is on the north bank of the middle reaches of the Jinjiang River. It is one of the nine counties in Jian'an Prefecture. In 700 of the Wu Zhou Dynasty, Wurong Prefecture was established with its government moved from Fengzhou Town of Nan'an County to the current location of ancient Quanzhou City. The South Street was opened up as a market in front of the government office, and a city began to be built in the administrative area, which was so-called "Tangcheng". In 711, Wurong Prefecture was renamed Quanzhou, which marked the establishment of Quanzhou City. It was an important period for the rapid development of Quanzhou as a prefecture from the Five Dynasties Period to the Yuan Dynasty. Quanzhou City gradually transformed from a regional political center before the Tang Dynasty to the largest port city for trade in the country during the Song and Yuan Dynasties. The change in its nature and the economic prosperity of the city prompted the rapid development of urban construction, giving rise to several large-scale urban reconstructions and expansions.

具有 1,300 年历史的西街，见证了泉州的古今繁荣与历史文化。（吴刚强 摄）
With a history of 1,300 years, West Street bears witness to the ancient and modern prosperity as well as history and culture of Quanzhou. (Photo by Wu Gangqiang)

唐代始建子城

公元700年，州治从丰州迁到现址后，开始兴建衙署。作为地方政府办公场所，衙署的建筑相对一般民宅来说更为高大、结实、威严，由此形成衙城。开元六年（718），除了州衙外，开始建成城郭，即在周边的街坊、民居外也建设围墙将其包围起来。贞元九年（793），建六曹都堂（即工、仓、户、兵、法、士等六个部门的办公场所），重修郡城北城墙，古城形制基本完备。唐代末年，王潮、王审邽、王审知三兄弟入闽攻下泉州后，在原来古城之内衙城之外，加筑一道城垣，是为子城。子城周围三里，设有城门四个，即东门行春门、西门肃清门、南门崇阳门和北门泉山门。城市形状根据中国传统建城方式，为规则的四方形。城内有十字街道与四个城门相连通，平时城门打开，可作为城乡交流的重要交通要道，动乱时期，关闭城门，可据城防守。

五代拓建罗城

五代时，随着城市经济发展，人口增长，泉州城也随之进行拓建。先是王延彬于唐天祐年间权知军州事，其妹为西禅寺尼，拓城西地以包寺。五代南唐保大年间，清源军节度使留从效因“泉州城市旧狭窄，至是扩大仁风、通淮等数门，教民间开通衢，构云屋”，将城市向四周扩展，并新建城墙，建成的城墙周长20里，城门由4个增加为7个，原子城四门改为鼓楼。官府还教城内民众开通道路，构建货栈，商住两用街区逐渐形成。这一时期拓建的城池部分，史称“罗城”。

泉山门为唐代泉州子城的北城门。（陈英杰 摄）

Quanshan Gate is the North Gate of Quanzhou Zicheng in the Tang Dynasty. (Photo by Chen Yingjie)

Initial Construction of Zicheng (Minor Wall) in the Tang Dynasty

In 700 of the Tang Dynasty, the construction of the government office began after the prefecture government moved from Fengzhou to the current site. As a local government office, the buildings were relatively taller, stronger, and more majestic than ordinary houses. Thus, a city of government office came into being. In 718, in addition to the government office buildings, the city began to enclose the surrounding neighborhoods and houses with walls, which formed the enceinte of the city. In 793, *Liucao Dutang* (that is, the offices of the six departments which are Works, Warehouses, Revenue, War, Justice, and Scholars) was built, and the northern city wall was rebuilt, which made the ancient city basically complete in shape. At the end of the Tang Dynasty, after the three brothers, Wang Chao, Wang Shengui, and Wang Shenzhi, entered Fujian and conquered Quanzhou, they built additional city walls (i. e. Zicheng) outside the government office buildings and inside the original ancient city, which was 1.5km long with four city gates, namely, Xingchun Gate in the east, Suqing Gate in the west, Chongyang Gate in the south and Quanshan Gate in the north. The shape of the city is a regular square based on the traditional Chinese way of building a city. Inside the city, there are cross streets which are connected to the four city gates. Usually the city gates are open and can be used as an important traffic thoroughfare for urban-rural communications. In times of turmoil, the city gates can be closed for defense.

Expanded Construction of Luocheng (Enveloping Wall) During the Five Dynasties Period

During the Five Dynasties Period, the urban city of Quanzhou expanded in accordance with the economic development and population growth. First, during the Tianyou Period (904—907) of the Tang Dynasty, Wang Yanbin, the Governor of Quanzhou, expanded the city in the west to include Xichan Temple because his younger sister was a nun in the temple. During the Baoda Period (943—957) of the Southern Tang Dynasty, Liu Congxiao, the Military Commissioner of Qingyuan Army, stated, "The gates such as Renfeng Gate and Tonghuai Gate are newly built because the urban city of Quanzhou is still narrow and small. The people are taught to build thoroughfares and construct tall and large houses". He expanded the city around and built a new city wall with a total length of 10km, increasing the four city gates to seven and changing the previous four gates of Zicheng into drum towers. The government also taught the people in the city to build roads and warehouses. The commercial and residential mixed-use blocks were gradually formed. The part of the city expanded during this period was known as Luocheng in history.

宋代改筑罗城、加筑翼城

入宋以后，泉州对罗城进行过多次增筑重修。宋乾德初，清源军节度使陈洪进推动扩城：以城东松湾地建崇福寺，并拓展周边地界。此时泉州城北的东西隅稍宽，城向东北方向突出，形似葫芦，俗号“葫芦城”。元祐二年（1087），朝廷在泉州南城镇南门界外设置市舶司，以便利外商。宣和二年（1120），泉州城由砖城改为石城“外砖内石，基横二丈，高过之”，城垣高度、厚度均得到了提高。南宋，泉州城曾经有六次重修五代罗城。绍兴二年（1132）郡守连南夫主持重修，绍兴十八年（1148）郡守叶廷珪主持重修，并疏浚八卦沟，淳熙、绍熙中，郡守邓祚、张坚、颜师鲁相继对城池加以修缮。嘉定四年（1211），郡守邹应龙号召外国商人捐资，以捐资款项对城墙进行一次较大规模的重修。这一时期，建城技术有很大的进步，在土城垣的内外，以砖石加衬内外壁和基础部分，使得城墙更加坚固结实。南宋泉州的海外贸易持续发展，镇南门内外所谓“南关”，成为番商聚集和交易的主要场所。《晋江县志》引元代庄弥邵《罗城外壕记》：“一城要地，莫盛于南关，诸番琛贾，皆于是乎集。”这一带是宋元时期泉州城对外贸易最繁荣的地方，因在城市的南部，被称为“泉南”或“城南”。

南宋时期针对罗城还有一次大规模的扩建。绍定三年（1230），为了防止水患，太守游九功在各个城门口增筑用砖石砌成拱顶的瓮城门，从西南的临漳门起，沿江筑石城，长 438 丈，高 1 丈有余，基础宽 8 尺，把城南部分包围起来，形成翼城。至此，泉州城画坊八十，百姓安居乐业，人口大幅增长，与福州、广州一起成为浙江以南三个最大的城市。

临漳门是古代泉州古城通往漳州的唯一通道。（傅捷雄 摄）
Linzhang Gate is the only passage from the ancient city of Quanzhou to Zhangzhou in the old days. (Photo by Fu Jiexiong)

Reconstruction of Luocheng and Addition of Yicheng (Affiliated City Walls) in the Song Dynasty

After entering the Song Dynasty, Luocheng was extended and reconstructed many times in Quanzhou. At the beginning of the Qiande Period (963—968) of the Song Dynasty, Chen Hongjin, the Military Commissioner of Qingyuan Army, promoted the expansion of the city, that is, to build Chongfu Temple in the area of Songwan in the east of the city and to expand the surrounding boundaries. At this time, the east and west corners of the northern part of Quanzhou City were slightly wider, and the city protruded to the northeast, which looked like a gourd and was commonly known as "Gourd City". In 1087, the imperial court set up the Maritime Trade Office outside Zhennan Gate of the southern town of Quanzhou to facilitate foreign businessmen. In 1120, Quanzhou was changed from a brick city to a stone city with city walls consisting of bricks outside and stones inside, the base of which was 6.7m wide, and the height more than 6.7m. Both the height and thickness of the city walls have been increased. In the Southern Song Dynasty, reconstructions were carried out six times for Luocheng of the Five Dynasties. In 1132, Prefect Lian Nanfu presided over the reconstruction; in 1148, Prefect Ye Tinggui hosted the reconstruction and dredged the Bagua Ditch; the prefects Deng Zuo, Zhang Jian, and Yan Shilu successively repaired the city walls during the Chunxi Period (1174—1189) and the Shaoxi Period (1190—1194). In 1211, Prefect Zou Yinglong called on foreign businessmen to donate money for a large-scale reconstruction of the city walls. During this period, great progress had been achieved in the technology of city wall construction, that is, to reinforce the earthen city walls with bricks and stones inside, outside and in the foundation parts, which made the city walls stronger. In the Southern Song Dynasty, Quanzhou's maritime trade continued to develop, and the inside and outside areas of Zhennan Gate, known as the "South Gate", became the main place where foreign merchants gathered and made trades. As *Local Chronicles of Jinjiang County* quoted *The Records of the Area Outside Luocheng* by Zhuang Mishao in the Yuan Dynasty, "As a key place in the city, there is none as prosperous as the South Gate where businessmen from many foreign countries gather to make trades." This area was the most prosperous place in the foreign trade of Quanzhou during the Song and Yuan Dynasties. It was known as "Quannan" or "Chengnan" for its location in the south of the city.

There was another large-scale expansion of Luocheng during the Southern Song Dynasty. In order to prevent floods, Prefect You Jiugong added the brick-and-stone arched urn gate to each gate of the city in 1230. Along the Jinjiang River and from Linzhang Gate in the southwest, he built stone city walls of 1,460m long and more than 3.3m high, with the foundation of 2.7m wide. The stone city walls enclosed the southern part of the city to form Yicheng. So far, there were eighty blocks in Quanzhou City where people enjoyed a good and prosperous life and the population increased significantly. Together with Fuzhou and Guangzhou, Quanzhou became the three largest cities to the south of Zhejiang Province.

元代建成鲤鱼形的城垣

至正十二年（1352），因淮西（今安徽省江淮地区）地方武装起义纷起，朝廷命各地州郡修浚城墙，于是监郡偰玉立召集僚属讨论，确定城东、西、北三面仍旧按原来罗城城墙的位置，南面按翼城旧址进行加固拓建，并废罗城之镇南门与通津门，改南门曰德济，又于临漳、德济两门之间增建南薰门。拓修后的城墙高二丈一尺，周围三千九百三十八丈；东西城基广二丈四尺，外墙皆用石头砌筑；南城基广二丈，内外城墙墙基和城门皆用石头砌筑，使城垣更加坚固。此次拓修后泉州城周长达 30 里，奠定了新罗城的规模。城门共有七座，分别为：东门仁风门、西门义成门、南门德济门、北门朝天门、东南侧通淮门、西南临漳门及濒溪水门南薰门。门上各有楼，城门外环以壕沟，壕沟阔三丈七尺，深一丈八尺，可通潮汐。

自此，泉州古城格局基本定型，从城垣工程的规模和质量上来看，是越扩越大，越增越高，越增越厚，材质也越变越坚固。

朝天门为泉州古代七城门之一。（吴云轩 摄）
Chaotian Gate was one of the seven ancient city gates in Quanzhou. (Photo by Wu Yunxuan)

Carp-Shaped City Walls Built in the Yuan Dynasty

Because armed uprisings constantly broke out in Huaixi area (Jianghuai region of Anhui Province nowadays), the imperial court ordered the prefectures and counties to repair the city walls in 1352. So Xie Yuli, Prefect of Quanzhou, convened a discussion with his staff and determined to reinforce and expand the city walls according to the original positions of Luocheng city walls in the east, west and north sides, and the old Yicheng site in the south side. Meanwhile, Zhengnan Gate and Tongjin Gate of Luocheng were abandoned. The South Gate was renamed Deji Gate, between which and Linzhang Gate, Nanxun Gate was added. After the reconstruction and expansion, the city walls were about 7m high, 13km long. The city wall bases in the east and west were about 8m wide, the outer walls of which were built with stones. The city wall base in the south was about 6.7m wide. The bases of the inner and outer city walls, together with the gates, were all built with stones to make the city walls more solid. After this expansion, there were city walls with the perimeter of 15km in Quanzhou City, laying the foundation for a new scale of Luocheng. There were seven gates in total then, namely, Renfeng Gate in the east, Yicheng Gate in the west, Deji Gate in the south, Chaotian Gate in the north, Tonghuai Gate in the southeast, Linzhang Gate in the southwest, and Nanxun Gate beside the river as a water gate. There were towers on each gate, the outer ring of which was surrounded by a moat. The moat was about 12.3m wide, and 6m deep, which was wide and deep enough for the tides to pass through.

Till then, the shape of ancient Quanzhou City was basically finalized. From the perspectives of scale and quality, the city walls were lengthened, heightened, thickened and reinforced in material.

明代加以修缮

入明以后，地方官员也对城墙与城门相继进行修葺。明洪武初，泉州卫指挥同知李山对城垣增高五尺，城基广二丈四尺，内外皆砌石，建六座瓮城、一百四十个窝铺，城门各修筑城楼。又于仁风、通淮之间辟小东门。从清源山上俯瞰全城，因城形似鲤鱼，遂称鲤鱼城，即明代方志学家何乔远《闽书》所记载的："小东门，其门直东湖之嘴，早日初升，湖光潋滟，如鱼饮湖水者然，因号为鲤鱼城。"嘉靖三十七年（1558），倭寇煽乱，对沿海一带城市不断进行骚扰，甚至越来越猖獗，直接拥众直抵泉州城下，于是各个城门日夜戒严，加强守卫。这一年德济门因灾损毁，知府熊汝达重建德济门，又改通淮门为迎春门、南薰门为通津门，并对各个瓮城进行重修，同时重新疏浚外壕沟。当时负责泉州防务的万民英疏浚外壕，使之深阔可通舟楫。万历三十二年（1604），泉州发生大地震，城墙多有损坏，兵备副使姚尚德、知府姜志礼加以修缮，城墙上原有用砖的地方，全部改用以石。

Repairs in the Ming Dynasty

After the ushering in of the Ming Dynasty, local officials also repaired the city walls and gates one after another. At the beginning of the Hongwu Period (1368—1398) in the Ming Dynasty, Li Shan, Sub-Prefect of Quanzhou Defending Military System, increased the city walls in height by about 1.7m, widened the bases at about 8m with stones both in inner and outer city walls, built 6 barbicans and 140 temporary camps, constructed towers on city gates, and opened up a small East Gate between Renfeng Gate and Tonghuai Gate. Overlooked from Qingyuan Mountain, the whole city looks like a carp, so it is also called Carp City. As recorded in *The Book of Min* by He Qiaoyuan, a local chronicler of the Ming Dynasty, "The small East Gate, facing directly the mouth of the East Lake, is like a fish drinking water from the lake which shines with the early sunrise. That's why the city is named Carp City." In 1558, the Japanese pirates instigated riots and continued to harass the cities along Chinese coast. Later, they became more and more rampant and directly swarmed to Quanzhou, so the gates of Quanzhou City was under martial law day and night. In the same year, Deji Gate was damaged due to a disaster. Prefect Xiong Ruda rebuilt Deji Gate, and renamed Tonghuai Gate as Yingchun Gate, Nanxun Gate as Tongjin Gate. He also rebuilt the barbicans and re-dredged the outer trenches. Wan Minying, the official in charge of the defense of Quanzhou then, dredged the outer trenches to make them deep and wide enough for ships. In 1604, a strong earthquake occurred in Quanzhou and destroyed many city walls. In repairing them, Deputy General Yao Shangde and Prefect Jiang Zhili replaced all the original bricks on the city walls with stones.

清代加固城墙

清顺治十五年（1658），提督马德功、兴泉道叶灼棠、知府陈秉直等按照关东式对城垣进行改造，拆补城垣三百八十九丈，周城筑石台，垒垛墙二千三百八十六堵，盖空心炮楼六角，葺城楼六座，炮门炮台一百七十五，开朝天门，瓮城加六尺，因城北羊马墙故址拓翼城四处。康熙十七年（1678），因海寇围城，德济门一带颇多坍塌，知府张仲举、知县沈朝聘重修之。道光十五年（1835），提督马济胜、兴泉永道周凯、知府崇福又率士绅等捐修城垣。至此泉州城内以城墙为基本范围，城下设隅，隅下设铺，铺下设境，即民间所谓的“铺境”，城内共分为东、西、南、北四隅，三十八铺，有街道二十二条、巷子八十六条、集市二十一处。城内主干道有顶、中、下三个十字街，七个城门六条街道可直达周围各县，出城后东可至洛阳江，西到丰州，北到朋山岭，东南可通晋江入海。

Strengthening the City Walls in the Qing Dynasty

In 1658, General-in-Chief Ma Degong, Military Commissioner Ye Zhuotang, and Prefect Chen Bingzhi reconstructed the city walls according to Guandong (Northeast China) style. They demolished and repaired the city walls for about 1,297m. They also built stone platforms around the city walls, along with 2,386 piles of buttress walls, 6 hollow turrets, 6 towers, 175 forts, opened up Chaotian Gate, heightened the barbicans for about 2m, and increased 4 Yicheng along the old site of Yangma Wall (a kind of military defense wall outside the city walls) in the north of the city. In 1678, the pirates sieged and attacked Quanzhou, resulting in much collapse of the city walls in Deji Gate area. Prefect Zhang Zhongju and Magistrate Shen Chaopin rebuilt them. In 1835, General-in-Chief Ma Jisheng, Military Commissioner Zhou Kai, and Prefect Chong Fu called on local gentry to donate to repair the city walls. So far, within the city walls the community in the rank order of "Yu > Pu > Jing" had been formed, with so-called "Pu Jing" system by the folk. There were 4 "Yu"s, East Yu, West Yu, South Yu and North Yu, containing 38 "Pu"s, with 22 streets, 86 alleys and 21 markets inside the city. The main roads in the city included top, middle, and lower crossed streets, on which there were seven city gates and six streets directly leading to the surrounding counties. After leaving the city, people can reach the Luoyangjiang River in the east, Fengzhou in the west, Pengshan Hill in the north, and the Jinjiang River in the southeast which flows into the sea.

民国后拆墙辟路

民国初，随着城市建设的推进，泉州城墙出现残缺不全。20 世纪 20 年代泉州开始拆城辟路，并在城墙的位置修建现代道路。

泉州州城自武周久视元年（700）迁移到现址，至清顺治十五年（1658）对城垣进行改造扩建，900 多年间历经 8 次扩城。现泉州古城范围东至温陵路与城市新区接壤，东北、北、西北均为环城河，西南为晋江，据比例尺为 1：5000 的泉州市区图测算，唐代泉州子城周长 13.2 里（约 6.1 千米），城区面积将近 3 平方千米；唐末五代罗城周围 17.2 里，面积约 4 平方千米；元代定型的翼城周长 23 里，面积约 6.2 平方千米；清代拓翼城，此时环城 24 里，城区面积近 6.8 平方千米。

Disassembling City Walls and Paving Roads During the Republic of China

At the beginning of the Republic of China, with the advancement of urban construction, the city walls of Quanzhou were gradually damaged. In the 1920s, the city walls began to be demolished and modern roads were paved where the city walls were.

Quanzhou City has undergone eight times of expansion in more than 900 years, dating from Quanzhou City's moving to the current location from the year of 700 in the Wu Zhou Dynasty to the rebuilding and expansion of the city walls in 1658 of the Qing Dynasty. Now the ancient city of Quanzhou is bordered by Wenling Road in the east which connects with the new urban area, surrounded by rivers in the northeast, north, and northwest, and by the Jinjiang River in the southwest. According to the map of Quanzhou City with the ratio of 1:5000, it is estimated that the length of Quanzhou Zicheng in the Tang Dynasty is 6.1km long, with an urban area of nearly $3km^2$; the length of Luocheng in the Five Dynasties at the end of the Tang Dynasty is 8.6km long, with an area of about $4km^2$; Yicheng, finalized in the Yuan Dynasty, is 11.5km long, with an area of about $6.2km^2$; the extended Yicheng in the Qing Dynasty is 12km long, with an area of nearly $6.8km^2$.

坪山上的巨型郑成功雕像和山下的泉州城。（陈英杰 摄）
The giant statue of Koxinga (Zheng Chenggong) on Pingshan Hill and Quanzhou City at the foot of the hill. (Photo by Chen Yingjie)

清源山天池。（陈英杰 摄）
The heavenly lake of Qingyuan Mountain. (Photo by Chen Yingjie)

泉州城市建设特点

城市沿江向海发展

泉州在唐代就是全国四大港口城市之一，五代时期第一次大规模扩建，正是在唐代发展基础上的延续。南宋时，泉州一跃成为全国第一对外商贸大港。城市经济的发展和对外贸易的需要，促使泉州多次重修罗城，乃至向南扩建翼城。此后泉州城市规模基本定型，再无大的发展变化。

城市经济发展方向决定了泉州城的发展从规则的矩形到不规则形状。泉州城的建设，共筑有衙城、子城、罗城、翼城等不同时期的城垣。唐代衙城与子城都修筑有相对方正的城垣；五代罗城及宋元时期新拓的翼城，则就地势变化沿江修筑城垣。城市的扩建从晋江北侧的高地向外围扩展，发展方向自西北向东南，自内地向海边，从北边清源山向南边晋江边发展。唐初因海外贸易的需要，州治从丰州迁移到泉州，从晋江中游迁向晋江下游。五代到宋元时期城市经历三次扩大，特别是南宋游九功修翼城，最终使泉州城南扩至晋江江边，而城的东、西、北三面再无大发展，可见泉州城市向南往江海的扩展最为明显。

Features of Quanzhou's Urban Construction

River-Bound and Ocean-Oriented Development of the City

Quanzhou was one of China's four major port cities in the Tang Dynasty. The first large-scale expansion of the city during the Five Dynasties was a continuation of the city's development in the Tang Dynasty. In the Southern Song Dynasty, Quanzhou thrived to become the country's largest foreign trade port. The development of the city's economy as well as the needs of foreign trade prompted Quanzhou to rebuild Luocheng many times and to expand Yicheng southward. Since then, the scale of Quanzhou City has basically been set without any major development or change.

The direction of urban economic development determines the area development of Quanzhou City from a regular rectangle to an irregular shape. The city walls of Yacheng, Zicheng, Luocheng and Yicheng were built in different periods during the construction of Quanzhou City. In the Tang Dynasty, Yacheng and Zicheng were built with relatively square walls. The city walls of Luocheng in the Five Dynasties and the newly developed Yicheng in the Song and Yuan Dynasties were built along the river according to the changes of the terrain. The expansion of the city extended from the highland on the north side of the Jinjiang River to the periphery, from the northwest to the southeast, from the mainland to the coast, and from Qingyuan Mountain in the north to the Jinjiang River in the south. In the early Tang Dynasty, due to the need of maritime trade, the state government moved from Fengzhou to Quanzhou, and from the middle reaches to the lower reaches of the Jinjiang River. From the Five Dynasties to the Song and Yuan Dynasties, the city experienced three times of expansion. Especially in the Southern Song Dynasty, the south of Quanzhou City was expanded to the Jinjiang riverside when Prefect You Jiugong built Yicheng, but there was no more major development in the east, west, and north of the city. It can be seen that the southward, river-bound and ocean-oriented expansion of Quanzhou City is the most evident.

晋江大桥连接着晋江两岸。（陈英杰 摄）
Jinjiang Bridge connecting both sides of the Jinjiang River. (Photo by Chen Yingjie)

城市布局合理、功能齐全

纵观泉州古城内现有历史建筑，虽然自唐至元，泉州城市规模扩大了六倍多，但泉州衙署核心区主要还是集中在西北、东北，即以今东街、西街以北的中部区域为行政区。历代政府衙署等地方管理机构主要分布在这一区域，教育机构也大致分布在这一区域，贡院和县学临近衙门区。翼城兴建后，泉州府学靠近南门，位于古城的中心位置，文运随之兴盛起来。宗教庙宇中，佛教、道教和民间信仰所建的庙宇也主要位于城市中偏北部。东街、西街以南为传统生活区与商业区，唐代商坊在泉州子城十字街以南；五代，商业中心改在东门、涂门；北宋逐渐移到涂门、南门、新门一带；南宋商业区则移到水门、南门一带。城南地区因与海外交通便利，成为泉州最重要的商业核心区，而工业和手工业产业则主要分散在内陆地区，城内仅存一些小型作坊。泉州城市合理的功能分布，使得泉州得以儒商并重，在宋元时期不仅是海滨邹鲁、朱子过化之地，还一跃成为世界级的港口城市。泉州城市的发展明显反映了古代工商业贸易港口城市发展的特点，这一特点在宋代乃至在中国古代的城市发展中都具有重要的代表意义。

泉州府文庙是宋元中国规制最高的州府级文庙。（田米 摄）

Quanzhou Confucian Temple was the prefect-level Confucian temple with the norme superieure in Song-Yuan China. (Photo by Tian Mi)

Appropriate Urban Layout and Comprehensive Functions

Among the existing historical buildings in the ancient city of Quanzhou, it can be found that although the city of Quanzhou has expanded by more than six times from the Tang Dynasty to the Yuan Dynasty, the core area of Quanzhou government office is still distributed mainly in the northwest and northeast, that is, the central area to the north of today's East Street and West Street as the administrative area. Local administrative institutions such as government offices in previous dynasties are mainly distributed in this area, and educational institutions are also roughly distributed here, with former provincial examination hall and county schools close to this administrative district. After the construction of Yicheng, located in the center of the ancient city, the prefectural school of Quanzhou was established close to the South Gate, so the culture prospered accordingly. Among religious temples, those built in Buddhism, Taoism and folk beliefs are also mainly located in the north-central part of the city. Traditionally, to the south of the East Street and the West Street is the living and commercial areas. In the Tang Dynasty the commercial area is to the south of the Cross Street of Zicheng in Quanzhou. In the Five Dynasties, the commercial center shifted to the East Gate and the Tumen Gate, and gradually moved to the area of the Tumen Gate, the South Gate and the New Gate in the Northern Song Dynasty, then to the area of the Water Gate and the South Gate in the Southern Song Dynasty. Thanks to the convenient transportation with overseas countries, the southern part of the city has become the most important core business district of Quanzhou, while the industry and handicrafts are mainly scattered in the inland areas, with only a few small workshops remained in the urban city. The reasonable distribution of different functional areas in Quanzhou City made it possible to attach equal importance to its cultural and business development. During the Song and Yuan Dynasties, Quanzhou became not only a coastal land of rich culture and a place where Zhu Xi lived and taught, but also a world-class port city. The development of Quanzhou City clearly manifests the characteristics of the development of ancient industrial and commercial port cities, which are significantly representative in the city development in the Song Dynasty and even in ancient China.

元妙观是道教传入泉州后所建的第一座道观，也是道教传入福建后的第一座道教宫观。（黄善哲 摄）
Yuanmiao Temple is the first Taoist temple built after the introduction of Taoism both to Quanzhou and to Fujian Province. (Photo by Huang Shanzhe)

城市中多元文化和谐共存

据南宋泉州市舶司提举赵汝适所著《诸蕃志》记载，其时有 58 个海外国家和地区的商人到泉州，大量外国商客集中侨居在泉州城最繁华的城南地区，在城南形成外国人聚居区——番坊。其中有的人通过商贸活动发家致富后定居泉州，在城内建有大型豪华府第，并在城南兴建了多处外来宗教庙宇如清真寺、番佛寺等，在城市东北郊外还有专门的外国人墓葬区。此外在泉州还发现遗留有婆罗门教、印度教、基督教等宗教的石刻。多元文化的和谐共存、共同发展，使泉州出现"市井十洲人""涨海声中万国商"的繁荣景象。

泉州城内随处可见多元文化和谐共处的实证。（傅捷雄 摄）
Evidences of harmonious coexistence of diverse cultures can be seen everywhere in Quanzhou City. (Photo by Fu Jiexiong)

Harmony and Coexistence of Multiple Cultures in the City

As recorded in *Records of Foreign Countries*, a book written by Zhao Rukuo, Supervisor of Quanzhou Maritime Trade Office in the Southern Song Dynasty, businessmen from 58 overseas countries and regions came to Quanzhou at that time, and a large number of foreign merchants inhabited in the most prosperous southern part of Quanzhou City, forming a residential area of foreigners, named *Fanfang* (the lane of foreigners). Some of them settled in Quanzhou after acumulating capital through trade. They built large luxurious houses and many foreign religious temples in the south of the city, such as mosques, *Fanfo* temples (foreign Buddhist temples), etc. There are also burial areas specially for foreigners in the northeast suburbs of the city. In addition, the relics of religious stone carvings of Brahmanism, Hinduism, and Christianity have also been found in Quanzhou. With the harmonious coexistence and common development of multi-cultures, Quanzhou has witnessed the prosperity of "people from all over the world gathering in Quanzhou" and has become "the emporium for worldwide merchants".

泉州城内发现了多种宗教石刻。（成冬冬 摄）
Stone carvings of diverse religions have been found in Quanzhou City. (Photo by Cheng Dongdong)

德济门遗址及其价值

德济门的建造与发展

德济门的建造与发展，与 10—13 世纪泉州海外贸易的繁荣密切相关。当时沿晋江的城南一带，外商云集、商品交易发展繁荣，因而人烟阜盛，但每年江水泛滥时则尽成泽国。南宋绍定三年（1230），郡守游九功于濒江一线建设了兼具防洪功能的城墙，开设两门。其中之一就是位于南端的德济门，这里成为进入城市南部商业区的交通要道。德济门门址在元至正十二年（1352）进行了拓建，明代增建瓮城，清代重修加固瓮城的墙基，沿用至 20 世纪中期。此后，随着泉州近代城市的发展建设，德济门不再使用，又于 1948 年毁于火灾，历时 700 余年。2001 年，经过考古发掘，德济门遗址完整呈现了 13 世纪以来多次营建的遗迹。相关部门现在原址上实施遗址保护措施，并对遗址的历史信息进行了系统的阐释与展示，使这一承载了丰富历史信息的古城门遗址重新呈现在世人面前。

德济门遗址

经考古发掘的德济门遗址由不同时期的遗迹叠合而成。遗址坐北面南，面积近 2,000 平方米，由花岗岩条石、废旧石建筑构件等砌筑而成，局部以白灰灌浆加固。遗存年代涵盖南宋、元、明、清，各时期建筑叠压打破关系基本清晰。遗址由北向南分别由南宋城墙遗迹、内壕沟及古拱桥、元明城墙及城门、明代瓮城、外壕沟等遗迹组成，整体呈现出由北向南扩建的趋势。

德济门遗址是我国现存使用时间最长、面积最大的石构古城门遗址之一。（吴云轩 摄）

Site of Deji Gate is one of the oldest and largest extant sites of ancient stone city gate in China. (Photo by Wu Yunxuan)

Site of Deji Gate and Its Values

Construction and Development of Deji Gate

The construction and development of Deji Gate are closely related to the prosperity of Quanzhou's overseas trade in the 10th—13th centuries. At that time, the southern part of the city along the Jinjiang River was densely populated because many foreign businessmen gathered there for commodity trades, but it was flooded every year when the river overflowed. In 1230 of the Southern Song Dynasty, Prefect You Jiugong built city walls with flood control functions along the riverside and set up two gates, one of which was Deji Gate at the southern end, which became the traffic hub for entering the southern business district of the city. The site of the gate was expanded in 1352 in the Yuan Dynasty. In the Ming Dynasty, a barbican was constructed for the gate, and the wall foundation of which underwent repairs and reinforcement in the Qing Dynasty. Up until the middle of the 20th century, the gate remained in regular use. Since then, with the urban development and construction of Quanzhou in modern times, Deji Gate was no longer in use and was destroyed by fire in 1948, giving it a history of over 700 years. Archaeological excavations in 2001 fully revealed the remains of various phases of construction on the site from the 13th century. Relevant departments are now implementing protection measures on the original site, and have systematically interpreted and displayed the historical information of the site, exposing this ancient city gate site with rich historical information to the world.

Site of Deji Gate

The archaeologically excavated site of Deji Gate is composed of relics from different periods. Facing southwards and covering an area of 2,000m^2, Deji Gate is made of granite slabs and waste stone building components, etc., and partially reinforced with lime grouting. The relics in Deji Gate range from the Southern Song, Yuan, Ming Dynasties to the Qing Dynasty, and the stacks of buildings in each period are basically clear. From north to south, the site consists of the remains of the Southern Song Dynasty city walls, the inner moat and the ancient arch bridges, the city walls and gates of the Yuan Dynasty and the Ming Dynasty, the barbican of the Ming Dynasty, and the outer moat, etc., which shows the trend of expansion from north to south as a whole.

南宋城墙遗址：南宋绍定三年（1230）所建翼城的遗存，沿宋代晋江岸线呈弧状东西向延伸，城墙以南的壕沟在此时已经使用。考古发掘揭露长度 31.5 米，墙宽 7.2—7.6 米，墙体外壁用条石丁顺分层砌筑，墙心填土及少量碎石并稍加夯筑而成。

元代德济门及壕沟：元至正十二年（1352）偰玉立主持建造。遗迹包括东西向城墙基址、壕沟、壕沟北侧石壁以及架于壕沟上的拱桥。壕沟初为宋代城墙南侧的外城壕。元至正十二年南扩城墙至壕沟以南，并改砌壕沟侧壁及沟底，作为内壕沟使用。壕沟考古发掘揭露长度 47.2 米，宽 1.93—2.88 米，深 2.5—2.75 米。壕沟两侧壁由条石丁顺分层砌筑。

明代城墙与瓮城：明洪武初在元代城墙基础上修建城墙及瓮城，现留存城垣、门楼基础、门道、瓮城等遗迹。明代城墙位于宋代城墙及壕沟南侧，东西向延伸，考古发掘揭露长度 43.1 米，残高 0.5—1 米，基宽 4.8—5.45 米。墙体外壁用条石丁顺分层砌筑，墙心填土及少量碎石并稍加夯筑而成。城门门道南窄北宽，平面呈"凸"字形，北端东西两侧保存有城楼墩台遗迹。门道铺架五条石桥板横跨于内壕沟之上。瓮城西墙内侧还保留有清代为加宽和加固明代瓮城而增补的一段城墙。

德济门遗址内还出土了南宋修城官砖、宋元外来宗教石刻、明末"盘诘奸细"石碑、明清铁炮、铁弹丸、古钱币，以及瓦当和瓷器碎片等文物。其中一方古基督教石刻非常特别，石刻一端是基督教的十字架与莲座，另一端刻有伊斯兰教"云月"图案。这可以证明宋元时期泉州政府对各宗教采取兼容并蓄的政策，反映了基督教与伊斯兰教之间融合的现象。

德济门遗址出土的明末"盘诘奸细"石碑以及明清铁炮。（成冬冬 摄）

The stone stele of "Interrogating Enemy Agents" in the late Ming Dynasty and the iron cannons of the Ming and Qing Dynasties unearthed at the Site of Deji Gate. (Photo by Cheng Dongdong)

City wall ruins of the Southern Song Dynasty are the remains of Yicheng built in 1230 of the Southern Song Dynasty. It extends east-west in an arc along the river bank of the Jinjiang River in the Song Dynasty. The trench to the south of the city wall was already in use at this time. Archaeological excavations revealed a length of 31.5m and a width of 7.2—7.6m of the city wall. The outer side of the wall was built with strips of stone in English bond (a pattern formed by laying alternate courses of stretchers and headers), and the core of the wall was stuffed and rammed with earth and a small amount of gravel.

Deji Gate and the moat of the Yuan Dynasty were built under the direction of Prefect Xie Yuli in 1352. The relics include the base of the east-west city wall, the moat, the stone wall on the north side of the moat, and the arch bridge over the moat. The moat was originally the outer trench on the south side of the city wall in the Song Dynasty. In 1352, the city wall was expanded to the south of the trench; at the same time, the side wall and the bottom of the trench were rebuilt to make the trench an inner moat. The archaeological excavation of the moat revealed its length of 47.2m, a width of 1.93—2.88m, and a depth of 2.5—2.75m. The two side walls of the moat were built with strip stones in English bond.

The city wall and the barbican of the Ming Dynasty were built at the beginning of the Hongwu Period (1368—1398) in the Ming Dynasty, whose base is the city wall constructed in the Yuan Dynasty. There are the city wall, foundation of the gate, doorways, barbican and other relics remained. The city wall of the Ming Dynasty extends from east to west on the south side of the city wall and the moat of the Song Dynasty. Archaeological excavations exposed its length of 43.1m, a residual height of 0.5—1m, and a base width of 4.8—5.45m. The outer side of the wall is built with strips of stone in English bond, and the core of the wall is stuffed and rammed with earth and a small amount of gravel. The doorway of the city gate is narrow in the south and wide in the north, appearing in a shape of " 凸 "(convex) from a horizontal perspective. There are ruins of gate tower piers and abutments on the east and west sides of the north end of the doorway. The doorway is paved with 5 stone bridge slabs across the inner moat. On the inner side of the west wall of the barbican, there is still a section of the city wall remained which was added in the Qing Dynasty to widen and strengthen the barbican in the Ming Dynasty.

The Site of Deji Gate also unearthed official bricks for city wall repairing in the Southern Song Dynasty, stone inscriptions of foreign religions in the Song and Yuan Dynasties, stone steles of "Interrogating Enemy Agents" in the late Ming Dynasty, as well as the cultural relics of the Ming and Qing Dynasties, such as iron cannons, iron bullets, ancient coins, eave tiles and porcelain fragments. Among the relics, there is an ancient Christian stone carving which is quite special, with a Christian cross and rosette at one end, and an Islamic "cloud and moon" pattern at the other end. This stands testament to Quanzhou government's inclusive policy towards various religions during the Song and Yuan Dynasties, which leads to the fusion between Christianity and Islam.

德济门壕沟遗址。（陈英杰 摄）
The site of the moat at Deji Gate. (Photo by Chen Yingjie)

德济门遗址的价值

德济门作为泉州古城的南门、沟通城内外的主要通道，其遗址的历史信息非常丰富。通过考古，研究人员发现城门在宋、元、明、清各时期的遗存历史发展脉络清晰，从中可见泉州城市建设发展历史的完整演变过程。德济门考古发掘证实了宋元时期在海洋贸易促进下，在自然和人文因素的影响下，泉州城市不断向南部沿江区域拓展的发展史实，明显反映了宋元以来泉州城南一带在江岸线变迁和海外商贸活动繁盛的共同作用下形成商业区的城市发展轨迹，以及宋元泉州地方政府对海洋贸易和城市商业发展的行政保障。

Values of the Site of Deji Gate

As the South Gate of the ancient city of Quanzhou and the main thoroughfare to connect the inside and outside of the city, Deji Gate contains rich historical information in its site. According to the archaeological excavations, researchers find that there is clear historical development of the city gate relics in the Song, Yuan, Ming and Qing Dynasties, which shows the complete historical evolution process of Quanzhou's urban construction and development. The archaeological excavation of Deji Gate proves the developmental history that under the promotion of maritime trade in the Song and Yuan Dynasties, and with the influence of natural and cultural factors, Quanzhou City continued to expand southward to the riverside. It clearly reflects the urban development route of the commercial district formed in the southern part of Quanzhou City since the Song and Yuan Dynasties under the joint effects of the changing riverside and the prosperous overseas business activities. It also stands testament to Quanzhou's local government's administrative assurance for the development of maritime trade and urban commerce.

毗邻晋江的聚宝街一带曾是泉州对外贸易最集中的地方。（吴云轩 摄）
Adjacent to the Jinjiang River, the area of Jubao Street was once the most concentrated place for Quanzhou's foreign trade. (Photo by Wu Yunxuan)

千帆齐聚刺桐——泉州设立市舶司及其遗址

Thousands of Sails Gathered in Zayton: Establishment of the Maritime Trade Office in Quanzhou and Its Site

市舶司是我国古代国家在特定海港城市设置的专门掌管涉外船舶、对外贸易、征税缉私和接待外国使节等海外贸易事务的行政机构，其基本职能类似于今天的海关。北宋元祐二年（1087），福建路市舶司在泉州设立。其设置标志着泉州正式成为开放的国家对外贸易口岸，对宋元时期泉州的经济繁荣、文化交流以及海洋贸易各参与方的共同发展有至关重要的意义。市舶司遗址于 2019—2022 年进行科学考古发掘，现以遗址形态对外进行展示，在“泉州：宋元中国的世界海洋商贸中心”系列遗产中是海洋贸易管理保障的代表性遗产。

泉州市舶司从设立到迁往福州延续了 400 余年。（陈英杰 摄）
Quanzhou Maritime Trade Office lasted for over 400 years from its establishment to its relocation to Fuzhou. (Photo by Chen Yingjie)

Maritime trade office is an administrative agency set up by the ancient Chinese regimes in a specific port city to manage maritime trade affairs relating to foreign ships, foreign trade, tax collection, anti-smuggling, and reception of foreign envoys. Its basic functions are similar to those of today's customs. In 1087 of the Northern Song Dynasty, Fujian Regional Maritime Trade Office was established in Quanzhou, which marked the official designation of Quanzhou as a national foreign trade port. This was of vital importance to the economic prosperity, cultural exchanges, and the common development of all participants of maritime trade in the Song and Yuan Dynasties. After undergoing an archaeological excavation during 2019 and 2022, Quanzhou Maritime Trade Office is now displayed in the form of a site. It is a representative heritage of marine trade management guarantee in the cultural heritage series of "Quanzhou: Emporium of the World in Song-Yuan China".

市舶司遗址挖掘现场。（王俊 摄）
The excavation site of the Maritime Trade Office. (Photo by Wang Jun)

市舶司机构的历史沿革

“市舶”是中国古代对从事海外贸易商船的统称。市舶司简而言之就是专门管理海外贸易的机构。它在促进古代中国的海外贸易，增进同各贸易往来国人民之间的经济、文化交流，增加国家财政收入等方面都起了重要的作用。

草创于唐代

我国市舶司制度草创于唐代。唐朝出现贞观之治和开元盛世两个社会、政治、经济、文化、贸易空前繁荣的时期，吸引了西域诸国纷纷前来贸易通好。此时，陆上丝绸之路进入全盛时期，海上对外贸易也随之勃兴。为更高效便捷地管理对外贸易的各项事务，唐高宗显庆六年（661）朝廷首次在广州设置市舶使一职。唐玄宗开元十年（722）正式设立市舶使（院），这是我国古代最早设立的专门对海外贸易及番舶进行管理和征缴关税的监察机构。执掌市舶的官员称为市舶使，又称押番舶使或监舶使，当时广州市舶使由岭南节度使兼任。市舶使除掌管海外贸易事务外，还负责涉外事务，故又称“结好使”。唐代市舶使的设置为我国古代市舶制度的建立奠定了基础，此后市舶官制逐渐成为定制。

古代泉州货船模型。（成冬冬 摄
A model of cargo ships in ancient Quanzhou. (Photo by Cheng Dongdong)

Historical Evolution of the Maritime Trade Office

Shibo is the collective name for merchant ships engaged in overseas trade in ancient times. Generally speaking, *Shibosi* (the Maritime Trade Office) is an organization that specializes in the management of overseas trade. This institution played an important role in promoting ancient China's overseas trade, enhancing economic and cultural exchanges with people from various trading countries, and increasing national fiscal revenue, etc.

First Establishment in the Tang Dynasty

The initial period of China's maritime trade administrative system was in the Tang Dynasty, when there were two periods of unprecedented prosperity in society, politics, economy, culture and trade, i.e. Zhenguan Prosperous Era and Kaiyuan Flourishing Age, which attracted many countries in the Western Regions to come for commercial intercourse. At this time, the Silk Road entered its heyday, and maritime trade also flourished accordingly. In order to manage foreign trade affairs more efficiently and conveniently, the imperial court appointed a maritime trade commissioner in Guangzhou City for the first time in 661 during Emperor Gaozong's reign in the Tang Dynasty. In 722, Emperor Xuanzong of the Tang Dynasty officially established Maritime Trade Supervisorate which was the earliest supervisory agency in ancient China to specialize in the management of overseas trade, foreign ships and customs collection. The official in charge of the merchant ships engaged in overseas trade was called Maritime Trade Commissioner, also known as Foreign Trade Supervisor or Shipping Supervisor. At that time, it was the Military Commissioner of Lingnan area (the area to the south of the five mountains in Southern China) who held the concurrent post of the Maritime Trade Commissioner in Guangzhou. Besides overseas trade affairs, the Maritime Trade Commissioner was also responsible for foreign-related affairs, so he was also called Communication Commissioner. The establishment of Maritime Trade Commissioner in the Tang Dynasty laid the foundation for the establishment of the ancient maritime trade management system in our country. Since then, the official system for the maritime trade management has gradually become fixed.

成熟于宋元

宋代海外贸易的收入成为国家不可或缺的重要财源之一，所谓“经费困乏，一切倚办海舶”。所以在管理海外贸易方面，宋代基本承袭唐代的制度，在重要的对外通商口岸设置市舶司：开宝四年（971）在广南东路设置广州市舶司，端拱二年（989）和咸平二年（999）分别在两浙路设置杭州市舶司、明州（今宁波）市舶司，元祐二年（1087）在福建路设置泉州市舶司。南宋乾道二年（1166）撤销杭州市舶司、明州市舶司，只保留广州市舶司和泉州市舶司，这两地市舶司多被合称为“闽广两路舶司”或“泉广市舶司”。市舶使起初由州郡地方官兼领，元丰三年（1080）改由各路转运使兼领。宋徽宗时设置直接隶属户部统辖的专职机构——提举市舶司，其下属机构有市舶务和市舶场。宋代市舶司的职责较之唐代市舶使（院）更加明确，管理制度也更为完备。此外，为加强对海外贸易的管理，元丰三年朝廷出台《广州市舶条》，通过市舶司的查守执行和所在地方官的同行检视，把海外贸易置于政府的严格控制之下。

First Establishment in the Tang Dynasty

The income from overseas trade in the Song Dynasty became one of the indispensable and important financial revenues for the country, so there was a saying that "Maritime trade can be always counted on when lack of funds". Therefore, in terms of managing overseas trade, the imperial court of the Song Dynasty basically inherited the system of the Tang Dynasty, establishing maritime trade offices at important foreign trade ports. In 971, Guangzhou Maritime Trade Office was set up in the East of Guangnan Region (approximately Guangdong Province nowadays); Hangzhou Maritime Trade Office and Mingzhou Maritime Trade Office were set up in Liangzhe Region (approximately Jiangsu Province and Zhejiang Province nowadays) in 989 and 999 respectively; and Quanzhou Maritime Trade Office was set up in Fujian Region in 1087. In 1166 in the Southern Song Dynasty, Hangzhou and Mingzhou Maritime Trade Offices were abolished, and only Guangzhou and Quanzhou Maritime Trade Offices were retained, which were often referred to as "Minguang (Fujian-and-Guangdong) Regional Maritime Trade Offices" or "Quanguang (Quanzhou-and-Guangzhou) Maritime Trade Offices". At the first beginning, the maritime trade commissioners were concurrently held by the local officials of prefectures, but were later transferred to transport commissioners of respective areas in 1080. During Emperor Huizong's reign of the Song Dynasty, a full-time institution directly under the jurisdiction of the Ministry of Revenue was set up, namely, Maritime Trade Superintendency, the subordinate agencies of which included Maritime Trade Affairs and Maritime Trade Market. Compared with that in the Tang Dynasty, the responsibilities of the Maritime Trade Office in the Song Dynasty were more clear, and the administrative system was more complete. What's more, in order to strengthen the management of overseas trade, the imperial court issued *Guangzhou Maritime Trade Regulations* in 1080, which put overseas trade under the strict control of the government through both the inspection of the Maritime Trade Office and the supervision of the local officials.

元代，元世祖忽必烈统一全国后，下诏恢复海外贸易，并沿袭唐宋的市舶司制度，对海外贸易采取鼓励政策。元朝廷在上海、庆元（今宁波）、杭州、澉浦（今嘉兴）、温州、泉州、广州设置后来全国闻名的七大市舶司。朝廷同时推行"官本船"制度，即官府准备船只，提供本钱，委托商人经营的一种官本商办的海外贸易模式，权势之家不得用自己的钱入番为商，否则会被罚没家产。这一制度开创了由国家垄断海外贸易的行业管理模式。至元二十四年（1287），鉴于市舶管理体制日久生弊，朝廷裁冗整治，又增设行泉府司（户部泉府司的派出机构）统领行省镇抚司、市舶司、海道都漕运万户府等涉海管理机构。此后根据对外贸易和各港口的发展状况，市舶司时立时废，至元朝末年，还存有广州、泉州、庆元三个市舶司。为进一步完善市舶管理制度，元朝廷还于至元三十年（1293）正式制定《市舶抽分杂禁》，共二十二条，以按例抽解纳税并系统强化管理为基本原则，同时以法令形式允许包括出海使臣在内的权豪势要从事海外贸易。延祐元年（1314）又在原有基础上进行修订，即《延祐市舶则法》，其内容涉及市舶司的职责、船舶和货物的查验及税收、船舶进出口岸手续的办理，对外籍船只和商人的管理、对走私漏税及官员违法渎职的处罚，以及禁止出口产品等一系列原则性规定。这是我国古代现存最早、最系统的海外贸易单行法规，是对唐宋以来海外贸易管理实践的总结。

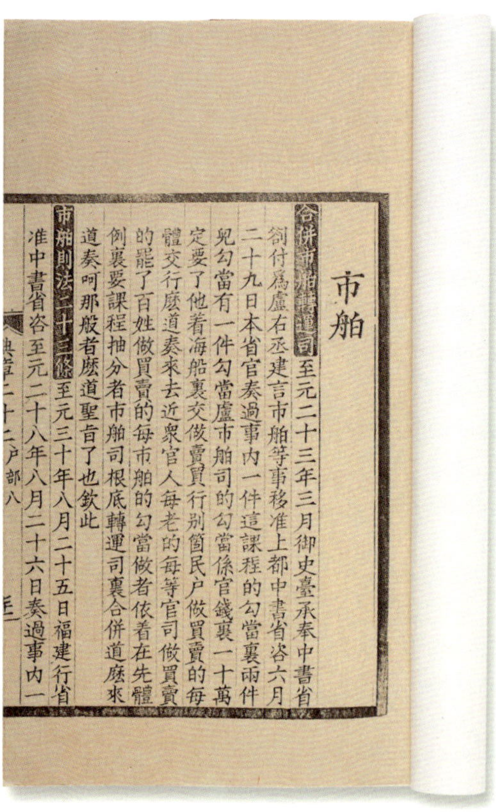
市舶

合併市舶轉運司 至元二十三年三月御史臺承奉中書省劄付爲盧右丞建言市舶等事移准上都中書省咨六月二十九日本省官奏過事內一件這課程的勾當裏兩件兒勾當有一件勾當盧市舶司的勾當係官錢裏一十萬定要了他着海船裏交做賣買行別箇民户做買賣的每體交行麽道奏來去近衆官人每老的每等官司做買賣的罷了百姓做買賣的每市舶的勾當做者依着在先體例裏要課程抽分者市舶司根底轉運司裏合併道麽來道奏呵那般者麽道聖旨了也欽此

市舶則法二十三條 至元三十年八月二十五日福建行省准中書省咨至元二十八年八月二十六日奏過事內一

典章二十二户部八

至元《市舶抽分杂禁》。（黄明珍 供图）

The *Maritime Trade Taxes and Various Prohibitions* in the Zhiyuan Period. (Courtesy of Huang Mingzhen)

In the Yuan Dynasty, Kublai Khan, the first emperor of the Yuan Dynasty, issued an imperial edict to resume overseas trade after unifying the country. Following the system of the maritime trade office in the Tang and Song Dynasties, he adopted an incentive policy for overseas trade. The imperial court of the Yuan Dynasty set up seven maritime trade offices in Shanghai, Qingyuan (Ningbo nowadays), Hangzhou, Ganpu (Jiaxing nowadays), Wenzhou, Quanzhou and Guangzhou, which turned out to be nationwide famous later. At the same time, the imperial court implemented a system of "official ship and capital", that is, an overseas trade mode according to which the government provided ships and capital, then entrusted merchants with overseas trade. Powerful families were not allowed to invest their own money in business in foreign countries, otherwise their property would be confiscated, creating an industry management mode in which the state monopolized overseas trade. In 1287 of the Yuan Dynasty, with the growing disadvantages of the maritime trade management system growing over time, the imperial court implemented redundancy rectification by adding Xingquan Fusi (a dispatched agency of Quan Fusi of the Ministry of Revenue), leading the administrative maritime agencies, such as the Regional Security Department, the Maritime Trade Office, and the Department of Water Transportation. Since then, the maritime trade offices were established or abolished from time to time in accordance with the development of foreign trade in different ports. By the end of the Yuan Dynasty, there were still three maritime trade offices which were in Guangzhou, Quanzhou, and Qingyuan. In order to further improve the management system of maritime trade, in 1293 of the Yuan Dynasty, the imperial court officially formulated the *Maritime Trade Taxes and Various Prohibitions* with a total of 22 articles, taking the tax collection and systematic strengthening of management as the basic principles, and at the same time, in the form of laws and regulations, allowing members of powerful and wealthy clans including the maritime envoys to engage in overseas trade. In 1314, based on the original version, it was revised to be *Yanyou Maritime Trade Regulations*, which covers a series of principles such as the duties of the maritime trade office, the inspection and taxation of ships and goods, the handling of ship entry and exit formalities, the management of foreign ships and merchants, the punishment of smuggling, tax evasion and official malfeasance, and the prohibition of export products. These were the earliest and most systematic specific regulations on overseas trade extant in ancient China, summarizing the overseas trade management practices since the Tang and Song Dynasties.

衰败于明清

明初，因东南沿海海疆不靖，明太祖朱元璋把“海禁”作为基本国策，严格限制海外贸易，申禁濒海之民私自出海与诸番互市。明成祖朱棣为了“示朝廷怀柔之意”，笼络周边国家，实行朝贡贸易制度，相继恢复明州、泉州、广州等地的市舶司。明中后期，沿海倭患不止，海禁愈演愈烈，海外贸易随之衰落。至明末仅存广州市舶司，其职责主要为查验番货进口批文真伪、检查登记船货并征税、监管商品交易、查禁沿海居民通番走私等，与宋元时期的市舶司机构性质已大不同。明初的海禁政策几乎与明王朝相始终，并且为清代所沿袭。

清初为了阻断台湾郑氏集团与大陆的联系，朝廷实行迁海令，沿海地区居民全部内迁 30 至 50 里，片帆不得下海。康熙皇帝收复台湾后，废除迁海令，于康熙二十四年（1685）在镇江、宁波、福州、广州等地设立江、浙、闽、粤海关，市舶司机构至此撤销。

Decline in the Ming and Qing Dynasties

In the early Ming Dynasty, because of the turmoil in the southeast coast, Zhu Yuanzhang, the first emperor of the Ming Dynasty, took the "*Haijin* policy (a ban on maritime activities)" as a basic national policy which strictly restricts overseas trade and prohibits people along the coast from going overseas and making trades with foreigners without permission. In order to "show the conciliation of the imperial court" and gain support from neighboring countries, Zhu Di, the Emperor Chengzu of the Ming Dynasty, implemented the tributary trade system, and successively restored the maritime trade offices in Mingzhou, Quanzhou, and Guangzhou, etc. In the middle and late Ming Dynasty, the ban on maritime activities intensified because of the continuous harassment of coastal Japanese pirates, so overseas trade declined accordingly. By the end of the Ming Dynasty, there was only Guangzhou Maritime Trade Office left, whose main duties were to check the authenticity of the import approval documents of foreign goods, to inspect and register the cargo and collect taxes, to supervise commodity transactions, and to prohibit the smuggling by coastal residents, etc., which was quite different from the nature of the maritime trade office in the Song and Yuan Dynasties. The time span of the *Haijin* policy in the early Ming Dynasty was almost the same as that in the Ming Dynasty, and the policy was followed by the Qing Dynasty.

In the early Qing Dynasty, in order to cut off the connection between Taiwan's Zheng Group (group of armed maritime merchants in southern Fujian and Taiwan led by Koxinga) and the mainland, the imperial court ordered the Great Clearance in Southern China, which involved moving the entire population of the coastal regions inland for 15km to 25km and allowing no sails to go overseas. After Emperor Kangxi regained Taiwan, he abolished the Great Clearance and established Jiangsu, Zhejiang, Fujian, and Guangdong Customs in the cities of Zhenjiang, Ningbo, Fuzhou, and Guangzhou respectively in 1685, and the Maritime Trade Office was revoked so far.

市舶司在泉州设立

位于中国东南沿海的泉州很早就与海外有频繁的交流往来。据唐代《续高僧传》卷一《拘那罗陀传》记载，南朝时期精于大乘佛法的印度高僧拘那罗陀就是通过海路最早到泉州弘法的外国高僧。当时拘那罗陀应梁武帝的邀请，从扶南（今柬埔寨及越南、老挝、泰国的部分地区）泛海到广州，然后到江苏、江西、浙江、福建等地。南陈天嘉二年（561）他又乘小船至梁安郡（今福建南安市），准备换乘大船返回印度。因本地太守及信众的极力挽留，在南安丰州镇等候季风出航时，拘那罗陀在九日山下延福寺译经弘法，开创了泉州佛教与海外交流的先河，留下了"翻经石"等遗迹。以上记载说明当时泉州港已出现了和马来半岛、印度的海上航线。此外，在泉州的考古工作中，考古人员发现了天监十一年（512）铭文、承圣四年（555）铭文及僧侣图案的墓砖。这些僧侣身披袈裟、双手合拢、鼻梁高挺，皆为异域人士模样。这也证明，此时泉州与海外已有较为频繁的交流。

九日山"翻经石"。（成冬冬 摄）
Stone of Sutra Scripture Translation on Jiuri Mountain. (Photo by Cheng Dongdong)

Establishment of the Maritime Trade Office in Quanzhou

Quanzhou, located on the southeast coast of China, has had frequent exchanges with overseas countries for a long time. According to "The Biography of Gunarata" in the volume 1 of *Continued Biographies of Eminent Monks* in the Tang Dynasty, Gunarata, an Indian eminent monk proficient in Mahayana Buddhism during the Southern Dynasty, was the first foreign eminent monk traveling to Quanzhou by sea to propagate Buddhism. At that time, at the invitation of Emperor Wu of the Southern Liang Dynasty, Gunarata traveled across the sea from Funan (Cambodia, and parts of Vietnam, Laos, and Thailand nowadays) to Guangzhou, and then to Jiangsu, Jiangxi, Zhejiang, Fujian, etc. In 561 in the Southern Dynasties, he went to Liang'an County (Nan'an City, Fujian nowadays) by a small boat in order to be shifted to a big ship for returning to India, but the prefect and local believers strived to ask him to stay. While waiting for the monsoon favorable for setting sail in the town of Fengzhou, Gunarata translated Sanskrit sutras and promoted Buddhism at Yanfu Temple at the foot of Jiuri Mountain, pioneering the exchanges of Buddhism between Quanzhou and overseas countries and leaving relics such as "Stone of Sutra Translation". The above records show that at that time there were already sea routes with the Malay Peninsula and India at Quanzhou Port. Besides, in the archaeological excavation of Quanzhou, archaeologists discovered the inscriptions in 512, the inscriptions and the tomb bricks with monk patterns in 555. With hands folded and noses prominent, these monks were dressed in Kasaya and all looked like foreigners. This is a testimony to Quanzhou's frequent exchanges with overseas countries at that time.

唐五代泉州海贸初兴

唐时，随着北方战乱，陆上丝绸之路受阻，向海外寻求发展，因此海上丝绸之路日渐兴盛。泉州凭借地利成为当时全国四大对外交通港口之一，城市随之发展起来，城里已出现“市井十洲人”的热闹场景。大和八年（834）二月，唐文宗下诏，要求包括泉州在内的地方官要经常过问关注海外贸易的相关事务，除了税收、宫廷采买番货、进献贡品外，允许外商自由来往交易，不得重加税率。诏书内容说明朝廷已经注意到泉州的海外贸易情况，要求地方主要官员来管理海外贸易事务。到会昌年间，已出现“秋来海有幽都雁，船到城添外国人”的诗句，泉州已是“南海番舶”常至、“岛夷斯杂”的港口城市。朝廷虽未在泉州设立市舶使，但鉴于泉州海上交通要冲的战略地位，就在泉州设置参军事，掌出使、赞导等职位，管理往来的外使和外商。这些朝廷优待政策的颁布和管理机构的设置，促进泉州海外贸易的进一步发展。

五代时期（907—960），闽国统治者王审知及其后统治泉州的王延彬、留从效和陈洪进等人重视海外贸易，施行“招徕海中蛮夷商贾”“多发蛮舶，以资公用”“尽去繁苛，纵其交易”的政策。1982 年，在泉州开元寺东侧一座宝箧印经塔基座里发现一座八角八面石质的经幢，由时任泉州刺史的王继勋建造于南唐保大四年（946），其中记录了“军事左押衙充海路都指挥使兼御史大夫陈匡俊”“榷利院使刘拯”和“光禄大夫检校尉持节泉州诸军事守泉州刺史御史大夫上柱国琅琊郡开国侯食邑一千户王继勋”等官名和机构。榷利院与同时期吴越的“博易务”、福州的“榷货务”类似，都是专门管理海外贸易的机构，可见五代时期地方统治者对海外贸易的重视。

泉州开元寺大雄宝殿及东侧宝箧印经塔。（陈英杰 摄）
Mahavira Hall and the Ashoka Pagoda on the east side of Quanzhou Kaiyuan Temple. (Photo by Chen Yingjie)

Initial Flourishing of Quanzhou's Maritime Trade in the Tang Dynasty and the Five Dynasties

In the Tang Dynasty, the Silk Road by land was blocked due to the chaos caused by wars in the north. Seeking maritime development, the Maritime Silk Road by sea was flourishing day by day. Taking advantage of its location, Quanzhou developed into one of the four national major foreign transportation ports in the country at that time. The city developed accordingly, in which there was a bustling scene of "people from all over the world". Emperor Wenzong of the Tang Dynasty issued an edict, requiring local officials including those of Quanzhou to frequently pay attention to the matters related to overseas trade in February, 834. Except for taxation, purchase of foreign goods by the imperial court, and tribute offerings, foreign businessmen were allowed to trade freely with low taxes. The imperial edict indicates that the imperial court requires the leading local officials to manage the overseas trade affairs in Quanzhou after noticing the situation of Quanzhou's overseas trade. By the time of the Huichang Period (841—846), as depicted in the poem "There are wild geese flying from the north towards the sea when autumn comes; there are foreigners coming to the city when ships arrive", Quanzhou had become a port city "frequently visited by foreign ships from the southern countries" and "inhabited by various foreigners and islanders". Although the imperial court had not set up a maritime trade commissioner in Quanzhou, in view of Quanzhou's strategic position as a maritime transport hub, staff officers were appointed to act as ambassadors and ceremony directors, managing overseas envoys and merchants. The promulgation of these imperial court's preferential policies and the establishment of the management institutions promoted the further development of Quanzhou's maritime trade.

During the Five Dynasties, Wang Shenzhi, the ruler of the empire of Min (mostly Fujian Province nowadays), and Wang Yanbin, Liu Congxiao, and Chen Hongjin, who ruled Quanzhou later, all attached great importance to overseas trade, and implemented the policies of "summoning merchants from the barbarian lands overseas", "sending more ships overseas for funding utilities", and "eliminating exorbitant taxes and levies and motivating trades". In 1982, an octagonal and octahedral stone sutra pillar was found at the base of the Ashoka Pagoda on the east side of Kaiyuan Temple. The stone sutra pillar was built by Wang Jixun, Prefect of Quanzhou at that time, in 946 of the Southern Tang Dynasty, where there are records of several official titles and institutions such as "Chen Kuangjun, Military, Maritime Commander and Concurrently Assistant Prime Minister", "Liu Zheng, Official of Maritime Trade Office", and "Wang Jixun, Grand Master for Splendid Happiness, the Prefect of Quanzhou, Censor-in-Chief, Dynasty-Founding Marquis of Langya County, Petty Tribal Chieftain". Similar to "Boyiwu" (Goods Exchange Institution) of Wuyue Kingdom (907—978) and "Quehuowu" (Monopoly Tax Commission) of Fuzhou in the same period, "Queliyuan" (Deliberating Academy) was an institution specializing in the management of overseas trade. This reflects local rulers' great emphasis on overseas trade in the Five Dynasties.

宋元海贸昌盛、地位凸显

宋代，海舶商人出海前，必须在所在州府提交申请，向市舶司详细呈报所载人、船、货物及目的地，并由本地殷实之户作保。市舶司经验查核实后，发给海商“公凭”（亦称公据），即为出海贸易许可证。据北宋崇宁四年（1105）的李充公凭可知，舶商在申请公凭时，被严厉告知：不许兴贩兵器、女人、奸细、逃亡军人，到海外经商的船舶，不得逃避税收，如有违者，船上货物没收，纲首、杂事、部领、艄公都要判刑两年。船舶临出发前，政府还要委派和市舶没有关系的官员前往检查核实，一经发现非法夹带者，将给予程度不等的处罚以至判刑。海商归国时，应将公凭上缴市舶司。市舶司就地抽解，征收市舶税。在泉州未设市舶司前，泉州船舶凡要出海经商，南下出航者须到广州市舶司呈报，领取“公凭”后才能出海，回航时也要在广州市舶司办理抽解（纳税）手续后才能把货物运回泉州；北上出航者则须到明州市舶司办理同样手续。此为宋代市舶管理制度的主要内容和一项重要的财政收入。

随着泉州海外贸易的不断发展，宋熙宁五年（1072），有臣僚请于泉州设置市舶司，宋神宗下诏让发运使薛向“创法讲求之”（也即建立制度实施），因遭反对而作罢。两年后的正月初一，朝廷下诏泉州、福州等沿海各州有南番海南的货物航船到达，应取公据验认。如已抽买税务并给到回引则放行，否则押赴附近市舶司勘验抽买，这说明泉州实际上已经获得了市舶司的部分权利。元丰三年（1080），泉州知州陈偁上疏指出：泉州不设市舶司，对泉州海商极为不利，也影响朝廷的财政收入，陈请在泉州设司，但上级没有上报其奏疏。元祐二年（1087）十月初六，在户部尚书李常的建议下，泉州正式设置市舶司。但这并不是一劳永逸，而是几经周折。由于朝廷政策的变化，泉州市舶司后又几经罢免，但旋即又恢复设置。大观三年（1109）七月二十日，泉州与两浙市舶司同时被罢废，归提举常平官兼摄，通判管理。政和二年（1112）五月二十四日，朝廷允福建路提点刑狱邵涛所奏请，泉州与两浙市舶司同时恢复旧制。建炎元年（1127）六月十三日，朝廷责市舶司多以无用之物、枉费国用、取悦权近，又于十四日罢泉州、两浙市舶司，并归转运司。次年五月二十四日，又因并废市舶司以来，士人不便，亏失数多，恢复泉州、两浙市舶司。

Prosperous Maritime Trade and Prominent Status of Quanzhou in the Song and Yuan Dynasties

In the Song Dynasty, before going overseas, maritime merchants had to register in the local prefectural government, report in detail to the Maritime Trade Office the men on board, ships, cargoes and destinations, and be guaranteed by local well-off households. After inspected and verified by the Maritime Trade Office, they would be issued an "official certificate" (also known as official receipt), which was the maritime trade license. According to the official certificate of a merchant named Li Chong in 1105 of the Northern Song Dynasty, it can be seen that when applying for the certificate, merchants were seriously informed that they were not allowed to peddle weapons, women, spies and fugitive soldiers. Merchant ships doing business overseas were not allowed to evade taxes. In case of violation, the cargoes on the ships would be confiscated, and the captain, support staff, department leaders, and boatmen would be sentenced to two years' imprisonment. Prior to the departure, the government would appoint officials who had nothing to do with the maritime trade to inspect and verify the ship. Once illegal entrainment was found, the merchants would be punished to varying degrees and even be sentenced. When maritime traders returned to the country, they should hand over the official certificate to the Maritime Trade Office which would *choujie* on the spot, that is, collect the maritime trade tax. Before the establishment of the Maritime Trade Office in Quanzhou, all the southbound merchant ships for overseas business had to report to Guangzhou Maritime Trade Office to get the official certificate before going overseas when returning, they must also go through the taxing procedures in Guangzhou Maritime Trade Office before shipping the cargo back to Quanzhou. Those who sailed northward should go through the same formalities at Mingzhou (Ningbo nowadays) Maritime Trade Office. These were the main contents for the maritime trade management system and the tax was an important source of fiscal revenue in the Song Dynasty.

With the continuous development and considerable profits of Quanzhou's overseas trade, in 1072 of the Song Dynasty, some officials petitioned to establish a maritime trade office in Quanzhou. Emperor Shenzong ordered Xue Xiang, the Transport Commissioner, to "build a viable system", which was opposed by other officials and finally turned out to be futile. Two years later, on the first day of the first lunar month, the imperial court issued an edict that there should be official certificate verification on the arrival of the cargo ships from the southern foreign countries to the coastal prefectures like Quanzhou, Fuzhou, etc. If they have been taxed and given the receipts, they can be permitted to pass through; otherwise, they will be escorted to the nearby Maritime Trade Office for taxation and verification. This indicates that Quanzhou has actually obtained part of the rights of the maritime trade office. In 1080, Chen Cheng, Magistrate of Quanzhou, reported that the absence of a maritime trade office in Quanzhou was extremely unfavorable and inconvenient not only to Quanzhou maritime merchants but also to the fiscal revenue of the imperial court. He sincerely requested to establish a maritime trade office in Quanzhou, but his superiors did not report it upward. On lunar October 6, 1087, at the suggestion of Li Chang, the Minister of Revenue, the Maritime Trade Office was officially established in Quanzhou, although which did not happen once and for all, but after several setbacks. During this period, Quanzhou Maritime Trade Office was dismissed several times due to the changes of the imperial court's policies, but after that it was restored once again. For example, on lunar July 20, 1109, Quanzhou and Liangzhe Maritime Trade Offices were dismissed at the same time, and the affairs were managed by the assistant sub-prefect who concurrently held the post of maritime trade supervisorate. On lunar May 24, 1112, at the request of Shao Tao, the Penal Superintendent of Fujian Region, the imperial court agreed to restore both Quanzhou and Liangzhe Maritime Trade Offices. On lunar June 13, 1127, the imperial court condemned the maritime trade offices for wasting national expenditure to buy useless goods to bribe the authority and powerful people, which was a waste of the court's money. Then, on lunar June 14, Quanzhou and Liangzhe Maritime Trade Offices were dismissed and the management affairs were shifted to the Transport Commissions. However, on lunar May 24, 1128, Quanzhou and Liangzhe Maritime Trade Offices were restored because it had been inconvenient for both scholar-officials and common people and there had been great financial loss since the abolishment of the maritime trade offices.

绍兴二十一年（1151）闰四月初四日，右中奉大夫直显谟阁知抚州李庄任提举泉州市舶一职。高宗皇帝认为提举市舶官员责任重大，如果委任非人，则措置失当，海商不至，由此可见当时朝廷对市舶司官员的任命是很慎重的。泉州市舶司的设立及其市舶管理制度的相对完善，保障了泉州地区海外贸易的有序开展。据载，南宋绍兴末年泉州港的市舶收入，每年在百万缗（一缗约一千文）上下，约占朝廷年财政收入的2.5%。宋高宗一再强调市舶有助于国用，且对中外商贾及市舶司有功官吏进行奖励，来贩外商有特殊贡献者，甚至加官晋爵。如绍兴六年（1136）泉州番船纲首蔡景芳，因招诱贩到货物，从建炎元年（1127）到绍兴四年（1134）七年的时间中，收净利钱九十八万余贯；另一位叫啰辛的大食商贾，因所贩乳香值三十万缗，也补授为承信郎。这些都是“承信郎”这个官职用来奖励招徕外商有功或海贸获利丰厚、给国家带来大量经济收入之人的极明显例证。

On the 4th day of leap April in 1151, Li Zhuang, Right Grand Master for Palace Attendance and Department Magistrate, took the position of Supervisor of Quanzhou Maritime Trade Office. Emperor Gaozong believed that it was crucial to appoint a qualified official for a maritime trade office. Otherwise, it would lead to serious consequences including no maritime merchants coming. It can be seen that the imperial court was very cautious in appointing officials of the maritime trade offices at that time. The establishment of Quanzhou Maritime Trade Office and its relative sound management system ensured the orderly development of overseas trade in Quanzhou area. According to the records, in the last years of the Shaoxing Period in the Southern Song Dynasty, the revenue from maritime trade at Quanzhou Port was one million *min* of copper coins annually, accounting for about 2.5% of the annual fiscal revenue of the court. Emperor Gaozong repeatedly emphasized the benefits of maritime trade to the national funds. He rewarded Chinese and foreign maritime merchants and the meritorious officials of the maritime trade offices, and even conferred official positions to those foreign merchants who have made special contributions. For example, in 1136, Cai Jingfang, the head of foreign freight fleets, received a net profit of more than 980 thousand *guan* of copper coins during the seven years from 1127 to 1134 due to the solicitation of maritime goods. Another one was an Arabic merchant named Luo Xin, who sold the mastix worth 300 thousand *min* of copper coins. Both of them were granted the official positions of Chengxin Councillor for their special contributions. These are obvious examples of the official positions like Chengxin Councillor used to reward those who have done meritorious work in attracting foreign investors or have made huge profits in maritime trade, or have brought large economic revenue to the country.

元代，朝廷高度重视泉州市舶司，其市舶管理制度不断完善。东南沿海的战事尚未结束，朝廷便于至元十四年（1277）下令首先在泉州设置市舶提举司。至元十八年（1281）朝廷又规定商贾市舶经泉州市舶司抽分后到其他地方进行贸易，只需要输税，不用再抽分。至元二十一年（1284）九月，将市舶司并入盐运司，立福建等处盐课市舶都转运司。同年，在杭州、泉州设市舶都转运司，施行"官本船"制，即官方自具舶给本，选人入番贸易诸货，所获以十分为率，官取其七，所易之人得其三。至元二十三年（1286）八月，朝廷以市舶司拨属泉府司，十二月复置泉州市舶提举司。之后朝廷下令市舶司按统一标准对舶货进行抽分，同时裁撤前代设置的禁榷、博买，设立征收现钱的舶税：粗货十五分取一分，细货十分取一分之外，又取三十分之一为税。舶税在泉州首先实施后，朝廷下令以泉州为定制，至元三十年（1293）推广到其他各市舶司。虽然市舶司在泉州几经罢废、复立，但因地理位置的重要性和海外贸易的成熟发展，它已成为政府招徕外商、组织海外贸易（尤其是与南海诸国交通贸易）的中心，泉州港进入其历史上的黄金时代。

In the Yuan Dynasty, the imperial court attached great importance to Quanzhou Maritime Trade Office, which continuously improved its management system. Before the war on the southeast coast was over, the imperial court ordered to first establish Supervisorate of the Maritime Trade in Quanzhou in 1277. In 1281, it was stipulated that after being taxed by Quanzhou Maritime Trade Office, the merchant ships would not need to be taxed on goods again when moving to other places for trade. In lunar September of 1284, Maritime Trade Office was merged into Salt Distribution Commission, and Salt Maritime Trade and Transport Commission was established in places like Fujian. In the same year, Maritime Trade and Transport Commissions were set up in Hangzhou and Quanzhou, and a policy of "Official Capital and Ship" was implemented, that is, the government provided the ships and capital, and selected some agents to sail to foreign countries for goods trade. The government would take 70% of the profit and the traders will keep 30%. In lunar August of 1286, the Maritime Trade Office was allocated to Quanfusi, and in lunar December, Quanzhou Maritime Trade Office was restored. Afterwards, the imperial court ordered the Maritime Trade Office to collect tax (known as *choufen*) according to a unified standard, and simultaneously removed the policy of *jinque* and *bomai* (official trade) set up by the previous dynasty, and established a maritime trade tax system which collected cash. The maritime trade tax system was first implemented in Quanzhou, which means collecting one-fifteenth of the profits of the cheap and plain goods, one-tenth of the delicate and fine commodities, and an extra one-thirtieth of the total as taxes. The imperial court promulgated the maritime trade tax in Quanzhou to be the standard and extended it to other maritime trade offices in 1293. Although Quanzhou Maritime Trade Office was abolished and re-established several times, Quanzhou, due to the importance of its geographical location and its mature development of overseas trade, had become the hub for the government to attract foreign investors, organize maritime trade, and especially transport to and make trade with the countries in the South China Sea. Quanzhou Port ushered in a golden era in its history.

明代后没落

因明朝的国策，明洪武三年（1370）朝廷设宁波、广州、泉州三市舶司，规定泉州通琉球，宁波通日本，广州通占城、暹罗、西洋诸国。泉州对外贸易航线的规模和范围大大缩小。至成化八年（1472），泉州市舶司机构迁往福州，完成其历史使命。

在前后近400年的时间里，泉州市舶司见证了泉州港海外贸易的繁荣、极盛和衰退。（陈英杰 摄）

Lasting for nearly 400 years, Quanzhou Maritime Trade Office has witnessed the prosperity,heyday and decline of the maritime trade in Quanzhou Port. (Photo by Chen Yingjie)

Falling after the Ming Dynasty

According to the national policy, three maritime trade offices were established respectively in Ningbo, Guangzhou and Quanzhou in 1370 of the Ming Dynasty. It was stipulated that Quanzhou could only trade with the Ryukyu Islands; Ningbo could only trade with Japan; and Guangzhou could only trade with Champa, Siam and Western countries. In this case, Quanzhou's foreign trade routes were greatly shortened. In 1472, Quanzhou Maritime Trade Office was transferred to Fuzhou, which marked the termination of its historical mission.

泉州市舶司的官员及职能

据《宋会要辑稿·职官》记载，市舶司的职责主要是："掌番货、海舶、征榷、贸易之事，以来远人，通远物。"通俗说来，就是主要承担发放商贸许可、查验商船、征收关税、代表官方采购舶货、储存或出售征得的货品、转运货品或货币至都城、接待外国使节等职责。南宋专置提举制下，市舶司设官员四名，分别为市舶提举司提举（市舶司的首长）、市舶监官（主管抽买舶货，收支钱物等）、勾当公事（主持市舶司的日常事务）、监门官（主管市舶库）。吏十一位，分管文字、孔目、手分、贴司、书表、都吏、专库、专秤、客司、前行、后行等负责具体日常事务。市舶司的职能主要是经济管理和行政管理两大类。

Officials and Functions of Quanzhou Maritime Trade Office

As stated in "The Officials" of *The Compilation of the Manuscripts of National Decrees and Regulations in the Song Dynasty*, the main duties of the Maritime Trade Office are "managing the affairs of foreign goods, maritime shipping, collecting taxes and making trades in order to attract foreigners to come and exchange commodities". Generally speaking, the Maritime Trade Office is mainly responsible for issuing trade licences, inspecting merchant ships, collecting tariffs, purchasing foreign goods on behalf of the government, storing or selling the collected goods, transshipping goods or currencies to the capital city, and receiving foreign envoys, etc. Under the system of supervisorate specially set in the Southern Song Dynasty, there are four officials in the Maritime Trade Office, namely, Inspector of the Maritime Trade Superintendency (the head of the maritime trade office), Supervisorate of the Maritime Trade (in charge of taxes from maritime goods, revenues and expenditures, etc.), Administrator of Public Affairs (in charge of the daily affairs of the Maritime Trade Office) and Supervisor of the Maritime Trade Storehouse (in charge of the storehouses). There are eleven minor officials who are in charge of specific daily affairs including document management, officials services, official document administration, etc. The functions of the Maritime Trade Office are mainly economic management and administrative management.

经济管理职能主要有：

阅货：当外国商船进入中国海域，市舶司官员及其他官员一同对装载货物进行检阅。

抽解：就是对船舶运来的诸国货物进行征税，又称"抽分"或"抽税"。抽解之后，舶货才可进行交易。

禁榷：即专买专卖。市舶禁榷制度是对舶货中宝贵、稀有的物品实行的专买专卖制度。北宋初年，普遍对舶货实行禁榷，由市舶司收购，并规定了严厉的禁榷刑律。

和买（博买）：海外贸易的舶货到岸后，禁榷品全由市舶司收购，其他货物除按比例抽解之外，市舶司还要将其中的宝货进行部分收买，称为"博买"。

解送（纲运）：舶货的解送任务在宋前期由朝廷特派使臣来完成，后来舶货解送的任务归到转运司管辖。专职市舶司提举设置后，解送之事归市舶司直接掌管。

行政管理职能主要有：

监察荐举：市舶司作为路一级政府机构中的一部分，属于宋代地方监司的组成部分。因而它具有互察职能，即监督本路各官员，同时还能监督下一级官员。另外，市舶司官员还有荐举官员的职权。

发放公据：公据，即宋代政府发放给进出口海舶的贸易许可证。舶商出海前，必须向市舶司呈报所有船员的姓名，所载货物的数量及目的地，并由所在州出富户三人作保，经验实后，市舶司发给公凭。船舶回舶之日，需将公凭呈交于原发舶之市舶司，并在此处抽解纳税。

执行禁令：市舶司规定船舶解缆前，由市舶司官员、转运司官员和另一名与市舶职事无关的官员"不干碍官"共同临场检查。船舶放行后，检查官员还须继续监视，直至船舶远离港口入洋面，以防止铜钱私装或海上铜钱走私。

管理番商：代表政府行使管理权，由番长传达官府政令，处理番坊的日常政事，管理外籍居民；协助官府管理港口的对外贸易；作为官府与海外商人之间的联系人，负责招徕海商；协助办理外交事务，促进中外双方政府之间的交流。

主持仪典：市舶司官员会到九日山进行祈风仪式，祈风以求航海平安。

The main economic management functions are as follows:

Cargo inspection: When a foreign merchant ship enters the waters of China, the officials of the Maritime Trade Office and other officials will inspect its cargo.

Choujie: It is to levy taxes on goods brought in by ships from various countries, also known as "*choufen*" or "*choushui*". The goods can be traded only after being taxed.

Jinque: It means officially monopolized buying and selling. The policy of *jinque* in maritime trade is a monopoly system for the exclusive purchase and sale of valuable and rare items among the shipping cargo. In the early years of the Northern Song Dynasty, shipping goods, purchased by the Maritime Trade Office, were generally monopolized, for which strict criminal laws of *jinque* were stipulated.

Hemai (*Bomai*): After the overseas trade goods arrive at the shore, all the monopolies will be taken over by the Maritime Trade Office. Other goods will be taxed according to a certain ratio. Besides this, some other valuable goods will also be purchased by the Maritime Trade Office, which is called *"bomai"*.

Jiesong (escorting and shipment): The transportation of maritime goods is completed by the specially appointed imperial envoy in the early Song Dynasty, and is later transferred to the Transport Department. After the establishment of the Maritime Trade Superintendency, the task of despatching cargo is charged by the Maritime Trade Office.

The main administrative management functions are as follows:

Supervision and recommendation: As a part of the province-level government agencies, Maritime Trade Office is an integral part of the local supervisory office in the Song Dynasty. Therefore, it has the function of mutual supervision, that is, to supervise the officials at the provincial level and below. What's more, the officials of the Maritime Trade Office also have the authority to propose officials for promotion.

Issue of official permit: Official permit is a trade license issued by the Song Dynasty government to the import and export ships. Before going overseas, maritime merchants have to report to the office in detail the crew list, the quantity of cargo and the destination, and be guaranteed by three well-off local households. After inspection and verification by the Maritime Trade Office, they will be issued an "official permit". On the date of return, the official permit must be submitted to the original Maritime Trade Office where the tax will be collected.

Enforcement of the prohibition: The Maritime Trade Office stipulates that before untying the rope and setting off, an on-site inspection will be jointly conducted by officials from the Maritime Trade Office, officials from the Transportation Commission, and another "non-interference official" who has nothing to do with the maritime affairs. After the ship is permitted to pass through, inspection officials shall continue to track its movements until the ship is far away from the port and enters the ocean so as to prevent illegal loading of copper coins or smuggling of copper coins at sea.

Management of foreign merchants: The Maritime Trade Office exercises its right of management on behalf of the government, conveying official decrees through the head of *Fanfang* (the lane of foreigners), handling daily government affairs of *Fanfang*, managing foreign residents, and assisting the government to manage foreign trade of the port. As an agent between the government and overseas businessmen, the Maritime Trade Office is responsible for attracting maritime merchants, assisting in handling foreign affairs, and facilitating communications between Chinese and foreign governments.

Presiding over ceremonies: The officials of the Maritime Trade Office will go to Jiuri Mountain to pray for the wind favorable for safe trip.

市舶司官员及其主持仪典的活动，在九日山摩崖石刻上有较为完整的记载："知州事方谷正叔、提举市舶章炳文叔虎、新下邳令林深之原叔同游，崇宁三年八月初辭。"这方石刻记载了1104年担任福建路市舶提举司提举的章炳文与知州方谷、下邳知县林深之同游九日山的事件。

泉州市舶司遗址

市舶司遗址

据明代《八闽通志》所记，泉州市舶司具体的地理位置"在府治南水仙门内旧市舶务址…… 南薰门，在旧市舶司之旁"。南薰门即水仙门，简称水门。这说明历史上的市舶司大致就在今泉州古城南部，南薰门内、镇南门外，其西侧临翼城城墙旧址，西北侧有水沟通达城市的城壕与晋江水系，东侧可通往镇南门。市舶司管理机构在此长达近400年，曾有清芬亭、仓库等配套建筑。市舶司迁至福州后，市舶司在泉州的原址已逐渐为民居和其他公共建筑所覆盖。

泉州市舶司遗址出土陶瓷器。（成冬冬 摄）
Ceramics excavated from the site of Quanzhou Maritime Trade Office. (Photo by Cheng Dongdong)

There are relatively complete records of the officials of the Maritime Trade Office and their presiding over ceremonies in the stone inscriptions on the cliff surfaces of Juri Mountain. For example, "Fang Gu, courtesy name Zhengshu, Prefect of Quanzhou Prefecture, Zhang Bingwen, courtesy name Shuhu, Inspector of Maritime Trade Superintendency, and Lin Shenzhi, newly assigned District Magistrate of Xiapi County, courtesy name Yuanshu, traveled together in early August of 1104". This stone inscription records these three officials' trip to Juri Mountain.

Site of Quanzhou Maritime Trade Office

Site of the Maritime Trade Office

According to *A General Gazetteer of Fujian* written in the Ming Dynasty, the specific geographical location of Quanzhou Maritime Trade Office is in the site of the Maritime Trade Affairs which is situated near Narcissus Gate to the south of the government office and Nanxun Gate is near the site of the Maritime Trade Office. Nanxun Gate is also called Narcissus Gate, or Shuimen for short. It indicates that the Maritime Trade Office in history is roughly located in the south of the ancient city of Quanzhou today, inside Nanxun Gate and outside Zhennan Gate. Its west side is adjacent to the former site of Yicheng City Wall; the northwest side is connected with the trench and the Jinjiang River system of the city through ditches, and the east side is connected with Zhennan Gate. As a management organization, the Maritime Trade Office has been here for nearly 400 years in Quanzhou, and there used to be matching buildings such as Qingfen Pavilion and warehouses. After being transferred to Fuzhou, the site of Quanzhou Maritime Trade Office has gradually been covered by residential buildings and other public buildings.

市舶司遗址旁有水门和南薰门两处水关，用来调节水流和管理舟楫的出入。市舶司建立以后，凡涉外贸易往来的船只货物，均可在江口码头更换小船，溯晋江而上，沿着破腹沟、通过水关，进入壕沟直达市舶司报关。遗址旁建有水仙宫，20 世纪 80 年代在水仙宫旁设立泉州市舶司遗址保护碑，在宫内还设置了泉州市舶司的专题展览。遗址范围内尚保留有舶司库巷、马坂巷等包含历史信息的地名。2019—2021 年，中国社科院考古研究所、福建博物院、泉州市海上丝绸之路申遗中心联合组成泉州城考古工作队对泉州市舶司遗址进行科学考古发掘。在 2019 年首次的考古发掘中，发现了泉州宋元市舶司遗址相关的铺砖地面和铺石等建筑遗迹，以及建筑构件、陶瓷器等出土遗物。2020 年第二次发掘揭露出了暗渠、石墙、石墩、铺砖地面、鹅卵石铺面、基槽、古井等宋元时期建筑基址相关遗迹，出土有脊兽、花卉纹瓦当等建筑构件和青瓷、卵白釉瓷器等陶瓷器。考古遗迹及出土器物都表明这里是一处宋元时期较高等级的大型官式建筑群。而一侧印有"（监）造市舶亭蒲"字样的铭文砖的发现，则进一步佐证了该建筑群就是泉州市舶司遗址。这里不仅出现了"市舶"两个字，还出现了一个姓蒲的人名。此人极有可能是蒲寿庚的家族成员，而蒲寿庚是元代"提举泉州舶司，擅番舶利者三十年"的阿拉伯裔海商。

根据历史文献记载，宋元时期市舶司提举的品级不超过从五品。与泉州市舶司同一级别的宁波市舶司遗址经考古确认，遗址范围约为 12,000 平方米。通过这一系列的考古调查和发掘工作，结合泉州市舶司遗址周围水系、道路的构成等因素，考古学者推测泉州市舶司遗址的范围大致是马坂巷、八卦沟、竹街、水门巷围合的这一区域。

Next to the site of the Maritime Trade Office, there are two water gates, Shuimen Gate and Nanxun Gate, which are used to regulate water flow and manage the entry and exit of boats. After the establishment of the Maritime Trade Office, all maritime ships and cargoes can be transferred to small boats at the Jiangkou Docks, going up against the Jinjiang River, along the Pofugou Ditch, passing through the water gates and entering the moat to the Maritime Trade Office for customs declaration. There is Narcissus Palace built next to the site. In the 1980s, a protection monument for the site of Quanzhou Maritime Trade Office was set up next to the palace, inside which there is a special exhibition of Quanzhou Maritime Trade Office. Within the scope of the site, there are still places whose names contain historical information, such as Bosiku Lane (Storehouse of the Maritime Trade Office Lane) and Maban Lane (Horses and Vehicles Transferring Cargoes Lane). From 2019 to 2021, the Institute of Archaeology at Chinese Academy of Social Sciences, Fujian Museum, and Quanzhou Maritime Silk Road Heritage Application Center jointly formed Archaeological Team of Quanzhou City to carry out scientific archaeological excavations of the site of Quanzhou Maritime Trade Office. During the first archaeological excavation in 2019, architectural relics such as brick floors or paving stones, as well as unearthed relics like architectural components and ceramics were discovered, which were related to the site of Quanzhou Maritime Trade Office in the Song and Yuan Dynasties. The second excavation in 2020 revealed relics related to building foundations in the Song-Yuan Period, such as underdrains, stone walls, stone piers, brick floors, cobblestone pavements, foundation trenches and ancient wells, and unearthed architectural components, such as ridge beasts or roof tiles with flower pattern, and ceramics like celadon and egg-white glazed porcelain. The archaeological relics and unearthed artifacts all indicate that this is a higher level large-scale official building complex in the the Song-Yuan Period. The discovery of an inscription brick with the words "Pu ... supervised the construction of Shibo (Maritime Trade) Pavilion" printed on one side further proves that the building complex is the site of Quanzhou Maritime Trade Office. There are records of not only the word "Shibo", but also a person surnamed Pu. This person is very likely to be a family member of Pu Shougeng who was an Arabic maritime merchant in the Yuan Dynasty, known as "Inspector of Quanzhou Maritime Trade Superintendency who is good at profiting from maritime business for thirty years".

According to historical documents, in the Song and Yuan Dynasties, the rank for the Inspector of Maritime Trade Superintendency did not exceed the sub-fifth-rank officials. As confirmed by archaeological findings, the site of Ningbo Maritime Trade Office, which is of the same level as the one in Quanzhou, covers an area of about 12,000m^2. Through this series of archaeological investigations and excavations, and combined with the factors such as the composition of the water system and the roads around the site of Quanzhou Maritime Trade Office, archaeologists speculate that the scope of the site is roughly the area enclosed by Maban Lane, Baguagou Ditch, Zhu Street, and Shuimen Lane.

市舶司对泉州的影响

市舶司在泉州的设置及不断完善，使泉州有了较为完备的海外贸易管理机构。泉州成为海上来往船只的法定登记港口，为泉州消除了地方出口贸易的制度性障碍。市舶司的设立还使泉州与海外贸易市场之间形成较为稳定的关系，这对泉州海上贸易和区域经济发展有深远的意义。随着泉州港海外贸易日益繁盛，与之贸易往来的国家和地区不断增多，成为中外经济文化交流和人民友好交往的重要门户。到宋代泉州已跟 50 多个国家通商有贸易往来。宋代的文献记载“若欲泛外国买卖，则自泉州便可出洋”“欲至泉州者，入自甲子门”。《诸蕃志》记载我国与东南亚诸国、印度、阿拉伯以及北非各国的航线距离、日数、方位，且多以泉州为起点。

元朝首先在泉州设立市舶司。因泉州长期同南海诸国保持良好贸易往来，泉州港成为招徕外商、组织海外贸易的中心。据两次跟随泉州船队出洋的汪大渊所作《岛夷志略》记载，至元代泉州已跟世界上 99 个国家有通商贸易往来。

元代四大著名旅行家马可·波罗、鄂多立克、伊本·白图泰和尼哥罗·康蒂要离开中国时，往往从泉州起航，若从海路来华，一般也从泉州登陆。他们在目睹了当时泉州港的繁盛景象后，纷纷惊叹并在游记中不惜笔墨地描绘泉州盛景。

泉州市舶司遗址 TG3G 探沟。（张红兴 摄）
Exploratory trench TG3G on the site of Quanzhou Maritime Trade Office. (Photo by Zhang Hongxing)

Influence of the Maritime Trade Office on Quanzhou

The establishment and continuous improvement of the Maritime Trade Office provided Quanzhou with a relatively complete overseas trade management institution. Quanzhou had become a legal port for registration of maritime vessels, which had eliminated institutional obstacles to Quanzhou's local export trade. The establishment of the Maritime Trade Office also enabled Quanzhou to form a relatively stable relationship with overseas trade markets, which had far-reaching significance for Quanzhou's maritime trade and regional economic development. With the increasingly prosperous overseas trade of Quanzhou Port, there were increasing countries and regions trading with Quanzhou, which enabled it to become an important gateway for Sino-foreign economic and cultural exchanges and friendly communications between people. By the Song Dynasty, Quanzhou had traded with more than 50 countries, which can be shown in documents written at that time, such as "if you want to do business overseas, you can start your journey from Quanzhou" and "those who want to travel to Quanzhou should come through Jiazi Gate". As recorded in *Records Of Foreign Countries*, the shipping distance, number of shipping days, and location of the routes between China and Southeast Asian countries, India, Arabia, and North African countries, are mostly based on the routes starting from Quanzhou.

In the Yuan Dynasty, the Maritime Trade Office was first established in Quanzhou. Due to the long-term good trade foundation between Quanzhou and the countries in the South China Sea, Quanzhou Port became a center for attracting foreign businessmen and organizing overseas trade. According to *A Brief Account of Island Inhabitants* written by Wang Dayuan, who went overseas with the Quanzhou fleet twice, Quanzhou had trade relations with 99 countries in the world in the Yuan Dynasty.

Marco Polo, Friar Odoric, Ibn Battuta and Nicolo Conti were four famous travelers in the Yuan Dynasty. When they left China, they usually chose Quanzhou as their last stop for departure or when they came to China by sea, Quanzhou was their first stop. After witnessing the prosperous scene of Quanzhou Port at that time, they were all amazed at the magnificent scenery of Quanzhou and spared no effort in depicting the prosperity of Quanzhou in their travel notes.

意大利旅行家马可·波罗要离开中国，从泉州港出发到波斯时写道："刺桐是世界最大的港口之一，大批商人云集于此，货物堆积如山，买卖的盛况令人难以想象。"意大利传教士鄂多立克曾由海路来到泉州，然后北上大都。他的游记中如此记载："我来到一个叫作刺桐的著名城市，此城中有大量各种生活必需品……该地系世上最好的地方之一，就其对人之生活所需说亦如此。"意大利传教士马黎诺里于至正二年（1342）受罗马教皇派遣奉使东方，他惊叹记下："刺桐城，这是一个令人神往的海港，也是一座令人惊奇的城市。方济各会修士在该城有三座非常华丽的教堂。"摩洛哥旅行家伊本·白图泰通过海路来到中国，他到的第一站便是泉州。他如此描述道："刺桐港是世界上最大的港口之一，甚至可以说就是最大的。我看到港内有百条大船，至于小船可谓多得不可胜数。"

市舶司的设置对宋元泉州的经济繁荣、文化交流以及海洋贸易的发展具有至关重要的意义。其遗址作为世界文化遗产"泉州：宋元中国的世界海洋商贸中心"的重要制度保障之一，为研究宋代我国南方官式建筑、泉州地区古代商贸管理制度和海洋贸易历史提供了珍贵的实物例证。

旧时可让船只直达泉州市舶司的河道如今只剩下狭窄的壕沟。（陈英杰 摄）
The river that used to allow ships to directly reach Quanzhou Maritime Trade Office is now reduced to a narrow trench. (Photo by Chen Yingjie)

When the Italian traveler Marco Polo was about to leave China and set off for Persia from Quanzhou Port, he wrote that "Zayton is one of the largest ports in the world, where a large number of merchants gather together and the goods are piled up like a mountain. The grand occasion of trading is unimaginable." The Italian missionary Friar Odoric came to Quanzhou by sea, and then went north to Kanbulu (Beijing nowadays), the capital of the Yuan Dynasty. As recorded in his travel notes, "I came to a famous city called Zayton where there are a lot of daily necessities available for purchase... It is one of the best places in the world because it can perfectly meet people's daily needs." The Italian missionary Giovanni dei Marignolli, who was sent by the Pope of Rome to the East in 1342, was amazed and recorded, "Zayton is a fascinating seaport and an amazing city. There are three magnificent churches for the Franciscans in the city." The Moroccan traveler Ibn Battuta also came to China by sea, whose first stop was Quanzhou. He described the scene he saw in this way, "Zayton Port is one of the largest ports in the world, even the largest ever. I saw hundreds of large ships and countless (small) boats in the port."

The establishment of the Maritime Trade Office is of great significance to the economic prosperity, cultural exchanges and the development of marine trade of Song-Yuan Quanzhou. As an important institutional guarantee for the world cultural heritage of "Quanzhou: Emporium of the World in Song-Yuan China", the site of the Maritime Trade Office provides valuable and vivid physical evidence for studying the official buildings in Southern China in the Song Dynasty, the ancient commercial and trading management system and the history of maritime trade in Quanzhou.

祈风护佑海贸——
祈风典礼及九日山祈风石刻

Praying for Wind Protection for Maritime Trade: Wind-Praying Ceremony and Jiuri Mountain Wind-Praying Inscriptions

九日山祈风石刻位于距离泉州古城约 7 千米的南安丰州九日山上。这是一组纪录宋代地方官员、市舶司官员、南外宗正司皇室后裔等人到昭惠庙、延福寺为商舶往来海外一帆风顺而举行祈风仪式，礼毕后到九日山上游览并留下题名纪年纪事的摩崖石刻，共有 10 方。这些珍贵的石刻真实记录了宋代海洋贸易与季风密切关联的运行周期等历史信息，体现了宋代政府对海外贸易高度重视，将通远王这一民间信仰纳入官方祭典，以官方力量来倡导和推动海外贸易的发展。通远王信仰作为宋元时期泉州海商从事海洋贸易的重要精神寄托，与真武庙的真武大帝信仰、天后宫的妈祖信仰一起构成泉州地区独具特色的海神信仰体系，反映出海神信仰对海外贸易活动的精神促进。九日山祈风石刻和泉州市舶司遗址、德济门遗址、真武庙和天后宫，在"泉州：宋元中国的世界海洋商贸中心"系列遗产中一同成为海洋贸易管理保障的代表性遗产。

九日山及山下的晋江。（成冬冬 摄）
Jiuri Mountain and the Jinjiang River at the foot of the mountain. (Photo by Cheng Dongdong)

Jiuri Mountain Wind-Praying Inscriptions are on Jiuri Mountain in Fengzhou Town, Nan'an County, about 7 kilometers away from the ancient city of Quanzhou. They are a series of cliff-face inscriptions recording the ritual ceremonies held by local officials, officials of Quanzhou Maritime Trade Office and descendants of the imperial clan of the Southern Clan Office in the Song Dynasty to pray in Zhaohui Temple and Yanfu Temple for favorable winds to aid voyages of merchant ships. After the ceremony, they went to Jiuri Mountain for a tour and left the inscriptions with chronicles of events and participants' names. There are 10 cliff inscriptions in total. These precious stone inscriptions are a historical archive providing an authentic record of such historical information as the operational cycles of maritime trade in the Song Dynasty, which were closely connected with the monsoons. They reflect that the government in the Song Dynasty attached great importance to maritime trade by including the folk belief of King Tongyuan into the scope of official ceremonies, and implementing state power to advocate and promote the development of maritime trade. As an important spiritual impetus for Quanzhou maritime merchants to engage in marine trade during the Song-Yuan era, the belief of King Tongyuan, together with the belief of Zhenwu Celestial Lord in Zhenwu Temple and the belief of Mazu in Tianhou Temple, constitutes the unique sea god belief system in Quanzhou area, reflecting the spiritual impetus of the belief in maritime deities to maritime trade activities. Together with the site of the Maritime Trade Office, the site of Deji Gate, Zhenwu Temple and Tianhou Temple, Jiuri Mountain Wind-Praying Inscriptions become the representative heritage of administrative assurance for maritime trade in the heritage series of "Quanzhou: Emporium of the World in Song-Yuan China".

九日山祈风祭典。（张清杰 摄）
Wind-praying ceremony on the Jiuri Mountain. (Photo by Zhang Qingjie)

九日山及其地理环境

闽南首邑

泉州境内水系发达，泉州的母亲河——晋江就是其中最主要的干流。晋江上游有东溪和西溪两大支流，东溪发源于永春县呈祥乡云路村，西溪发源于安溪县桃舟乡达新村。东溪、西溪在南安丰州交汇处形成一处天然良港——梁安港，这里水面宽阔，深度适宜，吐纳潮汐，舟楫可通于城下。三国吴永安三年（260）在此设立东安县，成为福建最早立县的县份之一，素有"闽南首邑"之称。晋太康三年（282）东安县改名晋安县，属晋安郡，南朝梁改为梁安县，治所均在今南安丰州一带。晋代永嘉年间，中原战乱频仍，部分士族南渡入闽，沿江聚居。因为怀念故土，他们将居住地旁的河流命名为"晋江"。随着中原士族而来的是先进的中原文化，掀起了闽南地区开发的高潮。

梁安港（位于今九日山下金鸡闸）是有史记载中国南方最早通商的口岸。（苏德辉 摄）
According to historical records Liang'an Port, which is located at Jinji Barrage at the foot of Jiu Mountain today, is the earliest trading port in Southern China (Photo by Su Dehui)

Jiuri Mountain and Its Geographical Environment

The First County of Southern Fujian

The water system in Quanzhou is well developed, among which the mother river of Quanzhou, the Jinjiang River, is the most important mainstream. There are two tributaries in the upper reaches of the Jinjiang River, Dongxi Stream and Xixi Stream, of which the former one originates from Yunlu Village, Chengxiang Township, Yongchun County, and the latter one starts from Daxin Village, Taozhou Township, Anxi County. Dongxi Stream and Xixi Stream intersect in Fengzhou, Nan'an to form a good natural harbor named Liang'an Port, where tide can be absorbed and drained and ships can go directly to the downtown owing to wide water surface and appropriate water depth of the port. In 260 during the Three Kingdoms Period, Dong'an County was established here, becoming one of the earliest counties in Fujian Province and known as "the first county in Southern Fujian". In 282 of the Jin Dynasty, Dong'an County was renamed Jin'an County under Jin'an Prefecture, and renamed Liang'an County in the Liang Period of the Southern Dynasty, with both administrative offices located in the area of today's Fengzhou, Nan'an. During the Yongjia Period of the Jin Dynasty, there were frequent battles in the Central Plains, so some gentry migrated south to Fujian and lived together along the river. In order to commemorate their native land, they named the river beside their residence "Jinjiang River". Along with the gentry of the Central Plains came the advanced Central Plains culture, which set off a climax of development in Southern Fujian.

南安丰州长期作为郡、州、县治所，是闽南的政治、经济、文化中心，享有闽南“治化最先”和“丰饶之州”的美誉。（陈英杰 摄）

Having long served as the prefecture, state and county administrative seat, Fengzhou Town of Nan'an County is the political, economic and cultural center of Southern Fujian, enjoying the reputation of "the earliest governance and cultivation of people" and "Land of Plenty" in Southern Fujian. (Photo by Chen Yingjie)

底蕴丰厚的九日山文化

九日山是南安丰州境内文化底蕴最为丰厚的名山，山因人而显，人因山而名，南渡的晋人每逢重九，登高远眺，寄托乡思，久而成习，便将此山称为“九日山”。这里地理位置优越、交通方便、土地肥沃，适宜人们生活、居住和生产发展。通过闽南地区 3 世纪之前的岸线图，可以看到九日山所在处是泉州湾进入晋江后江面最窄的位置，两岸有九日山、金鸡山夹峙，犹如天然门户。这里是泉州最早开发的地区之一，也是历代泉州城郊的风景胜地。泉州最早的佛教寺庙建筑——延福寺创建于九日山麓，这在北宋端拱年间泉州人曾会作的《重修延福寺碑铭》中有详细的描述：延福寺始建于西晋太康九年（288），东距郡城十五里，南离大海三十里，左侧是南安丰州的集市，前面是通潮汐的晋江……这份文献记载了延福寺始建于西晋，是福建最早的佛教寺院之一。

九日山分东、西、北三峰，山中古迹遍布，多数集中于西峰东坡和东峰南麓。自唐以来，文人墨客曾先后登临雅集或隐居于此。东峰因唐代宰相姜公辅贬谪栖隐于此，又称“姜相峰”，亦称“东台”。宋庆历四年（1044），同安人苏绅在此题刻“姜相峰”。西峰因唐代著名诗人秦系栖隐于此，故称“高士峰”，亦称“西台”。庆历六年（1046），福建提点刑狱苏舜元登游九日山时，留题“高士峰”三字于西峰。

Jiuri Mountain Culture with Rich Heritage

With the richest cultural heritage, Jiuri Mountain is a famous mountain in Fengzhou, Nan'an. The Jin people who migrated south climbed the mountain to express their nostalgia for the Double Ninth Festival (also known as Chongyang Festival, held on the ninth day of the ninth lunar month), which gradually forms a custom over time. The mountain was thus named "Jiuri (Ninth Day) Mountain". The mountain and the people complement to each other in their fames. With its superior geographical location, convenient transportation and fertile land, it is suitable for people to live, reside, produce and develop. According to the coastline map of Southern Fujian before the 3rd century, it can be seen that Jiuri Mountain is located at the narrowest position of the river after the ship enters the Jinjiang River from Quanzhou Bay. There are Jiuri Mountain and Jinji Mountain on both sides of the river, which forms a natural gateway. This is one of the earliest developed areas in Quanzhou as well as a scenic spot in the outskirts of Quanzhou in the past dynasties. Yanfu Temple, the earliest Buddhist temple building in Quanzhou, was built at the foot of Jiuri Mountain. As described in detail in *Inscriptions on Rebuilding the Yanfu Temple* by Zeng Hui from Quanzhou in the Duangong era (988—989) of the Northern Song Dynasty, "Yanfu Temple was built in 288 of the Western Jin Dynasty, with 7.5km to the downtown of the prefecture in the east, 15km to the south of the sea, the market in Fengzhou, Nan'an on the left, and the Jinjiang River in the front which could accommodate tide...". This document records that Yanfu Temple, first built in the Western Jin Dynasty, is one of the earliest Buddhist temples in Fujian.

As for Jiuri Mountain's three summits, namely, Eastern Summit, Western Summit and Northern Summit, there are many historical sites, most of which are concentrated on the east slope of the Western Summit and the south foot of the Eastern Summit. Since the Tang Dynasty, literati have successively visited, gathered or lived here. The Eastern Summit is also known as "Jiangxiang Summit (Summit of Prime Minister Jiang)" or "Eastern Platform" because Jiang Gongfu, the prime minister of the Tang Dynasty, was exiled here. In 1044 of the Song Dynasty, Su Shen, a native of Tong'an County, inscribed "Jiangxiang Summit" here. The Western Summit is also known as "Gaoshi Summit (Summit of a Profound Scholar)" or "Western Platform" because the famous poet Qin Xi of the Tang Dynasty lived here in seclusion. In 1046, Su Shunyuan, the Penal Superintendent of Fujian, inscribed "Gaoshi Summit" on the Western Summit when he visited Jiuri Mountain.

九日山素以“山中无石不刻字”著称，在东峰和西峰保留有宋、元、明、清摩崖石刻77方以及其他文物古迹。西峰山顶有石佛岩，乾德三年（965），陈洪进在九日山西峰就巨岩雕刻阿弥陀佛像。佛像高4.5米，宽1.5米，袒胸盘坐于莲座上，衣纹流畅对称，为泉州最早的石雕造像。西台无等岩顶大石上，为唐代高僧无等禅师纪念塔，塔身有楷书阴刻“佛品塔”三字。

蔡襄于庆历四年与友人同游九日山，并留下九日山最早的游览题名石刻——“庆历四年二月二十四日，沈衡、蔡襄、庄夏、宋宜、邑宰夏化育、林□同游延福寺隐君亭”，其书法竖写右行，在书法史上十分罕见。宋代著名理学家朱熹曾两次游九日山，并题“九日山”三字勒于壁，后因年代久远湮没。清乾隆三十二年（1767），福建提督马负书游览九日山，怀着对朱熹的崇敬之情，重书“九日山”三字并刻于西峰。

九日山西峰阿弥陀佛像。（成冬冬 摄）

The statue of Amitabha Buddha on the Western Summit of Jiuri Mountain. (Photo by Cheng Dongdong)

Jiuri Mountain is famous for "no stone in the mountains without inscriptions". There are 77 cliff stone inscriptions in the Song, Yuan, Ming and Qing Dynasties and other cultural relics and historic sites remaining in the Eastern and Western Summits. There is a Stone Buddha on the top of the Western Summit. In 965, Chen Hongjin carved a statue of Amitabha Buddha on a huge rock on the Western Summit of Jiuri Mountain. The statue, which is the earliest stone sculpture in Quanzhou, is 4.5m high and 1.5m wide, sitting on a lotus seat with its chest bare and clothes patterns smooth and symmetrical. On the big stone on the top of Wudeng Rock in the Western Platform, there is a memorial pagoda for Master Wudeng, an eminent monk of the Tang Dynasty, with the three Chinese characters of "佛品塔" (Buddha Character Pagoda) engraved in regular script intaglio.

Cai Xiang visited Jiuri Mountain with his friends in 1044, and left behind the earliest stone traveling inscriptions with names on Jiuri Mountain, "On February 24, 1044, Shen Heng, Cai Xiang, Zhuang Xia, Song Yi, County Magistrate Xia Huayu, and Lin □ visited Yinjun Pavilion of Yanfu Temple". Its calligraphy was written vertically from left to right, which is very rare in the history of calligraphy. Zhu Xi, a famous Neo-Confucian philosopher in the Song Dynasty, visited Jiuri Mountain twice and inscribed the words "九日山" (Jiuri Mountain) on the cliff, which later vanished over time. In 1767, Fujian Provincial Commander-in-Chief Ma Fushu visited Jiuri Mountain and rewrote the three words "九日山" on the Western Summit in honor of Zhu Xi.

马负书所书"九日山"石刻。（成冬冬 摄）

"九日山" (Jiuri Mountain) inscription by Ma Fushu. (Photo by Cheng Dongdong)

通远王信仰及祈风典礼

人们对海神信仰的需求

民间信仰是人们在面对自然、社会或人生时，感到不能掌握自己的命运，认为在现实世界之外，有超自然的力量或实体存在，并认为他们能够影响人们的命运，因而产生敬畏和崇拜的思想感情。泉州民间信仰十分庞杂，信仰对象广泛，可大致分为两类：一类是自然信仰，比如信仰天地山川、日月星辰、风雨雷电、动植物等自然现象，展现古老的万物有灵的观点；一类是人鬼信仰，除了信仰自己的祖先以外，许多被神格化的历史人物和人格化的神仙鬼怪都成了被崇拜的对象，如关羽、岳飞、妈祖、吴夲、萧太傅、广泽尊王、清水祖师、通远王、田都元帅等。此外，还有分布在泉州城乡各个角落的大小城隍和铺境神。民间信仰早已植入泉州百姓的内心深处，成为当地人的一种生活方式。

蟳埔顺济宫里虔诚上香的信众。（吴刚强 摄）
Devout believers offering incense in Xunpu Shunji Temple. (Photo by Wu Gangqiang)

宋元时期，在世界海洋贸易蓬勃发展的历史进程中，泉州凭借着悠久的航海传统、市舶司的设立、优良的航海和造船技术及地理优势等，成为各国商旅纷至沓来、多元文化交相辉映的"东方第一大港"。浩瀚的海洋变幻莫测，时而波涛汹涌，时而风平浪静，既存在很多未知的风险，也蕴含着无限的可能。随着泉州港口发展及海外贸易的繁荣，渔民、商人及移民出于对海洋未知危险的恐惧与敬畏，同时为寻求精神抚慰和心理慰藉，对海神信仰的需求不断增加。泉州地方海神信仰逐渐兴盛起来，通远王就是泉州地区早期的地方海神信仰之一。

King Tongyuan Worship and Wind-Praying Ceremony

People's Desires for the Worship of Sea God

Folk beliefs are people's thoughts and feelings of awe and worship towards supernatural forces or entities outside the real world. When people face nature, society or life, they feel unable to control their own destinies, so they believe that there are supernatural forces or entities outside the real world which can affect people's destinies. With a wide range of belief objects, Quanzhou's folk beliefs are very complex, which can be roughly divided into two categories. One is the beliefs in nature such as heaven, earth, mountains, rivers, Sun, Moon, stars, wind, rain, thunder, lightning, animals or plants, which reflects the ancient view of animism; the other is the beliefs in humans and ghosts including not only human beings' own ancestors but many deified historical figures and personified gods and ghosts as well such as Guan Yu, Yue Fei, Mazu, Wu Tao, Xiao Wangzhi, King Guangze, Master Qingshui, King Tongyuan, and Marshal Tiandu and so on. In addition, there are various city gods and town gods distributed in all corners of Quanzhou. Folk beliefs have long been embedded in the hearts of Quanzhou people and become a way of life for them.

During the Song and Yuan Dynasties, in the historical process of vigorous development of the world's marine trade, Quanzhou has become "the largest port in the East" with numerous merchants coming from various countries and diverse cultures complementing each other, by virtue of its long-standing maritime tradition, establishment of the Maritime Trade Office, excellent technology in navigation and shipbuilding, and geographical advantages. Sometimes rough while sometimes calm, the vast ocean is unpredictable, suggesting many unknown risks and infinite possibilities. With the development of Quanzhou Port and the prosperity of maritime trade, there are increasing desires for the worship of the lord of sea among the marine fishermen, businessmen and immigrants who are in fear and awe of the unknown dangers of the sea and would like to seek spiritual or psychological comfort. Thus the local beliefs in the sea god in Quanzhou gradually flourished, and King Tongyuan was one of the early local sea gods in Quanzhou.

通远王信仰

通远王原为山神乐山王，民间俗称白须公。相传唐咸通年间，九日山下延福寺圮废后重建大殿，寺僧四处寻找巨木。有僧慕名前往乐山，在山上遇到一位白须翁，他指点寺僧找到建寺的巨木。但是，乐山和九日山相距甚远，交通不便，巨木如何运到丰州是一个大难题。白须公发挥神力，使延福寺重建的木料问题得到解决，于是当地人就在延福寺旁兴建昭惠庙供奉。蔡襄在主持修建洛阳桥时，昭惠庙曾分灵到洛阳桥头建庙镇海。北宋嘉祐五年（1060）春，当地干旱甚为严重。蔡襄到昭惠庙祈雨应验，使得昭惠庙声名大噪，朝廷赐封白须公为"崇应公"。此时，通远王已兼有降水的神通，被民众奉为水神。政和四年（1114），朝廷敕封其"通远王"并赐庙额"昭惠"。

随着政府的推崇加封及民众信仰的增多，通远王的神通逐渐多元化，对于水旱灾、病疫还有祈风都颇有灵验。朝廷累加敕封"善利""广福""显济"等封号，通远王由此成为中国东南沿海地区的第一代海神。在官方的推崇下，民众相信通远王威灵显赫，能保佑航海平安、风调雨顺。因此，泉州所属沿海港口与内河驿站，兴建了许多供奉通远王的庙宇，最远到达德化县域。此后泉州地方官在九日山为航海祈风，通远王完成了从山神、水神再到海神的角色转变，与真武大帝、妈祖等海神信仰共同为宋元时期从事海上贸易的商人提供精神寄托。

九日山昭惠庙里供奉着初代海神通远王。（成冬冬 摄）
The early sea god King Tongyuan is enshrined in Zhaohui Temple of Jiuri Mountain. (Photo by Cheng Dongdong)

Evolution of the Belief in King Tongyuan

King Tongyuan was originally the god of Leshan Mountain, popularly known as Bai Xu Gong (a white-bearded man). It was said that during 860 and 873 of the Tang Dynasty, Yanfu Temple at the foot of Jiuri Mountain was to be rebuilt after the destruction, so the monks of the temple tried their best to look for big woods. One builder went to Leshan Mountain in search of woods and met a white-bearded man. According to the man's direction, he found huge cedars. However, with Leshan Mountain and Jiuri Mountain being far apart, the transportation was inconvenient. How to transport the giant woods to Fengzhou was a big problem. The white-bearded man used magic power to help solve the problem of woods for the reconstruction of Yanfu Temple, so the local people built Zhaohui Temple beside Yanfu Temple to worship him. When Cai Xiang presided over the construction of Luoyang Bridge, the deity of Zhaohui Temple had been shared in building a temple at the head of Luoyang Bridge in order to protect maritime sailing. In the spring of 1060 in the Northern Song Dynasty, there was a severe drought. Cai Xiang went to Zhaohui Temple to pray for rain, and the god granted the request, which made Zhaohui Temple famous. The imperial court bestowed the title of "Duke Chongying" on Bai Xu Gong. At this time, the sea god already had the supernatural power of precipitation, and was regarded as the god of water by the people. In 1114, the imperial court conferred him the title "King Tongyuan" and granted the temple forehead "Zhaohui" at the same time.

With the promotion of the government and the increase of the believers, the supernatural powers of King Tongyuan have gradually diversified, including being quite effective for floods, droughts, diseases and wind praying. As a result, the imperial court conferred him the titles such as "Shanli", "Guangfu" and "Xianji", making King Tongyuan the first generation of sea gods in the southeast coastal area of China. Under official advocacy, people believed that King Tongyuan was prominent and efficacious in blessing safe navigation and favorable weather. Therefore, many temples dedicated to King Tongyuan were built in the coastal ports and inland river stations of Quanzhou, as far as Dehua County. Since then, with local officials of Quanzhou praying for wind protection of maritime trips at Jiuri Mountain, King Tongyuan successfully transformed from mountain god, water god to sea god, and provided spiritual sustenance for the merchants engaged in maritime trade during the Song-Yuan era together with the sea god beliefs of Zhenwu Celestial Lord and Goddess Mazu.

冬遣舶、夏回航

古泉州人民依海而生，出海和回航都需要顺应季风规律，泉州夏季刮东南风，船舶从南部海域回航；冬季刮西北风，船舶从泉州出海，即“冬遣舶、夏回航”。由于海外贸易对国家财政的巨大贡献，宋代官方极为重视海上贸易的发展，10 世纪末开始对海上贸易大力扶持，在沿海重要港口设立管理海上对外贸易的机构市舶司。宋元祐二年（1087），泉州设立市舶司，职能包括出海许可审查、检验货物、征税以及主持祈风祭海等。官方主导的航海祈风活动是国家力量倡导海贸发展、加强海贸管理的重要体现。至迟在 12 世纪中叶，九日山的祈风仪式已列入国家祭典。

根据九日山上的石刻记载，祈风典礼一般是在九日山下的昭惠庙，于冬十月至十一月举行遣舶祈风仪式，夏四月举行回舶祈风仪式，向海神祈求风信顺利、航行平安。古代对祈风祭祀的程序规范，包括立祈风坛、执事、祭品、礼乐、宣读祭文、焚化祭文等。九日山举行的“祈风仪典”属于官办典祀，春祈西南风，冬祈东北风。祈风的对象是无祷不灵、庇佑海舶航行安全的九日山海神通远王，祭祀规格属官府“大祀”之列。祈风参与者有泉州郡守（泉州地方最高行政长官）、市舶司提举（专掌海交贸易事务长官）、泉州通判（州府副职）、统军（统领一州军事长官）、南安县令，以及下属官员、地方士绅、海舶商人等。根据传统祭祀典礼，要设祭坛，陈列羊、猪、酒等祭品，然后上香，奏迎神曲，由市舶司提举或郡守宣读《祈风文》。南宋时期曾担任泉州知州、素有“真大儒”之称的真德秀曾作有《祈风祝文》和《海神通远王灵著王祝文》，这两篇祝文均是为了祈求海道安宁、海舶出航一帆风顺而作。史料曾记载祈风仪式的盛况：其时“舟船遮江，旗幡蔽日，香烟缭绕，鼓乐喧天”。祈风典礼完成后，参与者乘兴登上九日山，欣赏美景，并题写诗文纪事，然后将祈风的经过镌刻于山中的岩壁间，这就是“九日山祈风石刻”的由来。

Departing in Winter and Returning in Summer

Depending on the sea for a living, the people of ancient Quanzhou needed to comply with the law of monsoon when departing or returning in navigation. In summer, there is southeast wind in Quanzhou, so ships return from the southern sea; in winter, the northwest wind blows, thus ships sail overseas from Quanzhou, henceforth so-called "departing in winter and returning in summer". Due to the great contribution of maritime trade to national finance, officials of the Song Dynasty attached great importance to the development of maritime trade. At the end of the 10th century, they began to provide strong support to maritime trade, and set up maritime trade offices to manage overseas trade in important coastal ports. In 1087, Quanzhou started to set up the Maritime Trade Office with its stipulated functions including review of seagoing license, cargo inspection, taxation, and presiding over praying for favorable wind and offering sacrifices to the sea gods. Officially-dominated maritime wind-praying activities are an important manifestation of the national power to promote the development of maritime trade and strengthen the management of maritime trade. By the middle of the 12th century at the latest, the ceremony of praying for wind at Jiuri Mountain had been included in the national ceremonies.

According to the stone inscriptions on Jiuri Mountain, the wind-praying ceremony is generally held at Zhaohui Temple at the foot of Jiuri Mountain. In order to pray for the safety of maritime trips, the wind-praying ceremony for departure is held from October to November in winter, and the ceremony for returning voyages is held in April in summer. In ancient times, the procedural norms for wind-praying ceremonies included setting up the prayer altar, choosing deacons, preparing sacrifices, providing ritual music, reading aloud sacrificial texts, burning sacrificial texts, etc. The wind-praying ceremony held in Jiuri Mountain is an official ceremony, praying for southwest wind in spring and northeast wind in winter. The object of the wind-praying ceremony is King Tongyuan, the sea god of Jiuri Mountian, who is effective in all praying and protects the safe navigation of ships. The ceremony can be called one of the local official "grand sacrifices" because of its scale. The participants in wind-praying ceremony include Prefect of Quanzhou (the chief official of Quanzhou), Superintendent of the Maritime Trade Office (the official in charge of maritime trade affairs), Assistant Sub-Prefect of Quanzhou (the deputy executive of Quanzhou Prefecture), Commander-General (the chief executive of prefectural military affairs), District Magistrate of Nan'an County, as well as the subordinate officials, local gentlemen, and maritime merchants. According to the traditional sacrificial ceremony, it is necessary to set up an altar to display sacrifices such as mutton, pork, wine, etc., and then burn incense, play ritual music to welcome the god, and the Maritime Trade Superintendency or the Prefect will read out the *Wind-Praying Text*. During the Southern Song Dynasty, Zhen Dexiu, who served as Prefect of Quanzhou and was known as the "Real Scholar", once wrote *Prayers of the Wind-Praying Ceremony* and *Prayers to the Sea God King Tongyuan* in order to pray for peace of the sea route and smooth sailing of the seagoing ships. As recorded in historical materials, the grand occasion of wind-praying ceremony is that "boats and ships covering the river, flags and sails blocking the sun, smoke of incense lingering around, drums and pipes filling the air". After the wind-praying ceremony was completed, the participants climbed Jiuri Mountain to enjoy the beautiful scenery, wrote poems and chronicles, and then engraved the wind-praying process on the rock cliffs of the mountain, which is the origin of the Jiuri Mountain Wind-Praying Inscriptions.

九日山祈风石刻及其价值

九日山上现存的祈风石刻，一般记述了祈风时间、地点、参加者姓名和仪式结束后的活动等内容。这 10 方石刻所记录的 11 次祈风多数由地方政府主官主持，专职负责国家海洋贸易管理的市舶司官员偕同南外宗正司官员（皇族）、军队统帅等朝廷任命的军政要员联袂参与。这些代表国家力量的重要官员的广泛参与，反映了市舶制度下国家对海洋贸易的倡导和推动。

这些石刻分布于九日山东、西两峰的崖壁上，东峰 2 方，西峰 8 方，根据参观的顺序，10 方祈风石刻分别辑录如下：

东峰祈风石刻

记载一年两次的祈风石刻

石刻文云："舶司岁两祈风于通远王庙，祀事既毕登山泛溪，因为一日之款。淳熙戊申夏四月，会者六人：林枅、赵公迥、胡长卿、韩俊、折知刚、赵善采。冬十月，会者五人：赵不遏、胡长卿、韩俊、赵善采、郑颐孙。"

九日山东峰祈风石刻群。（陈英杰 摄）
Wind-praying inscriptions on the Eastern Summit of Jiuri Mountain. (Photo by Chen Yingjie)

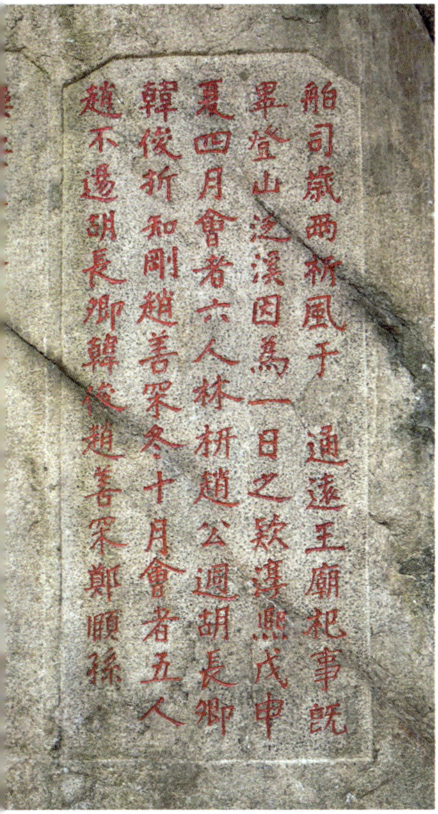

记载淳熙十五年（1188）夏四月和冬十月两次祈风的石刻。（成冬冬 摄）

The stone inscription recording the two wind-praying events in lunar April and October of 1188. (Photo by Cheng Dongdong)

Jiuri Mountain Wind-Praying Inscriptions and Their Values

The extant stone inscriptions of wind-praying on Jiuri Mountain generally record the information of the time, place, names of participants and activities after the ceremonies. Most of the eleven wind-praying ceremonies recorded in the ten stone inscriptions were presided over by the local government chief officials, and participated by the important officials appointed by the imperial court such as the officials of the Maritime Trade Office who were in charge of the national maritime trade management, the officials of the Southern Clan Office (belonging to the royal family), the military commanders, etc. The extensive participation of these important officials representing national power reflects the national advocation and promotion of maritime trade under the maritime trade system.

These stone inscriptions are distributed on the cliffs of the Eastern and Western Summits on Jiuri Mountain, among which two are on the Eastern Summit and eight on the Western Summit. According to the visiting order, the ten stone wind-praying inscriptions are listed as follows:

Wind-Praying Inscriptions on the Eastern Summit

The inscription recording wind-praying ceremonies twice a year

The stone inscription reads, "The Maritime Trade Office prayed for the wind at King Tongyuan Temple twice a year. When the ritual ceremony was completed, the participants climbed the mountain and rafted on the river. These are the norm activities on the day. In April of the summer in Wushen Year of the Chunxi Period (1188), six people attended the ceremony, who were Lin Ji, Zhao Gongjiong, Hu Changqing, Han Jun, Zhe Zhigang, and Zhao Shanshen. In October of the winter, there were five people involved, who were Zhao Buti, Hu Changqing, Han Jun, Zhao Shanshen, and Zheng Yisun."

这是一方记载夏四月和冬十月两次祈风的石刻，说明市舶司每年（夏、冬）两次到通远王庙举行祈风仪式。仪式完毕，众人登览九日山与泛舟金溪，因循旧例作为一天的招待。淳熙十五年（1188）夏季四月，与会者六人：福建转运判官兼知泉州林枅、知南外宗正司事赵公迥、泉州市舶司提举胡长卿、泉州左翼军统制韩俊、泉州通判折知刚、泉州添差通判代理州事赵善宷等人。冬季十月，参与祈风石刻的有：知南外宗正司事赵不逷、泉州市舶司提举胡长卿、泉州左翼军统制韩俊、泉州添差通判代理州事赵善宷、嘉定十三年（1220）进士郑颐孙。这是现存 10 方祈风石刻中，唯一记载了一年之中两次为海舶举行祈风仪式的石刻，尤显珍贵。

嘉泰元年（1201）冬季启航祈风石刻

石刻文云："嘉泰辛酉十有一月庚申，郡守倪思正甫、提舶余茂实腾甫，遵令典祈风于昭惠庙。既事，登九日山、憩怀古堂，回谒唐相姜公墓，至莲华岩而归。统军韩俊用章、同僚朱曾景参、戴溪肖望、钱箄仲渊、曾应定之、陈士龙云卿与焉。"

这是记载 1201 年十一月庚申日，泉州郡守倪思（字正甫）、市舶司提举余茂实（字腾甫），遵照法令在昭惠庙主持祈风仪式。祀事完毕，登临九日山在怀古堂休憩，并拜谒唐朝谪相姜公辅陵墓，游览到莲花岩然后返回。统军韩俊（字用章）、同僚朱曾（字景参）、戴溪（字肖望）、钱箄（字仲渊）、曾应（字定之）、 陈士龙（字云卿）同游。

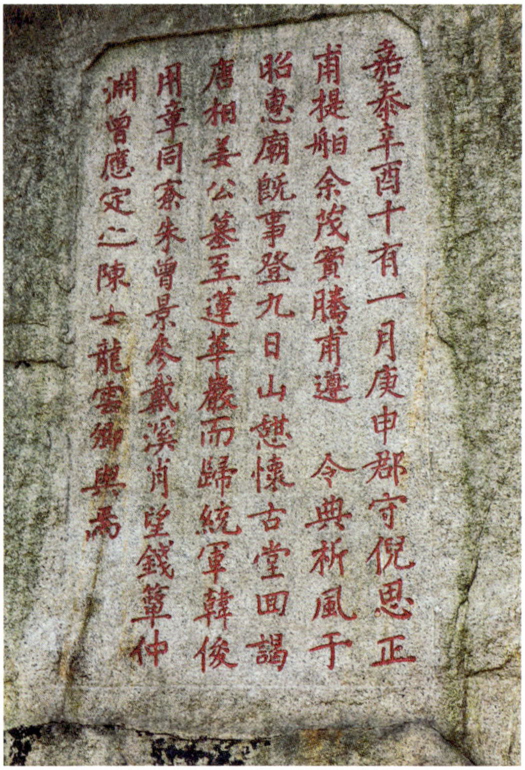

嘉泰元年冬季启航祈风石刻。（成冬冬 摄）
The wind-praying stone inscription for departing trips in the winter of 1201. (Photo by Cheng Dongdong)

This is a stone inscription recording two wind-praying ceremonies in lunar April and October, showing that the ceremonies were held semi-annually (in summer and winter) by the Maritime Trade Office in King Tongyuan Temple. After the ceremonies were over, all the participants visited Jiuri Mountain and went boating on the Jinxi River, which was the one-day reception event according to the old routine. In April of the summer in 1188, there were six participants, namely, Fujian Transport Commissioner and Prefect of Quanzhou Lin Ji, Administrator of the Southern Clan Office Zhao Gongjiong, Maritime Trade Superintendent Hu Changqing, Commander-General of the Left-Wing Army Han Jun, Assistant Sub-Prefect of Quanzhou Zhe Zhigang, and Deputy of Sub-Prefect of Quanzhou Zhao Shanshen, etc. In October of the winter in 1188, those who participated in the wind-praying stone inscriptions included Administrator of the Southern Clan Office Zhao Buti, Maritime Trade Superintendent Hu Changqing, Commander-General of the Left-Wing Army Han Jun, Deputy of Sub-Prefect of Quanzhou Zhao Shanshen, and Metropolitan Graduate in 1220 Zheng Yisun. This is the only stone inscription that records the semi-annual wind-praying ceremonies for safe maritime trips among the extant ten stone inscriptions, which makes it more precious.

The wind-praying stone inscription for departing trips in the winter of the 1st year in the Jiatai Period (1201)

The stone inscription reads, "On the Geng Shen Day (a day in ancient time for prayers) in lunar November of Xinyou Year in the Jiatai Period, the Prefect of Quanzhou Ni Si with his courtesy name Zhengfu, and Maritime Trade Superintendent Yu Maoshi with his courtesy name Tengfu, obeyed an order to hold a wind-praying ceremony in Zhaohui Temple. When things were done, they climbed Jiuri Mountain, rested at the Huaigu Hall, worshiped Jianggong Tomb (the tomb of prime minister Jiang Gongfu in the Tang Dynasty) on their way back, visited the Lianhua Rock and then returned. People who went together were the Commander-General Han Jun (courtesy name Yongzhang) and his colleagues Zhu Zeng (courtesy name Jingcan), Dai Xi (courtesy name Xiaowang), Qian Dan (courtesy name Zhongyuan), Zeng Ying (courtesy name Dingzhi), and Chen Shilong (courtesy name Yunqing)".

It is recorded that on the day of Geng Shen in lunar November, 1201, Quanzhou Prefect Ni Si (courtesy name Zhengfu), and Maritime Trade Superintendent Yu Maoshi (courtesy name Tengfu), presided over the wind-praying ceremony in Zhaohui Temple according to the decree. After the ceremony, they climbed Jiuri Mountain, rested at the Huaigu Hall, worshiped the tomb of the Prime Minister Jiang Gongfu in the Tang Dynasty, visited Lianhua Rock and then returned. The Commander-general Han Jun (courtesy name Yongzhang), and his colleagues Zhu Zeng (courtesy name Jingcan), Dai Xi (courtesy name Xiaowang), Qian Dan (courtesy name Zhongyuan), Zeng Ying (courtesy name Dingzhi), and Chen Shilong (courtesy name Yunqing) traveled together.

九日山祈风石刻群。（陈起拓 摄）
Wind-praying inscriptions of Jiuri Mountain. (Photo by Chen Qituo)

西峰祈风石刻

宝祐六年（1258）夏季回航祈风石刻

石刻文云："宝祐戊午四月辛卯，莆田方澄孙被旨摄郡兼舶，越十有八日戊申，祈风延福，寿阳纪智和、开封赵梦龙，三山彭樵、王广翁、赵时僣，豫章李宏模同会，遵故事也。时农望方切，并以雨祷，瓣芗才兴，霡霂随至，乃书于石以纪之云。"

这是1258年四月辛卯日，莆田方澄孙，接受圣旨代理泉州郡守兼市舶司提举，率领僚属祈风于延福寺通远王祠，寿阳纪智和，开封赵梦龙，福州彭樵、王广翁、赵时僣，豫章（今江西北部）李宏模等人按照以往惯例一同参与祈风。当时农夫望雨心情急切，祈风同时兼以祷雨。果品香花等祭品刚摆放，典礼才刚开始，蒙蒙细雨随之而来。于是众人在石上刻写以记录这件事。

Wind-Praying Inscriptions on the Western Summit

The wind-praying stone inscription for returning trips in the summer of the 6th year in the Baoyou Period (1258)

The stone inscription reads, "On the day of Xin Mao in lunar April of the Baoyou Period, Fang Chengsun of Putian City was ordered by the imperial court to act as Deputy of Quanzhou Prefect and Maritime Trade Superintendent and to pray for favorable wind in Yanfu Temple on the Wushen Day which was 18 days afterward. Ji Zhihe from Shouyang County, Zhao Menglong from Kaifeng City, Peng Qiao, Wang Guangweng, and Zhao Shifan from Sanshan (nickname of Fuzhou), and Li Hongmo from Yuzhang Prefecture (northern Jiangxi Province nowadays) met together, which was in accordance with the past routine. They prayed for both wind and rain because at that time farmers were eager for rain. It started to drizzle at the first beginning of the ceremony as soon as the offerings were placed, which was thus carved on the stone for recording."

This is to record that on the day of Xin Mao in lunar April, 1258, Fang Chengsun of Putian City accepted the imperial edict to act as Deputy of Quanzhou Prefect and Maritime Trade Superintendent, and led his staff to pray for favorable wind at King Tongyuan's Hall in Yanfu Temple. According to the past routine, Ji Zhihe from Shouyang County, Zhao Menglong from Kaifeng City, Peng Qiao, Wang Guangweng, and Zhao Shibo from Fuzhou City, and Li Hongmo from Yuzhang Prefecture participated in the ceremony together. They prayed for both wind and rain because at that time the farmers were eager for rain. As soon as the fruits, fragrant flowers and other offerings were placed, it started to drizzle at the first beginning of the ceremony, which was thus carved on the stone to record this event.

宝祐六年夏季回航祈风石刻。（成冬冬 摄）

The wind-praying stone inscription for returning trips in the summer of 1258. (Photo by Cheng Dongdong)

淳祐七年（1247）冬季启航祈风石刻

石刻文云："淳祐丁未仲冬二十有一日，古汴赵师耕以郡兼舶，祁风遂游。"

这是 1247 年十一月二十一日，泉州太守兼市舶司提举赵师耕到九日山祈风并游览的纪事石刻。这是文字最简洁的一方祈风石刻，仅用 24 个字就清晰记录了此次祈风仪式。

The wind-praying stone inscription for departing trips in the winter of the 7th year in the Chunyou Period (1247)

The stone inscription reads, "On the 21st day of lunar November of Dingwei Year in the Chunyou Period, Zhao Shigeng of the ancient Bianjing (Kaifeng City), the Prefect and Maritime Trade Superintendent of Quanzhou, prayed for favorable wind and then visited Jiuri Mountain."

This is the stone inscription of the chronicle that Zhao Shigeng, the Prefect and the Maritime Trade Superintendent of Quanzhou, came to pray for favorable wind and visited Jiuri Mountain on lunar November 21, 1247. This is the most concise wind-praying stone inscription, which clearly records the ceremony of wind-praying in only 24 words.

淳祐七年冬季启航祈风石刻。（成冬冬 摄）

The wind-praying stone inscription for departing trips in the winter of 1247. (Photo by Cheng Dongdong)

嘉定十六年（1223）夏季回航祈风石刻

石刻文云："嘉定癸未孟夏二十六日戊戌，东阳章梾敬则、寿春魏□叔子、山西杨进勋元功、三山林力行勉之、郡人留元圭持中、括苍何清德常之、合□陈亿曼卿、莆阳王彦广居之、清漳郑名卿坤辅、句水戚达先兼权、嘉禾陆相同甫、莆阳黄筌德言、即墨于达卿兼仲、天台应基子履、开封赵汝芪（茂）千里、三山赵与官清叟、三山南璒士登，以祈风于□昭惠祠下，因会于延福，登山瞻石佛，访隐君亭，少憩怀古而归，期而不至，浚仪赵善軿载卿、莆阳刘辉叔元览。"

The wind-praying stone inscription for returning trips in the summer of the 16th year in the Jiading Period (1223)

The stone inscription reads, "On the Wuxu Day in lunar April of Guiwei Year in the Jiading Period, Zhang Lai (courtesy name Jingze) of Dongyang Prefecture, Wei □ (courtesy name Shuzi) of Shouchun County, Yang Jinxun (courtesy name Yuangong) of Shanxi Province, Lin Lixing (courtesy name Mianzhi) of Sanshan (nickname of Fuzhou City), (Quanzhou) native Liu Yuangui (courtesy name Chizhong), He Qingde (courtesy name Changzhi) of Kuocang County, Chen Yi (courtesy name Manqing) of He □ , Wang Yanguang (courtesy name Juzhi) of Putian City, Zheng Mingqing (courtesy name Kunfu) of Qingzhang County (Pingding County in Shanxi Province nowadays), Qi Daxian (courtesy name Jianquan) of Jushui County (Yucheng County in Henan Province nowadays), Lu Xiang (courtesy name Tongpu) of Jiahe Prefecture (Jianyang District in Fujian Province nowadays), Huang Quan (courtesy name Deyan) of Putian City, Yu Daqing (courtesy name Jianzhong) of Jimo County, Ying Ji (courtesy name Zilyu) of Tiantai County, Zhao Ruqi (or Rumao) (courtesy name Qianli) of Kaifeng City, Zhao Yuguan (courtesy name Qingsou) and Nandeng (courtesy name Shideng) of Sanshan prayed for favorable wind in Zhaohui Temple, gathered in Yanfu Temple, and then climbed the mountain to see the Stone Buddha and visited Yinjun Pavilion, and finally returned after a short rest at the Huaigu Hall. Another two people were expected to come but did not arrive, who were Zhao Shanping (courtesy name Zaiqing) of Kaifeng City, and Liu Huishu (courtesy name Yuanlan) of Putian City."

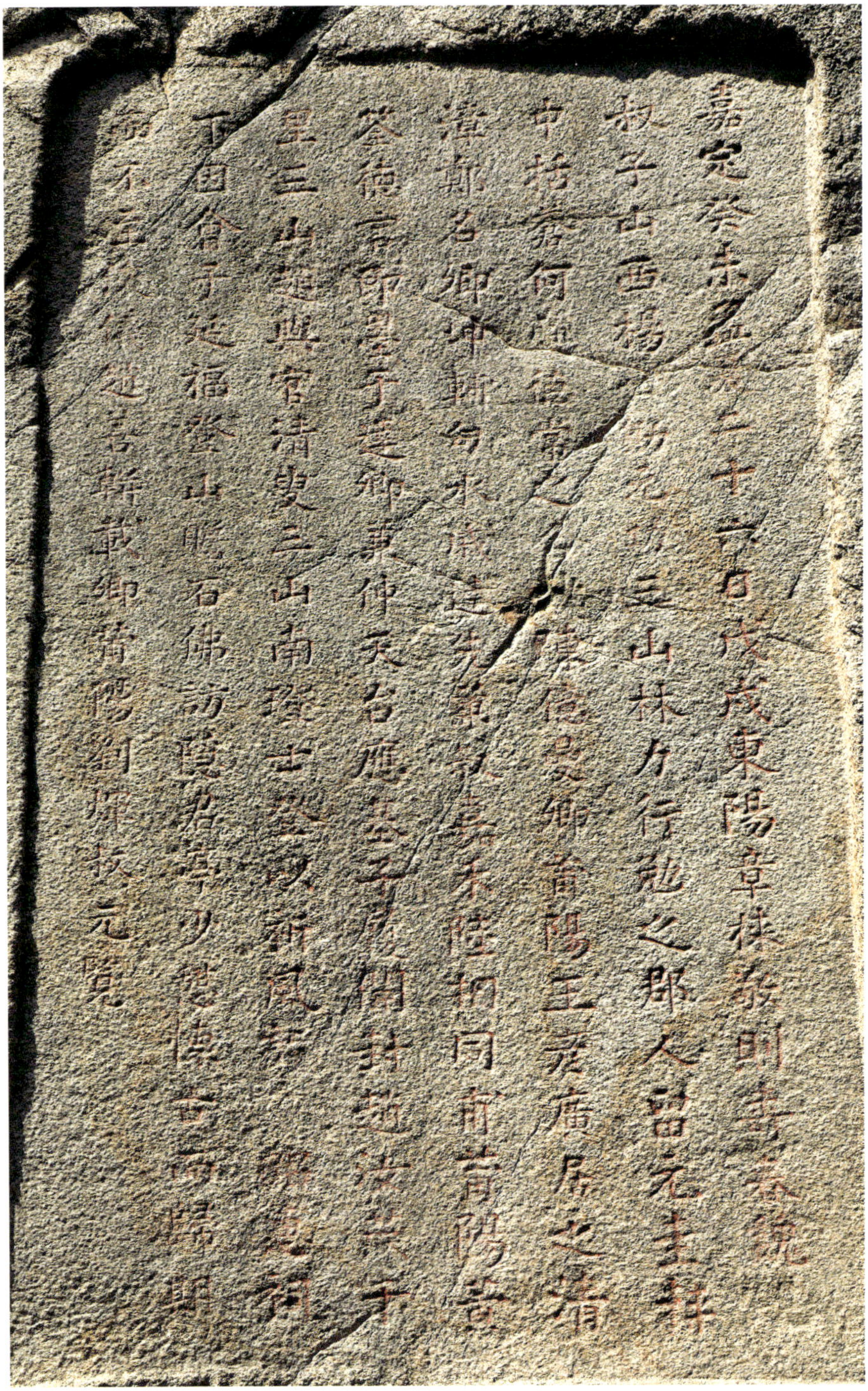

嘉定十六年夏季回航祈风石刻。（成冬冬 摄）
The wind-praying stone inscription for returning trips in the summer of 1223. (Photo by Cheng Dongdong)

这是记载 1223 年四月二十日，泉州太守东阳章梾（字敬则）于商船回舶的四月率同僚 16 人，分别为寿春魏□（字叔子）、山西杨进勋（字元功）、福州林力行（字勉之）、（泉州）郡人留元圭（字持中）、括苍何清德（字常之）、合□陈亿（字曼卿）、莆田王彦广（字居之）、清漳郑名卿（字坤辅）、句水戚达先（字兼权）、嘉禾陆相（字同甫）、莆田黄筌（字德言）、即墨于达卿（字兼仲）、天台应筌（字子履）、开封赵汝芪（字千里）、福州赵与官（字清叟）、福州南璒（字士登）等人，到昭惠庙祈风后，在延福寺聚会，再登山瞻仰石佛，寻访隐君亭，在怀古堂稍作休息后返回的纪事石刻。石刻还提到相约而没有到的人有：开封赵善軿（字载卿）、莆田刘辉叔（字元览）。

This is to record that on lunar April 20, 1223, the Prefect of Quanzhou, Zhang Lai (courtesy name Jingze) of Dongyang Prefecture, led 16 colleagues to pray for favorable wind in Zhaohui Temple, gathered in Yanfu Temple, and then climbed the mountain to see the Stone Buddha and visited Yinjun Pavilion, and finally returned after a short rest at the Huaigu Hall in April when the merchant ships returned. The colleagues included Wei □ (courtesy name Shuzi) of Shouchun County, Yang Jinxun (courtesy name Yuangong) of Shanxi Province, Lin Lixing (courtesy name Mianzhi) of Sanshan (nickname of Fuzhou City), (Quanzhou) native Liu Yuangui (courtesy name Chizhong), He Qingde (courtesy name Changzhi) of Kuocang County, Chen Yi (courtesy name Manqing) of He □ , Wang Yanguang (courtesy name Juzhi) of Putian City, Zheng Mingqing (courtesy name Kunfu) of Qingzhang County (Pingding County in Shanxi Province nowadays), Qi Daxian (courtesy name Jianquan) of Jushui (Yucheng County in Henan Province nowadays), Lu Xiang (courtesy name Tongpu) of Jiahe Prefecture (Jianyang District in Fujian Province nowadays), Huang Quan (courtesy name Deyan) of Putian City, Yu Daqing (courtesy name Jianzhong) of Jimo County, Ying Ji (courtesy name Zilyu) of Tiantai County, Zhao Ruqi (courtesy name Qianli) of Kaifeng City, Zhao Yuguan (courtesy name Qingsou) and Nandeng (courtesy name Shideng) of Sanshan. There were two people who were expected to come but did not turn up. They were Zhao Shanping (courtesy name Zaiqing) of Kaifeng City, and Liu Huishu (courtesy name Yuanlan) of Putian City.

淳熙十年（1183）冬季启航祈风石刻

石刻文云："淳熙十年，岁在昭阳单阏，闰月廿有四日。郡守司马伋、同典宗赵子涛、提舶林劭、统军韩俊，以遣舶祈风于延福寺通远、善利、广福王祠下，修故事也。遍览胜概，少憩于怀古堂，待潮泛舟而归。"

这是一方记载1183年闰十一月二十四日，泉州郡守司马伋，会同知宗正司事赵子涛、市舶司提举林劭、统军韩俊等人，到延福寺旁的通远、善利、广福王祠（即通远王祠）举行遣舶祈风仪式的石刻。此次祈风仪典是遵照旧的行事制度。众人祈风完毕遍览九日山美好景色，在怀古堂稍作休息，等待涨潮驾舟而归。

从这方石刻还能发现两个关键信息：一是"修故事也"，说明泉州地方官主持祈风仪式，是朝廷认可的官方行为，表明政府重视海外贸易的传统一直得到遵循。二是"待潮泛舟而归"，说明涨潮时，从九日山下可以直接乘船返回泉州城。

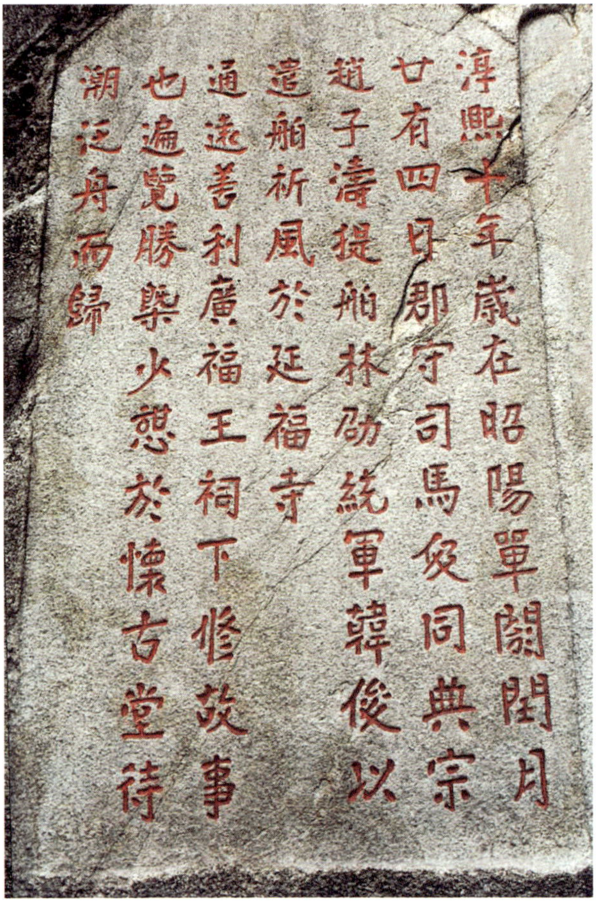

淳熙十年冬季启航祈风石刻。（陈英杰 摄）
The wind-praying stone inscription for departing trips in the winter of 1183. (Photo by Chen Yingjie)

The wind-praying stone inscription for departing trips in the winter of the 10th year in the Chunxi Period (1183)

The stone inscription reads, "On leap November 24 in the 10th year of the Chunxi Period, Quanzhou Prefect Sima Ji, together with Administrator of the Southern Clan Office Zhao Zitao, the Superintendent of the Maritime Trade Office Lin Shao, and the Commander-General Han Jun, etc., went to King Tongyuan Hall in Yanfu Temple to hold the wind-praying ceremony for the departure of ships. The ritual of this wind-praying followed the past routine. After the wind-praying ceremony, they enjoyed the beautiful scenery of Jiuri Mountain, took a short rest at the Huaigu Hall, and waited for the rising tide in order to return by ship."

This is a stone inscription recording that on leap November 24, 1183, Quanzhou Prefect Sima Ji, together with Administrator of the Southern Clan Office Zhao Zitao, Superintendent of the Maritime Trade Office Lin Shao, and Commander-General Han Jun, etc., went to King Tongyuan Hall in Yanfu Temple to hold the wind-praying ceremony for the departure of ships. The ritual of this wind-praying was in accordance with the old practice. After the wind-praying ceremony, they enjoyed the beautiful scenery of Jiuri Mountain, took a short rest at the Huaigu Hall, and sailed back when the tide rose.

Two key messages can also be found in this stone carving. The first one is, "followed the past routine" which shows that it was permitted by the imperial court for the local officials of Quanzhou to hold the ceremony of wind-praying, and indicates that the government had been following the tradition of attaching importance to maritime trade. The second is "waited for the rising tide in order to return by ship", which means that when the tide rose, people could return directly by ship from the foot of Jiuri Mountain to Quanzhou urban area at that time.

九日山上除了祈风石刻，还有许多古代名人留下的摩崖石刻。（田米 摄）
Besides the wind-praying inscriptions, there are also many cliff stone carvings left by ancient celebrities on Jiuri Mountain. (Photo by Tian Mi)

淳祐三年（1243）夏季回航祈风石刻

石刻文云："太守贰卿颜颐仲，祷回舶南风，遵彝典也。提舶寺丞刘克逊俱祷焉。重司存也。礼成，饮福，尚羊嵒壑，真胜践也。别驾卢同父、左翼权军陈世才、舶幙赵崇𥁕、邑令尹薛季良从与祠事也。宗正徽猷赵师恕，适拜开国命，弗果至也。时淳祐癸卯孟夏乙丑也。书者同父也。"

这是太守贰卿颜颐仲，在1243年农历四月，遵照常典，举行祈风仪式祈祷回舶南风，提舶寺丞刘克逊一起参与祷求的石刻。石刻写道，这是重视市舶司制度并使之存续下去的举措。典礼完成，众人在延福寺会饮，然后在山岚缭绕的山壑间闲游，感叹真是登临胜地！别驾卢同父、左翼权军陈世才、舶幕赵崇𥁕、南安县令薛季良跟从参与祭祀事务。担任知南外宗正司事且素有美德的赵师恕，恰好刚被赐授"开国男爵"的职衔，不能前来。1243年初夏乙丑日，书写者卢同父。

这方石刻记录的两位参加祈风仪式的人物，都在13世纪为泉州海上贸易发展做出了重要贡献：这次祈风仪式的主持人泉州太守颜颐仲在其任内减免外商税赋，为官清廉。参与祈风仪式的市舶司长官刘克逊，严禁盘剥外商，发布法令，鼓励外商前来泉州贸易，在其任内到泉州港的外国商船数量大增。

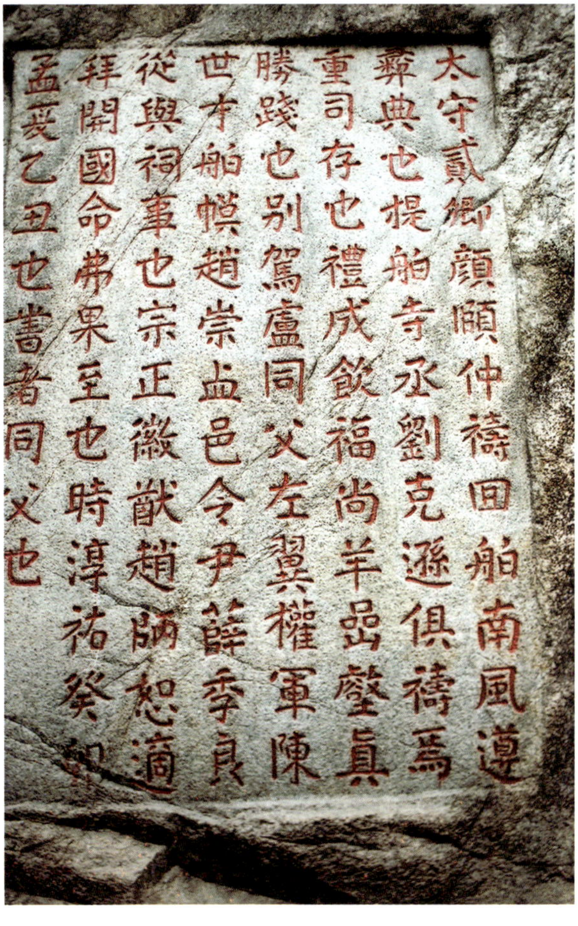

淳祐三年夏季回航祈风石刻。（陈英杰 摄）
The wind-praying stone inscription for returning trips in the summer of 1243. (Photo by Chen Yingjie)

The wind-praying stone inscription for returning trips in the summer of the 3rd year in the Chunyou Period (1243)

The stone inscription reads, "Following the routine ritual, Yan Yizhong, the Prefect of Quanzhou, held a wind-praying ceremony for the south wind to guard the safe return of ships. Liu Kexun, the Sub-Commissioner of the Maritime Trade Office, also participated in the praying together. The aim of this activity is to focus on and maintain the maritime trade system. After the ceremony, they drank at Yanfu Temple, and then strolled around among the hills which were fantastic. The Assistant Sub-Prefect Lu Tongfu, the Commander-General of the Left-Wing Army Chen Shicai, the Private Secretary of the Maritime Trade Office Zhao Chongqi, and Nan'an County Magistrate Xue Jiliang participated together in the sacrificial service. The Administrator of the Southern Clan Office Zhao Shishu could not arrive because he happened to have just been conferred a dynasty-founding title. This was written by Lu Tongfu on the Yichou Day in the early summer of Guimao Year of the Chunyou Period."

This is a stone carving recording that Yan Yizhong, the Prefect of Quanzhou, held a praying ceremony to pray for the south wind to guard the safe return of ships in accordance with the routine ritual in lunar April 1243. Liu Kexun, the Sub-Commissioner of the Maritime Trade Office, participated in the praying together. The stone inscription mentions that this was a measure to focus on and maintain the maritime trade system. After the ceremony, they drank at Yanfu Temple, and then strolled among the misty hills. They were amazed at the beautiful scenery of the mountain. The Assistant Sub-Prefect Lu Tongfu, the Commander-General of the Left-Wing Army Chen Shicai, the Private Secretary of the Maritime Trade Office Zhao Chongqi, and Nan'an County Magistrate Xue Jiliang accompanied to participate in the sacrificial service. The virtuous Zhao Shishu, who served as the Administrator of the Southern Clan Office, could not come because he happened to have just been conferred the title of "Dynasty-Founding Baron". This was written by Lu Tongfu on the Yichou Day in the early summer of 1243.

The two figures recorded in this stone inscription, who participated in the ceremony of wind-praying, made important contributions to the development of Quanzhou's maritime trade in the 13th century. Serving as a clean official, Yan Yizhong, the Prefect of Quanzhou who presided over the ceremony of wind-praying, reduced or exempted foreign business tax during his term of office. The Sub-Commissioner of the Maritime Trade Office Liu Kexun who participated in the ceremony of wind-praying, strictly prohibited the exploitation of foreign businessmen and issued a decree to encourage foreign businessmen to come to Quanzhou for trade. During his term, the number of foreign merchant ships to Quanzhou Port increased significantly.

宝祐五年（1257）冬季启航祈风石刻

石刻文云："宝祐丁巳仲冬下澣，郡守天台谢埴允道，因祈风昭惠庙，邀宗正天水赵师湇东之，及总管寿阳纪智和子常、别驾姑苏赵梦龙骧父、莆阳方澄孙蒙仲、晋江宰三山彭樵道夫、南安宰三山王广翁居安、权舶干三山卢文郁从周、监舶豫章李宏模希膺，陟西峰、探石穴、寻佛岩之遗迹，访君谟之旧游、觞咏于梅竹泉石间，竟日而归。"

这方石刻记录了1257年农历十一月下旬，泉州郡守天台谢埴（字允道），邀请宗正天水赵师湇（字东之）、总管寿阳纪智和（字子常）、别驾苏州赵梦龙（字骧父）、莆田方澄孙（字蒙仲）、晋江县令福州彭樵（字道夫）、南安县令福州王广翁（字居安）、权舶干福州卢文郁（字从周）、监舶豫章李宏模（字希膺）等人来昭惠庙祈风，后登上西峰，探找石穴，寻访石佛岩的遗迹，访求蔡襄旧日游踪，在梅竹泉石之间饮酒赋诗，游玩了一整天才归去。

宝祐五年冬季启航祈风石刻。（成冬冬 摄）
The wind-praying stone inscription for departing trips in the winter of 1257. (Photo by Cheng Dongdong)

The wind-praying stone inscription for departing trips in the winter of the 5th year in the Baoyou Period (1257)

The stone inscription reads, "In late lunar November of Dingsi Year in the Baoyou Period, Xie Zhi (courtesy name Yundao) of Tiantai County, Prefect of Quanzhou, prayed for favorable wind in Zhaohui Temple, when he invited the Administrator of the Southern Clan Office Zhao Shiyu (courtesy name Dongzhi) of Tianshui County, the Supervisor-in-Chief Ji Zhihe (courtesy name Zichang) of Shouyang County, the Assistant Sub-Prefect Zhao Menglong (courtesy name Xiangfu) of Suzhou City, Fang Chengsun (courtesy name Mengzhong) of Putian City, Jinjiang County Magistrate Peng Qiao (courtesy name Daofu) of Fuzhou City, Nan'an County Magistrate Wang Guangweng (courtesy name Ju'an) of Fuzhou City, the Maritime Trade Official Lu Wenyu (courtesy name Congzhou) of Fuzhou City, and Supervisor of the Maritime Trade Office Li Hongmo (courtesy name Xiying) of Yuzhang Prefecture (northern Jiangxi Province nowadays), etc. They then climbed the Western Summit to explore caves, searched for the remains of the Stone Buddha, visited Junmo's (courtesy name of Cai Xiang) formerly-visited places, drank and wrote poems among the beautiful landscapes. It took them a whole day before they went back."

This stone inscription records that in late lunar November, 1257, the Prefect of Quanzhou Xie Zhi (courtesy name Yundao) of Tiantai County, invited the Administrator of the Southern Clan Office Zhao Shiyu (courtesy name Dongzhi) of Tianshui County, the Supervisor-in-Chief Ji Zhihe (courtesy name Zichang) of Shouyang County, the Assistant Sub-Prefect Zhao Menglong (courtesy name Xiangfu) of Suzhou City, Fang Chengsun (courtesy name Mengzhong) of Putian City, Jinjiang County Magistrate Peng Qiao (courtesy name Daofu) of Fuzhou City, Nan'an County Magistrate Wang Guangweng (courtesy name Ju'an) of Fuzhou City, the Maritime Trade Official Lu Wenyu (courtesy name Congzhou) of Fuzhou City, and Supervisor of the Maritime Trade Office Li Hongmo (courtesy name Xiying) of Yuzhang Prefecture (northern Jiangxi Province nowadays), etc. to come to Zhaohui Temple for wind-praying, and then climbed the Western Summit to explore caves, searched for the remains of the Stone Buddha, visited Cai Xiang's formerly-visited places, drank and composed poems among the beautiful landscapes. It took them a whole day before they went back.

咸淳二年（1266）冬季启航祈风石刻

石刻文云："咸淳丙寅，南至后十日，祷风此山。知宗兼郡事古汴赵希悰安宅、提举缣事眉山王橚茂、领郡倦三嵎虞会和叔、三山郑君为瑞国、寮属番禺史霆声宏甫、天台卢应伯和、东嘉赵崇东旸卿、三山林起东景仁、黄以谦谦之、潘昌廷孔时、邑令三山陈梦发以道、陈山公仰卿。是日也，霜日熙明，溪山献状，登怀古，景先哲，宛然有得，彝典云乎哉！"

这是1266年冬至后十日祈风所留下的石刻。石刻记载了知宗正司事兼泉州郡守河南赵希悰（字安宅）、提举丝绸贸易事务眉山王橚（字茂悦）、领郡倦三嵎虞会（字和叔）、福州郑君为（字瑞国）、同僚广州史霆声（字宏甫）、天台卢应（字伯和）、温州赵东崇（字暘卿）、福州林起东（字景仁）、黄以谦（字谦之）、潘昌廷（字孔时）、南安县令福州陈梦发（字以道）、陈山公（字仰卿）共同参与祈风。这一天，霜后阳光明媚，溪山显露出优美的形态。众人登怀古堂，景仰先哲，颇有所得并留下石刻以纪事。时值南宋王朝风雨飘摇、岌岌可危之际。这也是宋代现存最晚的一方祈风石刻，此后九日山上再没留下记载祈风典礼的石刻。

咸淳二年冬季启航祈风石刻。（成冬冬 摄）
The wind-praying stone inscription for departing trips in the winter of 1266. (Photo by Cheng Dongdong)

The wind-praying stone inscription for departing trips in the winter of the 2nd year in the Xianchun Period (1266)

The stone inscription reads, "Ten days after the winter solstice of Bingyin Year in the Xianchun Period, wind-praying ceremony was held in this mountain. The participants were Administrator of the Southern Clan Office and Prefect of Quanzhou Zhao Xicha (courtesy name Anzhai) of ancient Bianjing City (Kaifeng City nowadays), Supervisorate of Silk Trade Affairs Wang Su (courtesy name Maoyue) of Meishan City, Executive of Prefecture Yu Hui (courtesy name Heshu) of Sanyu County (Chenggu County in Shaanxi Province nowadays), Zheng Junwei (courtesy name Ruiguo) of Fuzhou City, the colleagues Shi Tingsheng (courtesy name Hongfu) of Guangzhou City, Lu Ying (courtesy name Bohe) of Tiantai County, Zhao Dongchong (courtesy name Yiqing) of Wengzhou City, Lin Qidong (courtesy name Jingren) of Fuzhou City, Huang Yiqian (courtesy name Qianzhi) of Fuzhou City, Pan Changting (courtesy name Kongshi) of Fuzhou City, County Magistrate Chen Mengfa (courtesy name Yidao) of Fuzhou City, and Chen Shangong (courtesy name Yangqing). On that day, the sun was shining after the frost, and the mountains and streams showed their beauty. They went to the Huaigu Hall to admire the sages. Deeply impressed, they left stone carvings to record this event."

This is a stone carving of praying for favorable wind left ten days after the winter solstice in 1266. The stone inscriptions recorded the wind-praying participants including the Administrator of the Southern Clan Office and Prefect of Quanzhou Zhao Xicha (courtesy name Anzhai) of Henan Province, Supervisorate of Silk Trade Affairs Wang Su (courtesy name Maoyue) of Meishan City, Sub-prefecture Yu Hui (courtesy name Heshu) of Sanyu County (Chenggu County in Shaanxi Province nowadays), Zheng Junwei (courtesy name Ruiguo) of Fuzhou City, the colleagues Shi Tingsheng (courtesy name Hongfu) of Guangzhou City, Lu Ying (courtesy name Bohe) of Tiantai County, Zhao Dongchong (courtesy name Yiqing) of Wengzhou City, Lin Qidong (courtesy name Jingren) of Fuzhou City, Huang Yiqian (courtesy name Qianzhi) of Fuzhou City, Pan Changting (courtesy name Kongshi) of Fuzhou City, Nan'an County Magistrate Chen Mengfa (courtesy name Yidao) of Fuzhou City, and Chen Shangong (courtesy name Yangqing). On that day, the sun was shining after the frost, and the mountains and streams showed their beauty. People went to the Huaigu Hall to admire the sages. They were impressed and left stone carvings to record this event. It was a time when the Southern Song Dynasty was precarious and in danger. This is also the latest surviving stone inscription of praying for favorable wind in the Song Dynasty. Since then, there has been no stone inscription recording the ceremony of wind-praying on Jiuri Mountain.

淳熙元年（1174）冬季启航祈风石刻

石刻文云："淳熙元年，岁在甲午季冬朔，吴人虞仲房帅幕属洪子用、朱彦钦、赵德季、赵致孚，祈风于延福寺通远王祠下，修岁祀也。与者许称叔、吴景温、闻人应之、赵子张。"

这方石刻记载了 1174 年十二月初一日，市舶司提举杭州人虞仲房带领僚属洪子用、朱彦钦、赵德季、赵致孚等人到延福寺通远王祠祈风。这是遵照每年旧例举行祈风的祭祀仪式。参与者还有许称叔、吴景温、闻人应之、赵子张等人。这是现存祈风石刻中年代最早的一方。它与最后一方祈风石刻的年代相距 92 年。这方石刻也是一件难得的艺术珍品，它的书刻者虞仲房，不仅是一名清廉的地方官，也是当时著名的书法家。

The wind-praying stone inscription for departing trips in the winter of the first year in the Chunxi Period (1174)

The stone inscription reads, "On the first lunar day of December in Jiawu Year which is the first year of the Chunxi Period, Yu Zhongfang, a native of Hangzhou, led his subordinates Hong Ziyong, Zhu Yanqin, Zhao Deji, Zhao Zhifu to pray for favorable wind at King Tongyuan Hall of Yanfu Temple. This is an annual routine ritual of a wind-praying ceremony. Participants also included Xu Chengshu, Wu Jingwen, Wenren Yingzhi and Zhao Zizhang."

This stone inscription records that on the first lunar day of December, 1174, Superintendent of the Maritime Trade Office Yu Zhongfang, a native of Hangzhou, led his subordinates Hong Ziyong, Zhu Yanqin, Zhao Deji, Zhao Zhifu and so on to pray for favorable wind at King Tongyuan Hall of Yanfu Temple. This is an annual routine ritual of wind-praying. Participants also included Xu Chengshu, Wu Jingwen, Wenren Yingzhi, Zhao Zizhang, etc. This is the earliest one among the existing wind-praying stone inscriptions. It is 92 years away from the date of the last wind-praying stone inscription. This stone inscription is also a rare art treasure, because its carver Yu Zhongfang was not only an incorruptible magistrate but also a famous calligrapher at that time.

淳熙元年冬季启航祈风石刻。（成冬冬 摄）

The wind-praying stone inscription for departing trips in the winter of 1174. (Photo by Cheng Dongdong)

以上 10 方祈风石刻最早的为南宋淳熙元年（1174），最晚的为南宋咸淳二年（1266）。其中记载冬季启航祈风的石刻有 6 方，记载夏季回航祈风的有 3 方，还有 1 方同时记载了一年两季的祈风。碑文详细记载了历次参与祈风活动的市舶司官员、泉州地方军政要员、南外宗正司成员名单。石刻记录的几位泉州太守及市舶司长官，在促进泉州海上贸易发展中业绩突出，比如倪思疏浚河道，蔡襄兴建洛阳桥，韩俊维护治安，以及颜颐仲、刘克逊推行善待外商、鼓励贸易等举措。这些官员为推动泉州海外交通的兴盛与繁荣都作出了重大的历史贡献。

九日山祈风石刻是两宋时期（12—13 世纪）泉州地方官员和市舶司官员为"番舶"往返顺利而举行"祈风"祭祀活动的石刻文字记录，也是唯一现存古代中国官方有关航海事宜举行国家祭典的真实记录。它与市舶司遗址、德济门遗址等共同体现了宋代市舶制度下国家力量对海洋贸易的倡导和管控，也印证了宋代泉州港同东南亚、印度洋、波斯湾、红海和东非等地区的海上经济贸易和人民交往的史实。1991 年 2 月，联合国教科文组织"海上丝绸之路"国际考察团莅临实地考察九日山，对九日山摩崖石刻予以极高的评价，赞誉此处为考察路线全程最有世界意义的考察点。来自 37 个国家的 50 多位联合国考察团成员，特意用中英文留下一方象征友谊与对话的纪念石碑。碑文内容为："在九日山最后一次祈风典礼之后七百余年，我们，来自非洲、美洲、亚洲和欧洲的联合国教科文组织海上丝绸之路国际考察队员，乘坐阿曼苏丹提供的'和平号'考察船来到这里。作为朝圣者，我们既重温这古老的祈祷，也带来了各国人民和平的信息。这也正是联合国教科文组织丝绸之路——对话之路综合研究项目的最终目标。为此，特留下这块象征友谊与对话的石刻。"

联合国教科文组织官员考察九日山祈风石刻。（许兆恺 摄）

UNESCO officials were investigating the wind praying stone inscription on Jiuri Mountain. (Photo by Xu Zhaokai)

The earliest wind-praying stone inscription in the above ten inscriptions was carved in 1174, and the latest was carved in 1266 in the Southern Song Dynasty. Six of the inscriptions record wind-praying rituals for departing trips in winter, three for returning trips in summer and one records wind-praying rites in both summer and winter of the same year. The inscriptions record in detail the participant list of the maritime trade officials, local government and military officials and the Southern Clan Office members. The prefects of Quanzhou and the maritime trade officials recorded in the inscriptions have all made prominent achievements in promoting the development of Quanzhou's maritime trade. For example, Ni Si dredged the rivers; Cai Xiang took charge of the construction of Luoyang Bridge; Han Jun maintained the security and order of the society; Yan Yizhong and Liu Kexun took measures of being friendly to foreign businessmen and encouraging trade. These officials have made significant historical contributions to the prosperity of Quanzhou's maritime transportation.

Juri Mountain wind-praying inscriptions are the written inscriptive records of the wind-praying sacrificial activities held by Quanzhou local officials and the officials of the Maritime Trade Office in the Song Dynasty (12th to 13th centuries) for the smooth round trips of maritime ships. The stone inscriptions are also the only authentic official records in ancient China of national ceremonies on navigation matters. Together with the site of the Maritime Trade Office and the site of Deji Gate, it embodies the advocacy and control of maritime trade by state forces under the maritime trade system in the Song Dynasty, and also proves the historical facts of the maritime trade and people's exchanges between Quanzhou Port and the areas such as Southeast Asia, the Indian Ocean, the Persian Gulf, the Red Sea and East Africa in the Song Dynasty. In February 1991, the UNESCO Maritime Silk Road international delegation made field trips to Jiuri Mountain and highly praised the stone inscriptions on the cliffs of Jiuri Mountain, saying that it was the most meaningful investigation place with global significance during the whole route. More than 50 members of the UNESCO delegation from 37 countries left a monument in both Chinese and English to symbolize the friendship and dialogue. The content of the inscription is as follows: "More than 700 years after the last wind-praying ceremony on Jiuri Mountain, we, the members of the UNESCO Maritime Silk Road International Expedition from Africa, America, Asia and Europe, came here by the 'Peace' expedition ship provided by the Sultan of Oman. As pilgrims, we not only reviewed this ancient prayer, but also brought the peace message of people from all over the world. This is exactly the ultimate goal of the comprehensive research project on the UNESCO Silk Road—Road of Dialogue. For this reason, we specially left this stone inscription symbolizing friendship and dialogue."

从水神到海神——真武大帝信仰及泉州真武庙

From Water God to Sea God: Worship of Zhenwu Celestial Lord and Quanzhou Zhenwu Temple

泉州的真武大帝信仰

Worship of Zhenwu Celestial Lord in Quanzhou

真武庙的建筑形制

The Shape and Structure of Zhenwu Temple

真武庙的建筑特征

Architectural Features of Zhenwu Temple

法石真武庙。（郑文桂 摄）
Fashi Zhenwu Temple. (Photo by Zheng Wengui)

真武庙位于泉州城东部石头山上，既是古代法石港的重要地标，也是宋代官员祭祀泉州第二代海神——真武大帝的场所。真武大帝信仰是宋元时期泉州海商从事海洋贸易的重要精神寄托，在“泉州：宋元中国的世界海洋商贸中心”系列遗产中是海洋贸易管理保障的代表性遗产，与昭惠庙的通远王信仰、天后宫的妈祖信仰一起构成泉州地区独具特色的海神信仰体系，鼓舞着一代又一代的泉州人乘风远航、追逐梦想。

法石真武庙真武大帝塑像。（苏德辉 摄）

The statue of Zhenwu Celestial Lord in Fashi Zhenwu Temple. (Photo by Su Dehui)

Zhenwu Temple is located on the stone hill in the east of Quanzhou City. It is not only an important landmark of the ancient Fashi Port, but also a place where officials of the Song Dynasty worshiped Zhenwu Celestial Lord, the second generation of Quanzhou's sea god. The belief of Zhenwu Celestial Lord was an important source of spiritual support for Quanzhou merchants who engaged in maritime trade during the Song and Yuan period. It is a representative heritage of institutional guarantee for maritime trade management in the world cultural heritage series of "Quanzhou: Emporium of the World in Song-Yuan China". Together with the belief of King Tongyuan in Zhaohui Temple and the belief of Mazu in Tianhou Temple, it forms the unique belief system of the sea gods in Quanzhou area, inspiring generations of Quanzhou people to sail and pursue their dreams.

泉州的真武大帝信仰

真武大帝信仰

真武大帝，又称玄天上帝、真武、北极真君、元天上帝等。真武大帝信仰兴盛于宋代。在宋代建国之初，玄天上帝对国家统一和御敌等都有所帮助，所以自宋太祖起，宋朝历代皇帝大力提倡敬奉。宋真宗加封玄天上帝为“镇天真武灵应佑圣真君”，后来为避圣祖赵玄朗的名讳，将玄武的名称改为真武。元代则晋升其为“元圣仁威玄天上帝”。在道教神灵系统中，真武大帝本是镇守北方的水神，主风雨。因海以水为本，北方水神信仰传入泉州后，与当地悠久的海洋文明交融，真武大帝就很自然地被塑造成为具有镇海、保平安能力的“海神”。宋元时期供奉真武大帝的祠宇遍天下，其披头散发，身穿精铜盔甲、手持七星宝剑、光脚踩着龟蛇二怪的形象也在这一时期定型并广为人知。

Worship of Zhenwu Celestial Lord in Quanzhou

Worship of Zhenwu Celestial Lord

Zhenwu Celestial Lord is also known as Xuantian Shangdi (High Emperor of the Mysterious Heaven), Zhenwu, Beiji Zhenjun, Yuantian Shangdi, etc. The faith of Zhenwu Celestial Lord flourished in the Song Dynasty. At the beginning of the founding of the Song Dynasty, Xuantian Shangdi was helpful to the unification of the country and the defense of enemies. Therefore, successive emperors of the Song Dynasty vigorously advocated people to worship him since Emperor Taizu. Emperor Zhenzong of the Song Dynasty bestowed the title of Xuantian Shangdi as "Zhentian Zhenwu Lingying Yousheng Zhenjun". Later, the name of Xuanwu was changed to Zhenwu in order to avoid the taboo of the name of Zhao Xuanlang, the god of wealth. In the Yuan Dynasty, it was promoted as "Yuansheng Renwei Xuantian God". In the Taoist deity system, Zhenwu Celestial Lord was originally the water god who guarded the north and ruled wind and rain. After the water god belief in Northern China was introduced to Quanzhou, it was blended with the long-standing local maritime civilization because water was the source of sea. Thus, Zhenwu Celestial Lord was naturally shaped as the "sea god", with the ability to calm the sea and maintain peace. During the Song and Yuan Dynasties, temples dedicated to Zhenwu Celestial Lord were all over the country, whose image of exuding hair, wearing a fine copper armor, holding a seven-star sword, and stepping on the turtle and snake with bare feet was also finalized and widely known during this period.

深沪崇真殿始建于宋代，庙中祀北极玄天上帝，即真武大帝。（陈文丕 摄）
Shenhu Chongzhen Hall was first built in the Song Dynasty, where Beiji Xuantian Shangdi, also known as Zhenwu Celestial Lord, is enshrined. (Photo by Chen Wenpi)

泉州真武庙

宋代泉州供奉真武大帝的庙宇主要有泉州法石真武庙、晋江深沪崇真殿、晋江金井拱秀庙、晋江龙湖真如殿，市舶司旁建有玄天上帝宫，现与戏神田都元帅共居一庙，旁有巷子名曰“上帝宫巷”。这些庙宇中最著名的当数靠近江口码头的法石真武庙。法石真武庙建于控扼晋江入海口的石头山上，此处与晋江对岸的紫帽山、罗裳山遥相对峙，历史上是船舶从外港水域进入晋江的最窄处，于此可远眺泉州湾。石头山的西北向则山丘绵延，与清源山相接，护卫着刺桐古城。

历史上这个区域是著名的法石港，交通便利，码头密集，航运繁忙，又处在古城向东通往后渚港的干道沿线，便于出海人员的祭拜。据《晋江县志》记载：“真武庙，在三十六都郡城东南石头山上。庙枕山漱海，人烟辏集其下。”因为地理位置的重要性，南宋淳熙十三年（1186），知州真德秀在这里设置法石寨，城南置宝林寨，派军队守卫，与始置于乾道八年（1172）的永宁寨并称左翼水军三寨。对于法石寨的重要性，真德秀在《西山文集》中这样描述：“法石寨去城一十五里，水面广阔，寨临其上，内足以捍州城，外足以扼海道，合重屯以壮形势。”在古泉州外港与内港交界的关键性节点上，为祈求船舶顺风平安，建造了不少与海神有关的庙宇，真武庙就是其中最重要的一处。

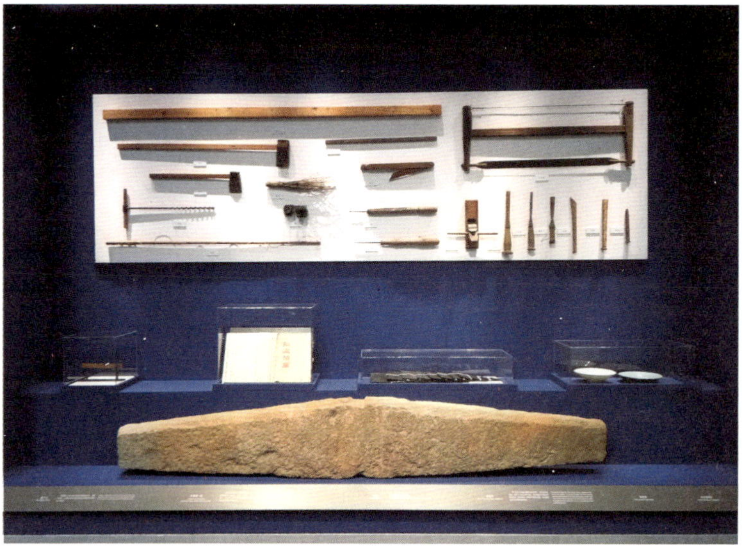

泉州法石古船遗址发现的碇石。（泉州海外交通史博物馆 供图）

The anchorage stone discovered at the site of ancient ship at Quanzhou Fashi Port. (Courtesy of Quanzhou Maritime Museum)

Zhenwu Temple in Quanzhou

The temples dedicated to Zhenwu Celestial Lord in Quanzhou in the Song Dynasty mainly included Fashi Zhenwu Temple in Quanzhou, Shenhu Chongzhen Hall, Jinjing Gongxiu Temple in Jinjiang and Longhu Zhenru Hall in Jinjiang. Next to the Maritime Trade Office, there is Xuantian God Palace which is now in the same temple as Marshal Tian Du (God of Drama). Beside the temple there is an ally named "God Palace Alley". The most famous one of these temples is Fashi Zhenwu Temple near Jiangkou Docks, which was built on the stone hill controlling the mouth of the Jinjiang River. This place faces Zimao Mountain and Luoshang Mountain on the opposite bank of the Jinjiang River, and is historically the narrowest place where ships enter the Jinjiang River from waters of the outer port. From here, people can overlook Quanzhou Bay. To the northwest of the stone hill, there are rolling hills which connect with Qingyuan Mountain, guarding the ancient city of Zayton.

This area was the famous Fashi Port in the history, with convenient transportation, dense wharves, and busy shipping. It is also located along the main road from the ancient city of Quanzhou to Houzhu Port to the east, making it convenient for maritime people to worship. According to the *Local Chronicles of Jinjiang County*, "Zhenwu Temple is located on the stone hill in the southeast of the 36th town. The temple rests on the hill and faces the sea, with many people gathering here." Owing to the significance of the geographical location, in 1186 in the Southern Song Dynasty, Prefect Zhen Dexiu set up Fashi Camp here and Baolin Camp in the south of the city, and sent troops to guard them. They were called "Three Left-Wing Navy Camps", together with Yongning Camp which was first set up in 1172. Regarding the importance of Fashi Camp, Zhen Dexiu described it in *Collected Works of Zhen Xishan*, "Fashi Camp is on the vast water 7.5km away from the city, which can defend the city inside and control the sea lane outside. It is necessary to be strengthened by garrison." At this critical junction between the outer port and the inner port of ancient Quanzhou, many temples related to the sea gods have been built in order to pray for safe sailing of ships, among which Zhenwu Temple is the most important one.

海神信仰与官方祭海

此时，真武大帝是国家认证的正统海神，真武庙是泉州官方祭祀海神的指定场所。真武庙作为海神信仰的重要场所，也是渔民、商人等海上航行者为祈求海上航行一帆风顺，从而在心理上战胜大风大浪的精神寄托。泉州太守和市舶司的官员每年都会到这里举行祭海活动，保障并鼓励泉州海洋商贸不断走向繁荣。

据乾隆版《泉州府志》载："石头山在万岁山之左，前与赤城山相连，山尽处有三山杰出，上有真武殿，宋时望祭海神之所。"每月望日（即农历十五）泉州郡守便到此祭拜海神，以祈求一切往来泉州的海船航行顺风吉利。南宋嘉定十年至十二年（1217—1219），真德秀担任泉州太守期间，曾多次到此祭祀海神真武大帝并撰写《真武殿祝文》。这篇祝文收录在传世史料《西山文集》中，描述了真太守在真武庙祭祀海神真武大帝，祈求真武大帝消除江海之上的灾害天气，保护商船、海舶航海平安。泉州郡守亲自定期向海神祷告保护航海平安，体现了政府对祭海仪式及对海洋贸易的鼓励与推动。

真德秀不仅多次前往真武庙祭拜真武大帝，祈求航海平安，他在泉州任上施行崇尚儒家文化风教、清除监狱冤假错案、严禁苛捐杂税、减轻赋税等利民惠民措施，还与市舶司提举赵崇度一起清除海外贸易管理制度上的弊端，极力招揽海外客商前来泉州港从事贸易，促进了泉州海外贸易的长足发展。

明清以来，法石真武大帝的信仰随着闽南人向外迁移的脚步，传播到我国台湾、香港地区和东南亚等地，比如印尼雅加达丹绒玄天上帝庙就是清代侨居印尼的泉州人修建的。至今，当地社区居民每逢农历正月二十九日，都会到此举行祭海祈福仪式。

法石真武庙祭典。（许兆恺 摄）
Sacrifice in Fashi Zhenwu Temple. (Photo by Xu Zhaokai)

Sea God Belief and Official Sea God Sacrifice

Zhenwu Celestial Lord was the orthodox sea god certified by the government then, and Zhenwu Temple was the designated place for official worship of sea god in Quanzhou. As an important place for sea god worship, Zhenwu Temple has been the spiritual sustenance for fishermen, businessmen and other seafarers to pray for smooth sailing on the sea so as to overcome the strong wind and waves psychologically. The Prefect of Quanzhou and officials of the Maritime Trade Office came here annually to hold sea god sacrifice activities to ensure and encourage the continuous prosperity of Quanzhou's maritime trade.

As stated in *Local Chronicles of Quanzhou Prefecture* compiled during Emperor Qianlong's reign, "The stone hill is on the left of Wansui Hill, and is connected to Chicheng Hill in its front. At the end of the hill, there are three prominent hills, with Zhenwu Temple on the top. In the Song Dynasty, that was the place for people to worship and offer sacrifices to the sea god." On the 15th day of every lunar month, the Prefect of Quanzhou came here to offer sacrifices to the sea god in order to pray for the safety of maritime trips to and from Quanzhou. From 1217 to 1219 in the Southern Song Dynasty, when Zhen Dexiu served as the Prefect of Quanzhou, he came here to worship the sea god Zhenwu Celestial Lord, and wrote *Prayer to Zhenwu Palace* in person. This prayer is included in the handed-down historical material *Collected Works of Zhen Xishan*, which describes that Prefect Zhen offered sacrifices to Zhenwu Celestial Lord in Zhenwu Temple, praying to him for eliminating the disastrous weather on the river and sea and ensuring the safety of merchant ships and maritime ships. The Prefect of Quanzhou personally prayed to the sea god regularly for the safety of navigation, which reflects the encouragement and promotion of sea sacrifice ceremonies and institutional management of maritime trade.

Zhen Dexiu went to Zhenwu Temple for many times to worship Zhenwu Celestial Lord and prayed for the safety of navigation. He also implemented measures to benefit the people during his tenure in Quanzhou, such as advocating Confucian culture and morality, clearing up unjust and wrong cases in prison, strictly prohibiting exorbitant taxes, and reducing taxes. Besides these, together with the Superintendent of the Maritime Trade Office Zhao Chongdu, he also proposed to remove the drawbacks of the maritime trade management system and tried to attract overseas merchants to trade in Quanzhou Port, which promoted the rapid development of Quanzhou's maritime trade.

Since the Ming and Qing Dynasties, the worship of Fashi Zhenwu Celestial Lord has spread to Taiwan, Hong Kong of China and Southeast Asia along with the outward migration of Southern Fujian people. For example, the Danrong Xuantian God Temple in Jakarta, Indonesia, was built by Quanzhou people who lived in Indonesia in the Qing Dynasty. So far, local community residents will hold the ceremony of sea god sacrifices to pray for blessings on every 29th of the first lunar month.

真武庙的建筑形制

依山面江，坐东朝西的法石真武庙始建于宋代开宝年间，此后历代有修葺。真武庙依山而筑，顺着山势逐步抬升，主体建筑包括山门、石阶、凉亭（拜亭）、大殿，占地面积 8,000 多平方米。

山门为四柱三间三楼牌楼式结构，面阔三间，进深三柱，重檐歇山顶，檐下施如意斗拱。山门正中悬黑底镏金行书“武当山”牌匾，两侧嵌着红砖雕，雕刻太上老君、吕洞宾、韩湘子、曹国舅、铁拐李、蓝采和、何仙姑、张果老、汉钟离等道教神仙以及“卍”字不断符。正中两根石柱上悬挂对联——上联：大道至易至简只在心上勤修炼；下联：玄机不难不烦唯于意中细悟参。两边墙石柱的楹联出自清代泉州翰林庄俊元的手笔——仰之弥高大观在上，过此以往联步而升。山门旁有一口古井，是明万历间泉州后城李氏妇人捐建。水井旁墙体上有石碑刻“在城宫后巷李奶奶喜舍 三蟹龙泉 万历四十四年八月吉旦”，此井水质清澈甘冽，为出海船队的重要淡水补给处。

山门通往真武圣殿的道路是依山坡砌筑的 24 级石阶，左右置有石扶栏，扶栏柱上雕有石狮，十分古朴。顺着石阶而上，可见尽头立有一方高 1.5 米、宽 0.5 米、厚 0.2 米的石碑。碑面正中阴刻大字楷书“吞海”，碑面右侧题款“赐进士第知晋江县事略子韩岳立”，左侧题款“大明嘉靖十二年岁次癸巳腊月之吉”。这方碑刻为韩岳担任晋江县令期间到真武庙祈福所立。韩岳在晋江任上整顿吏治，安抚民众，兴修水利，维护治安。

真武庙山门。（吴刚强 摄

The Mountain Gate c
Zhenwu Temple. (Phot
by Wu Gangqiang)

The Shape and Structure of Zhenwu Temple

Sitting east on the hill and facing the river in the west, Fashi Zhenwu Temple was initially built in the Kaibao Period (968—976) of the Song Dynasty, and has been repaired in successive dynasties since then. The main buildings of Zhenwu Temple include the Mountain Gate, stone steps, Worship Pavilion (Bai Pavilion), and the Grand Hall, which are built and gradually rise along the hill. It is built against the hill and gradually rises along with it, covering an area of more than 8,000m^2.

The Mountain Gate is a gateway of memorial-arch style with four columns and three archways. It is three-*chien* wide, three-pillar deep and three-floor high, with a double-eave gable, a hipped roof and Ruyi-shaped bracket sets placed under the eaves. In the middle of the Mountain Gate hangs a plaque of " 武当山 " (Mount Wudang) in black-bottomed gold-plated running hand. On both sides, it is inlaid with red brick carvings, carved with Taoist immortals, such as Lao Tzu, Lyu Dongbin, Han Xiangzi, Cao Guojiu, Tie Guaili, Lan Caihe, He Xiangu, Zhang Guolao, Han Zhongli, as well as the character of " 卍 " (Swastika). A couplet is hung on the two stone pillars in the middle, the first and second lines of which read "The greatest truth is the simplest which can be achieved by cultivating one's mind" "A profound theory is the easiest which can be understood by mediation". The couplet on the stone pillars on both sides of the wall was written by Zhuang Junyuan, Quanzhou Hanlin Academician in the Qing Dynasty, which reads "The temple seems taller when looking upwards; people go higher when crossing the Mountain Gate". There is an ancient well next to the Mountain Gate, which was donated by the wife of the Li family in Houcheng, Quanzhou during 1573 and 1620 of the Ming Dynasty. There is a stone inscription on the wall next to the well, "Grandma Li in the Hou Valley of the urban city is happy to donate this well name ' San Xie Long Quan' on lunar 1st of August in the 44th year of the Wanli Period." The water of this well is clear and sweet, which makes it an important fresh water supply place for the fleet going to sea.

The road from the Mountain Gate to Zhenwu Temple is built in 24 stone steps on the slope of the hill. There are stone handrails carved with stone lions on both sides of the steps, which is very quaint. Going up the stone steps to the end, people can find that there is a stone tablet 1.5m high, 0.5m wide, and 0.2m thick. On the center of the stele, there are two large characters " 吞 海 " (Devouring the Sea) engraved in regular script; on the right side, the inscriptions are "Erected by Jinjiang Magistrate Han Yue, Metropolitan Graduate with Honors (equivalent to doctor's degree)"; on the left side, the inscriptions are "On the 1st day of lunar December in the 12th year (Guisi Year) of the Jiajjing Period (1532—1535) in the Ming Dynasty". This stele was erected at Zhenwu Temple by Han Yue to pray for blessings when he served as the magistrate of Jinjiang County. When Han Yue was in office in Jinjiang, he rectified the officials, pacified the people, built water conservancy and maintained social security.

“吞海”石碑寓意真武大帝保佑海滨之民，吞海成桑田，使百姓可安居乐业，也寓意着泉州人民气可吞海、不怕艰难险阻的英勇气概。“吞海”石碑底座大石形似大龟的形状，另一边突出的部分像蛇头的形状。这一酷似龟蛇合体形象的大石符合真武大帝脚下踏着龟蛇的形象特征。另一方面通过与正殿的布局组合关系，附会了泉州民间信仰中真武大帝脚踏龟蛇、法力无边的传说，寓意镇住风浪，保佑航海船舶出入平安。

“吞海”碑刻左后侧有一座四柱八角角亭。平面呈四边形，边长 4.49 米，进深二柱，地面铺设条石，重檐攒尖顶，下檐为四角屋面，上檐为八角屋面，中间为八角形藻井，上有封板。角亭造型结构象征真武大帝钤用的印章。角亭石柱上书刻楹联“到此地静观自得　登斯亭少住为佳　同治庚午年仲夏”，这是清代同治庚午年（1870）修缮时留下的铭文。

角亭后方为真武圣殿。大殿始建于宋代，清代道光二十二年（1842）重修，两进五开间，为清代闽南传统宅院建筑格局及样式。前殿面阔五间，明间进深三柱，前侧为硬山式屋面，后侧为卷棚式梁架，歇山式屋面。次间进深二柱，为硬山式屋面。大门两旁石柱上有一副对联“罗紫双峰齐拱峙　溜浯一派尽朝宗”，两侧悬挂木对联“脱紫帽于殿前不整冠而正南面　抛罗裳于海角亦跣足以莅北朝”。对联中的“罗紫”即泉州四大名山中的罗裳山、紫帽山，“溜浯”则为泉州晋江流域中的溜石江和浯江。大门两旁墙体有青龙吐珠、猛虎下山的堆剪。殿内两侧石窗上有铭文“法石鱼帮弟子公立 道光壬寅仲春吉”“本境弟子郑定业敬 道光壬寅仲春吉”。两处铭文说明在 1842 年真武殿重修时，当地从事渔业及航运贸易的民众自发捐资倡修，可见泉州悠久的海外贸易传统一直影响着当地人们的生活、生产方式。

“吞海”石碑。（田米 摄）
The stele of " 吞海 " (Devouring the Sea). (Photo by Tian Mi)

The stele of " 吞海 " symbolizes that Zhenwu Celestial Lord blesses the people on the seashore by devouring the sea and turning it into fields so that the people can live and work in peace and contentment. It also embodies that Quanzhou people are brave enough to swallow the sea without being afraid of difficulties and obstacles. The large stone at the base of the stele is in the shape of a giant turtle, and the protruding part on the other side looks like a snake's head. This boulder, with the image of a turtle and a snake, is in line with the image characteristics of Zhenwu Celestial Lord stepping on a turtle and a snake. Additionally, through the combination with the layout of the Grand Hall, it is in accordance with the legend in Quanzhou folk beliefs that Zhenwu Celestial Lord with boundless mana steps on a turtle and a snake, implying calming the wind and waves and blessing the safety of sailing ships.

There is a four-pillar octagonal pavilion on the left back side of the " 吞海 " stele. Its plane is quadrangular with a side length of 4.49m, and its depth is two columns. With the ground paved with slats, the pavilion features double eaves and octagonal pyramidal roofs. The lower eaves are quadrangular roofs; the upper eaves are octagonal roofs; and the middle is octagonal caisson with a sealing plate. The shape and structure of the pavilion symbolize the seal used by Zhenwu Celestial Lord. A couplet is engraved on the stone pillars of the pavilion, which reads "Coming here to enjoy natural beauty by appreciating quietly; arriving at this pavilion to enjoy peace of mind by staying for a little while. Written in the midsummer of Gengwu Year in the Tongzhi Period (1870)". This is the inscription left by the renovation of Gengwu Year in the Tongzhi Period of the Qing Dynasty.

Behind the pavilion is the Main Hall of Zhenwu Temple. The Main Hall was first built in the Song Dynasty and rebuilt in 1842 in the Qing Dynasty, the architectural pattern and style of which is like the traditional houses in Southern Fujian in the Qing Dynasty, with two entrances and five *chiens*. The front hall is five *chiens* wide, and the main hall is three columns deep. The front side is flush gable roof, and the back side is rolling ridge beam frame with gable and hip roof. Two columns in depth, the side hall features flush gable roof. There is a couplet on the stone pillars on both sides of the gate, which reads "Luo Zi Mountains are standing opposite; Liu Wu Rivers are going across." A wooden couplet is hung on both sides, which reads "Taking off the purple hat in front of the hall and protecting the southern area without finishing clothes; throwing the fine clothes away and supporting the northern capital with bare feet". "Luo Zi" in the couplet refers to Luoshang Mountain and Zimao Mountain which are among the four famous mountains in Quanzhou, and "Liu Wu" refers to Liushi River and Wujiang River in the Jin River Basin of Quanzhou. On the walls on both sides of the gate, there are stack shears of "green dragons spitting pearls" and "a fierce tiger springing from the top of the mountain". There are inscriptions on the stone windows on both sides of the hall, one of which reads "Erected by the fishermen of Fashi in mid-spring of Renyin Year during the Daoguang Period", and the other of which reads "Built by the local disciple Zheng Dingye in midspring of Renyin Year during the Daoguang Period". The two inscriptions indicate that when the Main Hall was rebuilt in 1842, the local people engaged in fishing and maritime trade spontaneously donated money to advocate the restoration. It can be seen that the long tradition of maritime trade in Quanzhou has always been affecting the local people's way of life and way of production.

正殿为歇山式屋面，面阔五间，进深六柱，穿斗抬梁混合式木构架，梁枋、斗拱、雀替等木构件雕工十分精细。地面铺设条石、红砖。正殿两侧为连廊，连廊地面铺设红砖，屋面纵横交错，连廊与正殿由天井隔开。正殿正中供奉了着黑衣、仗剑、跣足踏龟蛇、执黑旗的真武大帝塑像，塑像下方石基座上保存有"承信郎□ 光觉奉舍"铭文。正殿正厅两旁立有马华光、赵公明、温峤、关羽四大元帅持戟握剑侍塑像。正殿上方横挂的"掌握玄机"鎏金大字匾额，为清乾隆年间善写大字的福建陆路提督马负书所书。殿内木构架上彩绘有八卦、仙鹤、麒麟、瑞草等图案，具有浓厚的道教特色。

在大殿的右侧，有一方清同治四年（1865）由官府立的示禁碑。碑上的文字内容，主要是禁止附近村民在庙宇周边开采山石，砍伐树木。这说明，至少在清代的时候，当地的官府和民众就已经非常注重保护真武庙周围的环境。而这种优秀的传统风俗一直延续至今，形成珍惜遗产、保护遗产的良好社会风气。

真武殿内外景。（罗春日、陈英杰 摄）
The interior and exterior scenes of Zhenwu Hall. (Photo by Luo Chunri and Chen Yingjie)

"掌握玄机"匾额。（罗春日 摄）
The plaque of " 掌握玄机 " (Mastering the Mystery). (Photo by Luo Chunri)

As for the Main Hall there is a gable and hip roof, with a width of five *chiens* and a depth of six columns. It is a mixed wooden structure with the combination of post-and-lintel and column-and-tie-beam construction. The wood components such as the girders, the bracket sets and the sparrow braces are finely carved. The ground is paved with strip stones and red bricks. There are corridors on both sides of the Main Hall. The ground of the corridors is paved with red bricks, and the roofs are crisscrossed. The corridors and the Main Hall are separated by courtyards. In the center of the Main Hall, a statue of Zhenwu Celestial Lord, dressed in black, holding a sword, stepping on a turtle and a snake with bare feet, and holding a black flag, is enshrined. The inscription "Donated by Chengxinlang □ Guangjue" is preserved on the stone pedestal of the statue. On both sides of the Main Hall, there are statues of Marshals Ma Huaguang, Zhao Gongming, Wen Qiao and Guan Yu holding halberds or swords. The large gilded plaque of " 掌握玄机 " (Mastering the Mystery) hanging horizontally above the Main Hall was written by Fujian Provincial Commander-in-Chief Ma Fushu, who was good at writing large characters during Emperor Qianlong's reign of the Qing Dynasty. The wooden frame in the hall is painted with patterns such as the Eight Trigrams, cranes, Kylins and auspicious grass, rich in Taoist characteristics.

On the right side of the Main Hall, there is a prohibition stele erected by the government in 1865 in the Qing Dynasty. The inscription is mainly to prohibit villagers near the temple from mining rocks and cutting down trees around the temple. This shows that at least in the Qing Dynasty, the local government and people had paid great attention to protecting the environment around Zhenwu Temple. And this excellent traditional custom has continued to this day, forming a good social atmosphere of cherishing and protecting heritages.

真武庙的建筑特征

法石真武庙作为供奉泉州第二代海神真武大帝的庙宇，其建筑体现了鲜明的道教庙宇特征和浓郁的海洋文化气息。

山门上雕刻的道教人物砖雕。（苏德辉 摄）

Brick carvings of Taoist figures on the Mountain Gate. (Photo by Su Dehui)

自然巧妙的依山建筑布局

真武庙依山而筑，顺着山势逐步抬升。山门雕刻太上老君、八仙等道教神仙。山巅台地有岩石状龟蛇，石“蛇”盘桓在庙前，石“龟”在庙前匍匐背驮明代所刻的“吞海”石碑，大埕前方竖立一把石刻“七星剑”等。整组建筑巧妙布局，利用位于沿江入海的石头山山形地势及山巅台地巨石的自然之性，顺其自然之势而建造，自然景观与人文景观和谐共处，将道家“崇尚自然”“讲究天人合一”的思想体现得淋漓尽致。

Architectural Features of Zhenwu Temple

As a temple dedicated to Quanzhou's second generation of sea god Zhenwu Celestial Lord, Fashi Zhenwu Temple embodies distinct architectural features of Taoism temples and rich flavor of maritime culture.

Natural and Ingenious Architectural Layout of Buildings Against the Hill

Zhenwu Temple is built against the hill and gradually rises along it. The Mountain Gate is carved with Taoist gods such as Lzo Tze and the Eight Immortals. There is a rock-shaped turtle and snake on the hill top terrace, with the stone "snake" hovering in front of the temple, and the stone "turtle" crawling in front of the temple with the " 吞海 " stele engraved in the Ming Dynasty on its back. There is a stone Seven Star Sword standing in front of the terrace. The whole group of buildings is ingeniously arranged and built according to the natural layout, taking advantage of both the natural features of the stone hill which is located along the river flowing into the sea, and the huge rocks on the hill top terrace. The harmonious combination of natural landscape and cultural landscape gives full display to the Taoist philosophy of "respect for nature" and "unity of people and nature".

"承信郎" 铭文。（成冬冬 摄）
The inscription of " 承信郎 "(Chengxinlang). (Photo by Cheng Dongdong)

显著的海洋文化特征

从建筑现存铭文可见真武庙建筑的发展与泉州海外贸易蓬勃发展历程息息相关，且海神信仰属性非常显著：

“承信郎”铭文。政和年间宋徽宗定武臣官阶五十三阶，其中第五十二阶为承信郎，是从九品的武阶官员。后来由于泉州的海外贸易获利丰富，能给南宋朝廷带来极大的收入，且当地雄厚海上力量给南宋帝国海防以坚实支持，南宋朝廷较前更积极经营对外贸易。宋高宗一再强调市舶之有助于国用，朝廷对中外商贾及市舶司有功官吏进行奖励；来贩外商有特殊贡献者，甚至加官奖励。真武殿真武大帝基座的这方石刻铭文“承信郎”，应该就是当时获得朝廷“承信郎”官职奖励的海商，捐资修建真武庙这座海神庙宇，以祈求行船经商一帆风顺、一本万利时所刻。

前殿两侧石窗上所刻铭文“本境弟子”“渔帮弟子”“道光壬寅”。这些铭文说明，在 1842 年真武殿重修的时候，当地从事渔业及航运贸易的民众捐资倡修。可见泉州悠久的海外贸易传统，一直影响着人们的生活生产方式。至今，真武庙附近的蟳埔村居民仍延续着祖辈们世代以传统捕捞业和滩涂养殖业为主的生活模式，当地的海鲜市场、海鲜酒楼比比皆是。在蟳埔，还有十分特别的蚵壳厝(闽南话中，厝乃房屋之意，蚵就是海蛎)。这些用海蛎壳和砖、石砌筑的建筑，因其独特的外墙造型，成为闽南沿海古民居的一道亮丽风景线。根据传说，蟳埔当地女性头上戴的“簪花围”也和泉州海商巨富蒲寿庚有关。漫步蟳埔，不时可见身上穿着独特服饰、头戴花围的蟳埔村老幼穿行在两旁皆是蚵壳厝的小巷。

蟳埔女头上的簪花围是一道移动的风景。（陈英杰 摄）

The flower hairpin on the heads of the local women in Xunpu is a beautiful moving landscape. (Photo by Chen Yingjie)

Notable Characteristics of Maritime Culture

From the existing inscriptions on the buildings, it can be seen that the architectural development of Zhenwu Temple is closely related to the development and prosperity of the maritime trade in Quanzhou and is distinctive in the attributes of sea god belief.

The inscription of "Chengxinlang". During the Zhenghe Period (1111—1118), Emperor Huizong of the Song Dynasty established fifty-three ranks of military officials, of which the fifty-second rank was Chengxinlang, who was a military rank official slightly below the ninth level. Later, the imperial court of the Southern Song Dynasty was more active in foreign trade than before because Quanzhou's maritime trade was profitable to bring great income to the imperial court, and also because the strong local maritime power provided solid support for the coastal defense of the empire. Emperor Gaozong of the Song Dynasty repeatedly emphasized the usefulness of maritime trade for the country, and the imperial court rewarded Chinese and foreign merchants and officials of the Maritime Trade Office. The foreign businessmen who made special contributions were even conferred on with official positions. The stone inscription of "Chengxinlang" on the pedestal of Zhenwu Celestial Lord in the Main Hall should be engraved by a maritime merchant who was awarded the official rank of "Chengxinlang" by the imperial court at that time, and donated money to build the sea god temple of Zhenwu Temple in order to pray for smooth sailing and great profit in business.

The inscriptions on the stone windows on both sides of the front hall are "Disciples of the Local Community", "Disciples of the Fishing Gang" and "Renyin Year in the Daoguang Period". These inscriptions show that when the Main Hall was rebuilt in 1842, local people engaged in fishing and shipping trade donated money to advocate the restoration. It can be seen that the long tradition of maritime trade in Quanzhou has always been affecting people's way of life and way of production. Up to now, the residents of Xunpu Village near Zhenwu Temple still continue their ancestors' traditional fishing and tidal flat breeding industry for generations. Local seafood markets and seafood restaurants are everywhere. In Xunpu, there is also a kind of special house called *Keqiao Cuo*, namely oyster shell house (in Southern Fujian dialect, *cuo* means the house, and *qiao* is the oyster). With the unique exterior wall shape, these buildings made of oyster shells, bricks and stones have become a beautiful landscape of ancient folk houses along the coast of Southern Fujian. According to the legend, the flower hairpin on the heads of the local women in Xunpu is also related to Pu Shougeng, a wealthy maritime merchant in Quanzhou. Strolling through Xunpu, people can see from time to time young and old wearing unique costumes and hairpins walking through the alleys with oyster shell houses on both sides.

有序的建筑历史传承

真武庙建于北宋，历代均有修缮，修缮情况虽未见文献明确记载，但从现存建筑的相关信息，可见其建筑历史传承有序。在 2016—2017 年对真武庙进行全面维修时，发现真武大帝塑像基座有“承信郎”铭文，承信郎是宋代的官职名称，一直沿用至 13 世纪后期。山门的石柱、扶栏上的石狮，皆有显著的宋代建筑特征。真武庙遗存有明代晋江知县韩岳所立的“吞海”石碑、李氏捐建的古井。真武庙保存的清代历史信息最为丰富：有乾隆十八年至三十二年（1753—1767）福建陆路提督马负书题写的“掌握玄机”，清代泉州翰林庄俊元题写的山门楹联，“道光壬寅”“本境弟子”“渔帮弟子”捐资修缮真武庙留下的铭文，同治四年（1865）官府树立的示禁碑，同治九年（1870）重修的四柱八角凉亭等。这一系列保存完好的宋至清代建筑遗存，共同构成了真武庙独特的建筑风格。

Sequential Historical Succession of Architecture

Zhenwu Temple was built in the Northern Song Dynasty and has been repaired in successive dynasties. Although there are no clear records of the repairs, the relevant information of the existing buildings shows that its architecture has been inherited in an orderly manner in history. During the comprehensive maintenance of Zhenwu Temple in 2016—2017, an inscription of "Chengxinlang" was found on the pedestal of Zhenwu Celestial Lord's statue. Chengxinlang was an official rank in the Song Dynasty and was used until the late 13th century. The stone pillars at the Mountain Gate and the stone lions on the railings all have obvious architectural features of the Song Dynasty. The " 吞海 " stele erected by Han Yue, the magistrate of Jinjiang County in the Ming Dynasty, and the ancient well donated by Mrs. Li have remained in Zhenwu Temple. Zhenwu Temple boasts the most abundant historical information of the Qing Dynasty, such as the plaque "Mastering the Mystery" written by Ma Fushu who was Fujian Provincial Commander-in-Chief from 1753 to 1767, the couplet of the Mountain Gate inscribed by Zhuang Junyuan who was the Hanlin from Quanzhou in the Qing Dynasty, the inscriptions of "Renyin Year in the Daoguang Period", "Disciples of the Local Community" and "Disciples of the Fishing Gang" carved after money donation to repair Zhenwu Temple, the prohibition stele erected by the government in 1865, and the four-pillared octagonal pavilion rebuilt in 1870. This series of well-preserved architectural remains from the Song to Qing Dynasties jointly constitute the unique architectural style of Zhenwu Temple.

山门后的台阶和扶栏后的狮子。（郑文桂 摄）
The steps behind the Mountain Gate and the stone lions behind the railings. (Photo by Zheng Wengui)

海洋有取之不尽用之不竭的资源，人们可以下海捕捞各种海洋生物，也可以扬帆出海从事商业活动，但行船走马三分险，于是人们寄希望于超自然力，祈求海神保佑他们扬帆出海可以平平安安。真武庙所承载的海神信仰是宋元时期商人群体从事海洋贸易的重要精神寄托。北宋元祐二年（1087）朝廷在泉州设立市舶司之后，泉州海贸渐兴，朝廷可从泉州市舶司得到非常可观的税金。面对如此巨大的经济利益，宋王朝也希望海外贸易能一帆风顺。朝廷官员以到真武庙祭海这种方式祈求海神对往来船只的护佑，客观上又促进了海外贸易的兴盛。现存真武庙的山门重檐歇山顶牌楼式，凉亭重檐八角，平面八卦形、大殿歇山式等建筑各具特色，1991 年成为联合国教科文组织海上丝绸之路考察团泉州考察点之一。2006 年 5 月，真武庙与江口码头、六胜塔、万寿塔、石湖码头 5 处文物古迹以“泉州港古建筑”之名由国务院公布为第六批全国重点文物保护单位。2021 年，真武庙成为“泉州：宋元中国的世界海洋商贸中心”系列遗产点之一，至今仍是当地从事海洋渔业的民众心中最重要的海神信仰庙宇。

The ocean has inexhaustible resources, where people can fish all kinds of maritime life and sail to engage in commercial activities. However, there are risks in sailing as well, so people place their hopes on the supernatural forces and pray for the sea gods to bless them with safety in sailing. The sea deity beliefs embodied by Zhenwu Temple was an important source of spiritual support for merchants who engaged in maritime trade during the Song and Yuan Period. After the imperial court established the Maritime Trade Office in Quanzhou in 1087 of the Song Dynasty, Quanzhou's maritime trade gradually flourished, and the imperial court could get a very considerable tax from Quanzhou Maritime Trade Office. Faced with such huge economic benefits, the imperial court also hoped that the maritime trade would be smooth. Officials prayed to Zhenwu Celestial Lord for protection of the ships by offering sacrifices to him in Zhenwu Temple, which objectively promoted the prosperity of maritime trade. The existing architecture of Zhenwu Temple, such as the Mountain Gate in memorial-arch style of gable and hip roof with multiple eaves, the octagonal pavilion with double eaves and the octagonal flat, and the Main Hall with gable and hip roof, have their own characteristics. In 1991, Zhenwu Temple became one of the inspection sites for the UNESCO Marine Silk Road delegation in Quanzhou. In May 2006, the five cultural relics and historic sites, Zhenwu Temple, Jiangkou Docks, Liusheng Pagoda, Wanshou Pagoda, and Shihu Dock, were announced by the State Council among the sixth batch of national key cultural relics protection units in the name of "Ancient Architecture in Quanzhou Port". In 2021, Zhenwu Temple became one heritage in the series of world cultural heritages of "Quanzhou: Emporium of the World in Song-Yuan China". Now it is still the most important temple of sea deity beliefs in the hearts of local people engaged in maritime fisheries.

从地方到世界——妈祖信仰及泉州天后宫

From Local Belief to Worldwide Religion: Mazu Worship and Quanzhou Tianhou Temple

妈祖信仰的形成

The Formation of Mazu Worship

泉州天后宫的建筑特征及其价值

Quanzhou Tianhou Temple's Architectural Features and Its Values

妈祖信仰的传播

Spread of Mazu Worship

天后宫全景。（吴云轩 摄）
The panorama of Tianhou Temple. (Photo by Wu Yunxuan)

天后宫位于泉州城南，是宋元时期朝廷官员祭祀泉州第三代海神——妈祖的场所。这里是外来商人、货物进入泉州城的第一站，也是出海的人祭祀海神妈祖之后，顺着晋江通往江口码头或者石湖码头前往海外贸易的第一站。妈祖信仰与昭惠庙的通远王信仰、真武庙的真武大帝信仰一起构成泉州地区独具特色的海神信仰体系，成为“泉州：宋元中国的世界海洋商贸中心”系列遗产中海洋贸易管理保障的代表性遗产。天后宫妈祖信仰是伴随宋元泉州海洋贸易而形成、发展的民间信仰。宋元官方对妈祖信仰的一再推崇使民间信仰与国家意志相结合，体现了国家力量对海洋贸易的推动。

妈祖原本是一位宋时泉州沿海的渔家女子，为人善良，熟悉海上风潮，多次在风浪中拯救乡民，受到人们的崇敬。妈祖去世后，被泉州沿海民众视为航海的保护神。10—13世纪，泉州九日山奉祀的“通远王”是出海人祈求信风的海神；真武庙奉祀的“真武大帝”是出海人祈求航行平安的海神；妈祖则是出海人遇险时祈求拯救生命的海神。三位海神各自承担不同的庇护功能，寄托着泉州航海人渴望航行平安、希望获得好收成的良好愿景。

天后宫作为宋元泉州南部商业性城区的重要地标，见证了海洋贸易发展和多元文化交融下泉州城市的发展和布局。（陈英杰 摄）

As an important landmark in the commercial area of Quanzhou's southern part in the Song-Yuan era, Tianhou Temple witnessed the development and layout of Quanzhou City along with the development of maritime trade and the integration of multiculturalism. (Photo by Chen Yingjie)

Located in the south of Quanzhou City, Tianhou Temple was the place where the government officials worshiped Mazu, the third generation of sea god in Quanzhou, during the Song and Yuan Dynasties. This is the first stop not only for foreign merchants and goods to enter Quanzhou City, but also for those who go overseas for trade from the Jinjiang River to Jiangkou Docks or Shihu Dock after worshiping the sea goddess Mazu. The belief in Mazu, together with the belief in King Tongyuan of Zhaohui Temple and the belief in Zhenwu Celestial Lord of Zhenwu Temple, constitutes the unique sea-god belief system in Quanzhou area, becoming the representative heritage of administrative assurance for maritime trade in the heritage series of "Quanzhou: Emporium of the World in Song-Yuan China". The belief in Mazu of Tianhou Temple is a folk belief formed and developed along with Quanzhou maritime trade in the Song and Yuan Dynasties. The continuous high praise of Mazu belief by the government in the Song-Yuan era combined the folk belief with the national will, reflecting the promotion of national power to maritime trade.

Mazu was originally a fisherwoman on the coast of Quanzhou in the Song Dynasty. Being familiar with sea waves, she was kind-hearted to rescue villagers in storms many times and was thus revered by people. After her death, Mazu was regarded as the patron saint of navigation by the people along the coast of Quanzhou. From the 10th to the 13th century, King Tongyuan enshrined in Quanzhou Jiuri Mountain was the sea god from whom people prayed for seasonal wind; Zhenwu Celestial Lord enshrined in Zhenwu Temple was the sea god from whom people prayed for safe sailing; and Mazu is the sea goddess from whom people prayed for life protection when in danger at sea. The three sea gods/goddess take on different protection functions respectively, entrusting the good vision of Quanzhou sailors for safe sailing and good harvests.

妈祖信仰的形成

妈祖，姓林名默，因出生时不哭，又称默娘，北宋清源军（后改名为泉州）莆田县湄洲屿人。据说林默生于建隆元年（960）三月二十三日，雍熙四年（987）九月初九日"羽化升天"。妈祖生前聪颖灵悟，能预知气象变化，有驱邪治病和泅水航海的本领，常"乘席渡海""翻飞水上"，救人于水厄海难。妈祖一生扶危救困，济世救人，备受人们的敬重和爱戴。她过世后"辄显灵应""海舟救护无数"，被尊为航海保护神，是历代船工、海员、旅客、商人和渔民共同信奉的神祇。人们在船舶启航前要先祭妈祖，祈求保佑顺风和安全，有的在船舶上还立妈祖神位供奉。南宋绍兴二十六年（1156），妈祖首次得到朝廷褒封。此后，历代统治者不断赐封号，共计 36 次，从夫人、妃、天妃、天后到天上圣母，妈祖至高无上的海神地位逐步确立。

妈祖庙由一个郡治县辖下的民间小庙登极至无上敕封的"天后宫"，林默娘这位渔家姑娘逝世后享有这般推崇，这与泉州作为世界海洋商贸中心的地位密不可分。从这个意义上讲，妈祖的"发迹"是在泉州。南宋绍定五年至绍定六年（1232—1233），真德秀第二次任泉州知州时，为驱逐海盗祈求妈祖庇佑，特作《圣妃祝文》，剿除海盗胜利后又作《圣妃宫祝文》。这是官方对泉州天后宫最早的祭文，从此，祭祀妈祖纳入官方祭典体系。

湄洲妈祖雕像。（林奕贤 摄）
The statue of Mazu in Meizhou Island. (Photo by Lin Yixian)

The Formation of Mazu Worship

Mazu, surnamed Lin and named Mo, also known as Moniang (a silent girl) because she did not cry aloud when she was born, was from Meizhou Island, Putian County, Qingyuan Military Prefecture (later renamed Quanzhou) in the Northern Song Dynasty. It is said that Lin Mo was born on lunar March 23, 960, and ascended to heaven on the 9th day of lunar September in 987, becoming an immortal. Being intelligent and enlightened during her lifetime, Mazu has the ability to predict weather changes, exorcise evil spirits, cure diseases, swim in the sea, and sail at the sea. She often "crossed the sea on a mat" and "flied over the water" to rescue people from disasters. Mazu helped people from danger and saved lives from shipwrecks, which made her highly revered and loved by the local people. After her death, Mazu "showed her mighty" and "rescued countless sea boats", and was revered as a tutelary deity of navigation, by seafarers, sailors, travelers, merchants and fishermen for generations. Before ships set sail, people worship Mazu first, praying for favorable wind and safe navigation, and some people set up the spirit tablets of Mazu on ships for worship. In 1156 of the Southern Song Dynasty, Mazu was honored by the imperial court for the first time. Since then, the rulers of successive dynasties have continued to confer titles on her for a total of 36 times, from Furen (Lady), Fei (Princess), Tianfei (Princess of Heaven), Tianhou (Queen/Empress of Heaven) to Tianshang Shengmu (Holy Heavenly Mother). Thus, Mazu's supreme status as the sea deity has gradually been established.

The reason for Mazu Temple's promotion from a small folk temple under the jurisdiction of a county to the supreme "Tianhou Temple", and the high admiration enjoyed by the seafaring girl Lin Moniang after her death, are greatly attributed to Quanzhou's status as the world's emporium. In this sense, Mazu's "prosperity" originates from Quanzhou. From 1232 to 1233 in the Southern Song Dynasty, Zhen Dexiu, serving as the Prefect of Quanzhou for the second time, prayed for Mazu's protection in order to expel the pirates and specially wrote *Prayers to Shengfei* . After achieving victory in eliminating the pirates, he also wrote *Prayers to Shengfei Temple*. This is the earliest official sacrificial writing to Tianhou Temple in Quanzhou. Since then, offering sacrifices to Mazu has been included into the official ceremonial system.

湄洲妈祖祖庙。（庄清贵 摄）
The ancestral temple of Mazu in Meizhou Island. (Photo by Zhuang Qinggui)

元朝政府出于海上漕运的顺利和海上贸易利益的考量，高度重视妈祖的海神作用。至元十五年（1278），元世祖下诏“制封泉州神女”，号“护国明著灵惠协正善庆显济天妃”，首次将妈祖这位民间信奉的女神擢升至朝廷制封的天神，这是妈祖信仰史上的重要转折点。三年后，元世祖再次下诏，遣正奉大夫宣德使、左副都元帅兼福建道市舶提举蒲师文册封妈祖为“护国明著天妃”，册封祭典就在泉州天妃宫里举行。元皇庆以后元朝官方开始遣使代祀天妃。据《元史》记载，妈祖因护海运特别灵应，被加封天妃的神号。直沽（今天津）、平江（今苏州）、周泾（今太仓）、泉州、福州、兴化（今莆田）等处，都有供奉天妃的庙宇。1312 年以后，开始派遣使者到这些庙宇进行祭祀，开了朝廷派官员在北方、南方举行天妃官祭的先河。元天历二年（1329）元文宗遣官从大都派出一支进香队伍，代表皇帝呈献祭文。从天津开始，队伍途经淮安、苏州、杭州、绍兴、温州、福州、湄州等重要港口，于十月二十五日抵达泉州天妃庙。他们沿途共拜谒 15 座妈祖庙，总行程近万里，耗时半年以上。在泉州天妃宫致祭祭文中元朝政府对泉州妈祖神位倍加颂扬，认定泉州妈祖庙为“闽南始发祥”之地位。如此高规格的祭祀在此后 20 多年间共举行 5 次。元政府最后一次加封妈祖的称号为“护国辅圣庇民广济福惠明著天妃”，名字之长超过以往所有封号，大幅提升了妈祖的海神地位。妈祖从一位区域性海神升格为全国性的海洋保护神，从妈祖信仰的传播，可以看出当年泉州港海外贸易的繁盛，印证了泉州港作为海上丝绸之路东方第一大港的历史地位。

The government of the Yuan Dynasty attached great importance to Mazu's role as the sea goddess for the sake of smooth marine transportation and the interests of maritime trade. In 1278, Kublai Khan, Emperor Shizu of the Yuan Dynasty, issued an edict to "confer the Goddess of Quanzhou" with the title of "Huguo Mingzhu Linghui Xiezheng Shanqing Xianji Tianfei" (illuminating Princess of Heaven who protects the nation), promoting Mazu from a goddess in folk beliefs to the goddess granted by the imperial court for the first time, which is an important turning point in the history of Mazu belief. Three years later, Emperor Shizu issued another edict, sending Pu Shiwen, the Senior Official and Pacification Commissioner, senior Vice-President of the Censorate, and Superintendent of Fujian Maritime Trade Office, to bestow Mazu with the title of "Huguo Mingzhu Tianfei", the ceremony of which was held in Tianfei Temple in Quanzhou. Since the Huangqing Period (1312—1313) of the Yuan Dynasty, the imperial court began to send envoys to worship Tianfei on behalf of the governments. According to *The History of Yuan*, Mazu was reconferred on the title of "Tianfei" because of her helpful response to the maritime protection. There are temples dedicated to Tianfei in Zhigu (Tianjin nowadays), Pingjiang (Suzhou nowadays), Zhoujing (Taicang nowadays), Quanzhou, Fuzhou, Xinghua (Putian nowadays), etc. Since 1312, envoys have been sent to these temples to offer sacrifices, setting the precedent for the imperial court to hold official sacrifices to Tianfei by government officials both in the north and in the south. In 1329 of the Yuan Dynasty, Emperor Wenzong dispatched officials to send a pilgrimage team from the capital Kanbulu (Beijing nowadays) to present sacrificial text on behalf of the emperor. Departing from Tianjin, the team passed the important ports in Huai'an, Suzhou, Hangzhou, Shaoxing, Wenzhou, Fuzhou, Meizhou and so on, and arrived at Tianfei Temple in Quanzhou on lunar October 25. They visited a total of 15 Mazu temples along the way, spending more than half a year to finish the journey of nearly 5,000km. In the prayers to Tianfei Temple in Quanzhou, the government of the Yuan Dynasty praised highly of the deity of Mazu in Quanzhou, recognizing Quanzhou Mazu Temple as "the flourishing birthplace of Mazu belief". Such high-level sacrifices were held five times in total during the next 20 years. The last title conferred on Mazu by the Yuan Government was "Huguo Fusheng Bimin Guangji Fuhui Mingzhu Tianfei". This title is longer than all the previous titles conferred, which greatly enhanced Mazu's status as the sea deity. Quanzhou Mazu has been promoted from a regional sea goddess to a national marine patron goddess. The prosperity of the maritime trade at Quanzhou Port at that time can be seen from the spreading of Mazu belief, confirming the historical status of Quanzhou Port as the largest port in the East on the Maritime Silk Road.

天后宫祭祀活动。（成冬冬 摄）
Sacrificial activities in Tianhou Temple. (Photo by Cheng Dongdong)

明朝，妈祖也多次获得朝廷的制封。洪武中封“昭孝纯正孚济感应圣妃”，永乐中封“护国庇民妙灵昭应宏仁普济天妃”等。据《泉州府志》记载，永乐五年（1407）出使西洋的三宝太监郑和，奏令福建镇守官重修此庙。明代凡派官出使琉球、暹罗（今泰国）、爪哇（今印度尼西亚爪哇岛）、满剌加（今马来西亚马六甲）等国，皆到天妃宫祭祀祷告，并于起讫点奉妈祖神像以求平安。永乐十三年（1415），郑和部属张谦从泉州出使到今天的加里曼丹岛一带，顺利返程后，认为是天妃的庇佑，于是上奏朝廷重修天妃宫。嘉靖庚子年（1540），天妃宫原建筑规模扩大，重建了寝殿七间、凉亭四座、西廊三十间、东西轩及斋馆二十八楹。

Mazu was also crowned with various conferred titles by the imperial court many times in the Ming Dynasty. For example, in the middle of the Hongwu and the Yongle periods, she was granted esteemed titles separately. According to *Local Chronicles of Quanzhou Prefecture,* Zheng He, Eunuch Sanbao who was commissioned to command the expedition to the West in 1407, requested the court to order the Governor of Fujian to rebuild the temple. In the Ming Dynasty, the officials dispatched to the countries like Ryukyu, Siam (Thailand nowadays), Java (Indonesian Java Island nowadays), Mancinga (Malacca, Malaysia nowadays) all went to Tianfei Temple to worship and pray, and enshrined the statue of Mazu at the departure place and the destination of the journey for safety. In 1415, Zhang Qian, one of Zheng He's subordinate who was dispatched from Quanzhou to the area of Kalimantan Island nowadays, requesting the imperial court to rebuild Tianfei Temple after the smooth return because he credited Tianfei for protecting the safe voyage. In 1540, the original building scale of Tianfei Temple was expanded by rebuilding seven-*chien* bedchamber hall, four pavilions, thirty rooms in west corridor, east and west windowed verandas and twenty-eight vegetarian halls.

泉州天后宫匾额。（吴松树 摄）
The plaques of Tianhou Temple in Quanzhou. (Photo by Wu Songshu)

至清代，妈祖地位更加显赫。康熙二十二年（1683），福建水师提督施琅东征台湾，胜利班师后奏知朝廷，谓天后显圣助阵。第二年，康熙皇帝下令褒封妈祖为"护国庇民妙灵昭应弘仁普济天后"，庙遂改名为"天后宫"。康熙五十九年（1720），朝廷特赐春秋二祭，奉行始入祀典。雍正元年（1723）雍正皇帝为天后宫御书匾额"神昭海表"（现在泉州天后宫内仍可见到此匾）。乾隆二年（1737）朝廷给妈祖的封号为"护国庇民妙灵昭应弘仁普济福佑群生天后"，第一次把"弘仁普济福佑群生"加入妈祖封号。"弘仁普济，福佑群生"成为清廷钦定的妈祖精神。嘉庆二十一年（1816），泉州知府徐汝澜重修天后宫并留下碑记，现立于天后宫拜庭东侧榕树下。道光年间朝廷晋封妈祖为"天上圣母"，随之天后宫名正式确立，并进行了大规模修建，备极殊荣。

泉州发达的海上交通贸易以及泉郡官员的大力推荐，对于妈祖由人至神，乃至于天妃、天后而圣母的褒封擢格，起到十分重要的作用，且历代褒封典祀，亦在泉州妈祖庙中。泉州天后宫在国内外众多妈祖庙中的地位因而最高。

The status of Mazu became even more prominent in the Qing Dynasty. In 1683, Shi Lang, the Admiral of Fujian Navy, marched eastward to Taiwan and gained victory. After he returned, he reported to the imperial court that Tianhou provided help to the battle. In 1684, Emperor Kangxi conferred Mazu with the title of "Huguo Bimin Miaoling Zhaoying Hongren Puji Tianhou", thus the temple was renamed "Tianhou Temple". In 1720, with the sacrifices in spring and in autumn specially granted, the ceremony started to become one of the official sacrificial rituals. In 1723, Emperor Yongzheng bestowed the plaque "Shen Zhao Hai Biao" (the Light of Goddess Shines on the Surface of the Sea) with his inscriptions to Tianhou Temple (the plaque can still be seen in Quanzhou Tianhou Temple today). In 1737, the royal title conferred on Mazu was "Huguo Bimin Miaoling Zhaoying Hongren Puji Fuyou Qunsheng Tianhou". With "Hongren Puji Fuyou Qunsheng" added to the conferred title of Mazu for the first time, it became the spirit of Mazu royally determined by the Qing Government. In 1816, Xu Rulan, the Prefect of Quanzhou, rebuilt Tianhou Temple and left a stele which is now standing under the banyan tree on the east side of the Worship Pavilion of Tianhou Temple. During the Daoguang Period (1821—1850), Mazu was granted the title of "Tianshang Shengmu" (Holy Heavenly Mother), then Tianhou Temple was confirmed in its name and was constructed on a large-scale, which was extremely honorable.

Quanzhou's well-developed maritime transportation and trade, and the strong recommendation of Quanzhou officials, played a very important role in the praise and promotion of Mazu from human being to goddess, and even to Tianfei, Tianhou, and the Holy Mother. What's more, all the conferment ceremonies in successive dynasties were carried out in Quanzhou Tianhou Temple. Therefore, Quanzhou Tianhou Temple enjoys the highest status among the numerous Mazu temples at home and abroad.

泉州天后宫内景。（罗春日 摄）
The interior view of Quanzhou Tianhou Temple. (Photo by Luo Chunri)

泉州天后宫的建筑特征及其价值

泉州天后宫始建于宋庆元二年（1196），位于内通城区、外连海港的显要位置，通过德济门，可就近抵达晋江。伴随历代官方和民间对妈祖信仰的推崇，天后宫历经营修、发展，现仍保存着 16 世纪之前已然形成的前殿后寝的布局特征。天后宫现存建筑群坐北朝南，总体呈中轴对称的院落式布局。中轴线上自南向北依次布局有山门、戏台、拜庭、天后殿、寝殿、梳妆楼，两侧东西厢房、轩房、斋馆和凉亭等附属建筑将院落围合。建筑群用地面积约 6,800 平方米，是海内外众多天后庙宇的建筑范本。

Quanzhou Tianhou Temple's Architectural Features and Its Values

Quanzhou Tianhou Temple was first built in 1196 of the Song Dynasty. It is located in a prominent position connecting the city inside and the harbor outside, from which people can reach the Jinjiang River nearby through Deji Gate. Along with the promotion of Mazu belief by both officials and folks in successive dynasties, Tianhou Temple, which experienced maintenance and development, is now still keeping the features of the layout with a hall in the front and bedchambers at the rear which had already came into being before the 16th century. Sitting north and facing south, the extant building complex is featured with a central axisymmetric courtyard layout as a whole. On the central axis, there are Mountain Gate, Theatrical Stage, Worship Pavilion, Tianhou Hall, Bedchamber Hall and Grooming Building from south to north. On both sides, there are ancillary structures such as the east and west wing rooms, bedrooms, vegetarian halls and pavilions, which enclose the courtyard. The building complex covers an area of roughly 6,800m^2 and is the architectural model of many Tianhou temples at home and abroad.

天后宫山门。（蒋长云 摄）
The Mountain Gate of Tianhou Temple. (Photo by Jiang Changyun)

拜庭是举行妈祖祭祀活动的场所：海内外信众一般在妈祖诞辰日（农历三月二十三）聚集此地，举行祭拜，祈求保佑。根据文献记载，每年春秋两季的祭祀妈祖仪式是在第二个月吉日举行。所需祭品为：白色帛一份、白瓷爵（古代祭祀盛酒容器）三个、铏（古代盛羹的小鼎）一个、簠（盛放黍、稷、粱、稻等饭食的方形器具）两个、簋（盛放熟食的器皿）两个、笾（盛果实、干肉等的竹编食器）四个、豆（盛放食物的器皿）四个、羊一只、猪一只等，仪式有奏礼乐、行三跪九叩礼、宣读祭文、焚化祭文等。

天后宫建筑中以正殿和寝殿最具特色。正殿又称大殿、天后殿，占地面积 625 平方米，是供奉妈祖圣像、信众祭拜妈祖的主要场所。正殿为重檐歇山顶，面阔五间 25 米，进深五间 25 米，殿内柱网排列规整，唯祭坛前减去两根金柱，以形成较宽阔的祭祀空间。为满足同样要求，又将中柱后移，使空间变化更为丰富。整个建筑的木构件以朱色为基调，台基高出地面 1 米。花岗岩砌筑的基座浮雕有鲤鱼化龙、八骏云火、鹤舞祥云、法器、花卉等中国传统吉祥图案，富有艺术感染力。拜廊明间有一对辉绿岩镂空透雕龙柱，气韵生动，工艺精湛，堪称闽南石雕龙柱的代表作。殿内后照壁保存一幅清代大型壁画《敕封天上圣母》，以写实的笔法描绘了当时湄洲岛天后宫的建筑格局，具有较高的历史与艺术价值。当年湄洲岛重修妈祖庙时，特地到此考察，借鉴壁画里展示的历史建筑信息，设计了湄洲妈祖祖庙重建的格局。湄洲岛是妈祖的出生地，曾经隶属泉州管辖。泉州天后宫绘制湄洲妈祖祖庙风光壁画，一是表示对妈祖出生地的尊敬，二是借助泉州港在海外交通中的地位以及泉州天后宫的文化影响力，扩大妈祖信仰文化的传播。

天后宫正殿。（陈英杰 摄）
The Main Hall of Tianhou Temple. (Photo by Chen Yingjie)

The Worship Pavilion is the place where sacrificial activities are held: believers at home and abroad usually gather here on Mazu's birthday (March 23rd of the lunar calendar) to hold worship and pray for blessings. According to records, the ceremony of offering sacrifices to Mazu is held on the 1st day of the second lunar month in both spring and autumn seasons each year. The sacrificial offerings required are as follows: a piece of white silk, three pieces of white porcelain *Jue* (the ancient wine container for sacrificing), one *Xing* (the ancient small tripod for soup), two *Fus* (the square utensil for holding millet, sorghum, rice and other food), two *Guis* (the utensil for holding cooked food), four *Bians* (the bamboo food utensil for holding fruit and dried meat), four *Dous* (the utensil for holding food), one cooked lamb, one cooked porket, and so on. The rituals include playing ritual music, performing kowtow ritual of "three kneelings and nine prostrations", reading aloud the sacrificial text, and burning the sacrificial text, etc.

Among the buildings of Tianhou Temple, the Main Hall and the Bedchamber Hall are the most distinctive. Covering an area of $625m^2$, the Main Hall, also known as the Chamber Hall or Tianhou Hall, is the main place where the statue of Mazu is enshrined and worshiped. The Main Hall features a double-eave gable with a hipped roof. It is five-*chien* wide of 25m, five-*chien* deep of 25m, inside which the pillars are regularly arranged to form a grid with two inner pillars subtracted from the front of the altar to form a broader sacrificial space. In order to meet the same need, the central columns are moved back in order to diversify the space. The color of the wooden components of the whole building is basically in vermilion, and the base is 1m above the ground. The base of the granite masonry is embossed with traditional Chinese auspicious patterns such as carp turning into dragon, eight colorful horses running quickly, auspicious dancing cranes, magic instruments, flowers, which are artistically appealing. There is a pair of diabase hollowed-out dragon pillars in the center of the Worship Pavilion, which is so vivid and exquisite in craftsmanship that it can be called the representative work of stone dragon pillars in Southern Fujian. A large-scale mural of the Qing Dynasty, *Conferment of the Holy Heavenly Mother*, is preserved on the rear wall of the Main Hall, depicting the architectural patterns of Tianhou Temple on Meizhou Island in a realistic way, which contains comparatively high historical and artistic value. When Meizhou Mazu Temple was being rebuilt, a special inspection was carried out here. Based on the historical architectural information displayed in the murals, the reconstruction pattern of Meizhou Mazu Temple was designed. Meizhou Island is the birthplace of Mazu and was once under the jurisdiction of Quanzhou. Painting the scenic murals of Meizhou Mazu Temple in Quanzhou Tianhou Temple aims to show respect to the birthplace of Mazu on one hand, and to expand the dissemination of Mazu belief on the other hand by virtue of the important overseas traffic status of Quanzhou Port and the cultural influence of Quanzhou Tianhou Temple.

《敕封天上圣母》壁画。（陈英杰 摄）
The mural of *Conferment of the Holy Heavenly Mother*. (Photo by Chen Yingjie)

寝殿位于正殿之后，又称后殿，地势比正殿高出 1.4 米，原为供奉妈祖父母的地方，现作为妈祖文物展示场所。该殿历代均有修缮，但结构和法式保留着明嘉靖时重修后的特征及当地的建筑风格。寝殿前檐设廊，硬山顶，面阔七间 36.7 米，进深四间 21.7 米，占地面积近 796 平方米。寝殿明间保存一对元代印度教十六角形辉绿岩石柱，是明代维修天后宫时移用至此。柱身外形呈十六角，突出上中下三部正方形画面。以圆光凸线作画面的轮廓线，圆光内有浮雕，其雕刻手法与开元寺大雄宝殿后回廊檐下的古代印度教石柱相同。不同的是，开元寺里的石柱雕刻有古代印度教神话故事，如“解放象王”“七女出浴”等，而这里石柱上雕刻的图案为四合如意及四季花卉等明显具有中国传统吉祥图案的艺术元素，见证了多元文化在泉州的交融。十六角形石柱上接木柱，正面刻有楹联一副“神功护海国 水德配乾坤”，高度颂扬了妈祖在保护航海方面的特殊贡献。

Located behind the Main Hall, the Bedchamber Hall, also known as the Apse Hall, is 1.4m higher than the Main Hall. It was originally a place where the parents of Mazu were worshiped, and now serves as a place to display cultural relics of Mazu. The hall was repaired in successive dynasties, but the structure and style retain the characteristics of the rebuilt buildings in the Jiajing Period (1522—1566) of the Ming Dynasty and the local architectural style. The Bedchamber Hall, equipped with flush gable roof and corridors under the front eaves, is seven-*chien* wide of 36.7m and four-*chien* deep of 21.7m, covering an area of nearly 796m^2. A pair of Hindu hexagonal diabase pillars of the Yuan Dynasty is preserved in the center of the Bedchamber Hall, which was moved here during the maintenance of Tianhou Temple in the Ming Dynasty. The shape of the pillar body is hexagonal, highlighting the square pictures in the upper, middle and lower parts. With the circular convex lines as the contour line of the picture, there are reliefs inside the circular light. This carving technique is the same as that of the ancient Hindu stone pillars under the eaves of the corridor behind the Main Hall of Kaiyuan Temple. The difference is that the stone pillars in Kaiyuan Temple are engraved with ancient Hindu myths, such as "The Liberation of Gajendra (the Elephant King)" and "Seven Girls Coming Out of the Bath", etc., while the patterns carved on the stone pillars here are "Sihe Ruyi" (pattern of four Ruyi, indicating good wishes) and flowers in four seasons, obviously characterized with artistic elements of traditional Chinese auspicious patterns, which witnessed the blending of multiple cultures in Quanzhou. The hexagonal stone pillars are connected with the wooden pillars in the upper whose front sides are engraved with a couplet, "Maritime protection with magic power; universal salvation with magnanimous kindness", which highly praises the special contribution of Mazu in navigation protection.

天后宫寝殿。(陈英杰 摄)
The Bedchamber Hall of Tianhou Temple. (Photo by Chen Yingjie)

寝殿明间一对辉绿岩元代印度教十六角形石柱。（罗春日 摄）
A pair of Hindu hexagonal diabase pillars of the Yuan Dynasty in the center of the Bedchamber Hall. (Photo by Luo Chunri)

现在天后宫主要供奉妈祖，同时供奉道教神仙及地方王爷神。东西两庑各供奉十二司，合为二十四司，据说是辅助天后的二十四路神仙，如北斗星君负责航海方向，雷声普化天尊司风雨雷电，水德星君司四季水的调节，四海龙王司江河湖海的潮汐，五显灵官大帝司天庭，文昌帝君司文运，哪吒太子司青少年成长，七娘妈司少儿成长，临水夫人司婴幼哺育和产妇安康，文武尊王司忠义，福德正神司财运及地方安宁，元帅王府司代天巡狩、查察人间善恶。其他还有纪王府、朱王府、池王府等，各有其名，亦各有所司。这些神仙形成一个系统，都归天后管辖。1988 年，泉州天后宫由国务院公布为第三批全国重点文物保护单位，这是大陆妈祖庙中第一座全国重点文物保护单位。

宋元以来，泉州和世界上一百多个国家和地区有经贸文化往来，“凡使海外，率皆制祭”。元代实行春秋两祀，成为国家彝典，且多次将国家祭典设在泉州天后宫举行。泉州天后宫见证了中国东南沿海悠久的航海传统，反映了 12 世纪末至 14 世纪泉州海外贸易发展和海神崇拜体系的演变特征。

Tianhou Temple is now mainly dedicated to the worship of Mazu, as well as Taoist immortals and local gods. There are twelve division rooms respectively for enshrining gods in the east and west wing rooms, making twenty-four divisions in total which are said to enshrine the twenty-four gods who assist Mazu, including Beidou Xingjun (Ursa Major) responsible for the navigation direction, Leisheng Puhua Tianzun (the Supreme Daoist God of Thunder) in charge of wind, rain, thunder, and lightening, Shuide Xingjun (Water Deity) responsible for the regulation of water in four seasons, the Dragon Kings of the Four Seas in charge of the tides of rivers and seas, Wuxian Lingguang Dadi (God of Wealth) in charge of the celestial court, Wenchang Dijun (Imperial Sovereign Wenchang) responsible for culture and literature, Nezha Taizi (Marshal of the Central Altar) responsible for the growth of teenagers, Qiniangma (Lady of Seven Stars) in charge of the growth of children, Linshui Furen Chen Jinggu (Lady at the Water's Edge) responsible for the infant feeding and maternal well-being, Wenwu Zunwang in charge of loyalty and justice, Fude Zhengshen (Righteous God of Virtue and Blessing) responsible for prosperity and local peace, Yuanshuai Wangfu (Marshals and Lords) in charge of imperial envoys inspecting goods and evils in folk. Besides these gods, there are still Ji Wangfu, Zhu Wangfu, Chi Wangfu and so on, each with its own name and responsibilities. All these gods form a system under the jurisdiction of the Queen of Heaven. In 1988, Quanzhou Tianhou Temple was announced by the State Council as one of the third batch of national key cultural relics protection units, which is the first national key cultural relics protection unit among all Mazu temples in mainland China.

Since the Song-Yuan era, there has been economic, trade and cultural exchanges between Quanzhou and more than 100 countries and regions in the world. "Before ships going abroad, sacrifices have always been offered to gods." In the Yuan Dynasty, national rituals were held twice a year in spring and autumn, among which many were held in Quanzhou Tianhou Temple. Quanzhou Tianhou Temple has witnessed the long-standing seafaring tradition along the southeast coast of China, reflecting the development of Quanzhou's overseas trade and the evolution of the sea deity worship system from the end of the 12th century to the 14th century.

天后宫妈祖。（陈英杰 摄）
The statue of Mazu in Tianhou Temple. (Photo by Chen Yingjie)

妈祖信仰的传播

宋元以来，随着泉州人海外贸易的足迹不断延伸，发祥于泉州的妈祖信仰在世界各地广泛传播。泉州地区众多妈祖宫庙，均从泉州天后宫分灵，如始建于宋代的金井东宫古地、始建于元大德年间的美山天妃宫、始建于元至正六年（1346）的暗林顺济宫、始建于明万历年间的蟳埔顺济宫、始建于明天启二年（1622）的霞洲妈祖宫、始建于明永乐年间的崇武天后宫、始建于清同治六年（1867）的法石长春妈祖宫等。明清时期随着闽南人过台湾、下南洋，妈祖信仰随之传到我国台湾及东南亚等地区。

"温陵妈祖会"千人踩街活动。（陈英杰 摄）

The "Wenling Mazu Parade" event involves thousands of people participating in folk performance on the street. (Photo by Chen Yingjie)

Spread of Mazu Worship

With the continuous extension of Quanzhou people's footprints in their maritime trade, the worship of the sea goddess Mazu, originating from Quanzhou, has been widely spread all over the world since the Song and Yuan Dynasties. Many Mazu temples in Quanzhou are divisions from Quanzhou Tianhou Temple, such as Donggong Gudi in Jinjing Town built in the Song Dynasty, Meishan Tianfei Temple built in the Dade Period (1297—1307) of the Yuan Dynasty, Anlin Shunji Temple built in 1346 of the Yuan Dynasty, Xunpu Shunji Temple built in the Wanli Period (1573—1620) of the Ming Dynasty, Xiazhou Mazu Temple built in 1622 of the Ming Dynasty, and Chongwu Tianhou Temple built in the Yongle Period (1403—1424) of the Ming Dynasty, Fashi Changchun Mazu Temple built in 1867 in the Qing Dynasty, etc. During the Ming and Qing Dynasties, with the people from Southern Fujian crossing Taiwan Straits and going to Southeast Asia, Mazu belief spread to Taiwan at home and Southeast Asia and so on.

蟳埔顺济宫妈祖圣驾入殿就位仪式。（吴云轩 摄）
The ceremony of Mazu holy statue's entering Xunpu Shunji Temple. (Photo by Wu Yunxuan)

泉州作为台湾汉族同胞的主要祖籍地之一，与台湾一衣带水。两地有着悠久的历史渊源，台湾在设府之前，一直隶属于泉州府。泉台两地地缘相近、血缘相亲、文缘相承、商缘相连、法缘相循。大约从两宋开始，大陆向台湾移民，但人数甚少。明中叶以后，移居澎湖、台湾者逐渐增多。明崇祯元年（1628），郑芝龙接受明朝招抚，适逢闽南大旱，饥民甚众，郑芝龙招纳泉州、漳州灾民数万人，许诺“人给银三两，三人给牛一头”，目的是将这些灾民用海船运到台湾垦荒。至此，大陆居民的迁台活动由分散无组织的民间行为转为有组织、有计划地向台湾大量移民。郑成功克荷复台后，清政府为切断郑氏政权与大陆的经济往来，实行“海禁”“迁界”政策，把各省沿海 30 里居民一律迁居内地，并禁止船只出海。清政府还派兵在沿海地区戍守，致使泉州沿海居民流离失所者众多。郑成功在台湾一方面实行军屯，一方面招徕泉州、漳州等沿海地区的失业、失地民众，向他们提供优惠的经济政策，鼓励他们到台湾垦荒，泉州再次出现迁台高潮。康熙、雍正年间，清政府统一台湾后，开放海禁，闽台两地实现通航对渡，泉州向台湾的移民活动出现了第三次高潮。“台湾之人，漳、泉为多，约占十之六、七。”1984 年“台湾当局”公布的台湾地区人口数字表明，福建籍人口占台湾人口 82.5%，其中 44.8% 是泉籍移民。

早期移民渡海至台时，为祈求平安，大多迎请故乡地方神祇，随身携带祖籍地神明的分香进行祀奉。这些随身携带的香火或神像，一般供在船上，一旦平安抵达，皆归因为神明的庇佑。他们在台湾扎根之后，就在聚居地修建庙宇供奉这些神灵，妈祖信仰就是这样跟随着移民的脚步，传播到台湾的。明天启四年（1624），澎湖建起了第一座妈祖庙，这是台湾地区历史上最早的一座妈祖庙。

位于台北市繁华市区西门町的台北天后宫。（成冬冬 摄）
Taipei Tianhou Temple is located in Ximending, the bustling downtown area of Taipei City. (Photo by Cheng Dongdong)

As one of the main ancestral homelands of the Han compatriots in Taiwan, Quanzhou is separated from Taiwan by Taiwan Straits. There is a long history between the two places. Before established as a prefecture, Taiwan had always been subordinate to Quanzhou Prefecture. Quanzhou and Taiwan have close links in five areas, specifically in geographical location, blood ties, cultural features, commercial exchanges and historical government administration. Since about the Song Dynasty, people started to migrate from the mainland to Taiwan, but the number was still small. After the middle of the Ming Dynasty, the number of people who moved to Penghu and Taiwan gradually increased. In 1628 in the Ming Dynasty, Zheng Zhilong accepted the imperial court's amnesty and enlistment. It happened that there was a severe drought in Southern Fujian, which caused many people suffered from famine. With the promise of "three *liangs* (150g) of silver ingots for each person; a head of cattle for three people", Zheng Zhilong recruited tens of thousands of drought victims from Quanzhou and Zhangzhou in order to transport them by ship to Taiwan for land reclamation. From then on, the nature of mainland residents' migration activities to Taiwan has transformed from a scattered and unorganized civil behavior to an organized and planned mass migration. After Zheng Chenggong defeated Dutch colonists and recovered Taiwan, the Qing Government implemented the policies of *Haijin* (a ban on maritime activities) and "Great Clearance" in order to cut off the economic exchanges between Zheng's regime and the mainland. All residents within 15km of the coast in each province were moved inland, and ships were prohibited from going to sea. In addition, the Qing Government also sent troops to garrison the coastal areas, resulting in a large number of coastal residents destitute and homeless in Quanzhou. Zheng Chenggong implemented military settlements in Taiwan on the one hand, and on the other hand, he recruited unemployed and landless people from coastal areas such as Quanzhou and Zhangzhou, provided them with preferential economic policies, and encouraged them to reclaim wasteland in Taiwan, which led to another climax of migration in Quanzhou. After the Qing Government unified Taiwan, with the abolishment of the "*Haijin* policy", the free transportation between Fujian and Taiwan was realized and the migration from Quanzhou to Taiwan reached the third climax during the reigns of Emperors Kangxi and Yongzheng. "Most of the people in Taiwan are from Zhangzhou and Quanzhou, accounting for about six to seven out of ten." According to the population figures of Taiwan released by the Taiwan authorities in 1984, the population from Fujian Province accounted for 82.5%, of which 44.8% were migrants from Quanzhou.

When the early migrants crossed the sea and went to Taiwan, most of them carried with them the incense ashes taken from the local gods in their hometowns to enshrine and worship for safety. These incense ashes or statues carried with them were generally enshrined on the ships. Once they arrived safely, they attributed to the gods' blessing. After they took root in Taiwan, they built temples in their habitations to worship these gods. It is in this way that Mazu belief spread to Taiwan along with the migrants' footsteps. In 1624 in the Ming Dynasty, the first Mazu temple was built in Penghu, which is the earliest Mazu temple in Taiwan history.

随着时间的推移和台湾本岛的不断开发，妈祖庙在台湾也纷纷建立起来。目前，台湾地区历史较早、规模较大的妈祖庙宇大部分是由泉州籍移民建造或倡建的，如创建于清初的鹿港天后宫（又名旧祖宫或圣母宫）。雍正三年（1725），施世榜献地迁建鹿港天后宫。嘉庆十九年（1814），庙宇倾颓，包括泉郊在内的鹿港八郊及地方士绅、船户、铺户相继响应，捐资重修。重修工程自同年农历九月开工，并于次年农历三月完工，嘉庆二十一年（1816）地方士绅将此次重修的缘由始末镌刻在《重修鹿溪圣母宫碑记》中。碑文中记载到包括木材、石材、砖瓦在内的重修鹿港天后宫的许多建筑材料大多从泉州加工好后运到台湾。清中后期至民国时期，则大量聘请泉州崇武的木匠、石雕工匠前往台湾修建天后宫等庙宇，而这些庙宇之后也大多成为台湾重要的名胜古迹。

据统计，台湾现有妈祖庙 1,000 多座，信众占总人口的四分之三，堪称妈祖信仰的极盛之地。台湾民众信仰妈祖之虔诚、祭祀妈祖仪式之盛大热烈，以至于在妈祖生日的农历三月，出现了“三月疯妈祖”的俗语。

泉台两地因共同的妈祖信仰而开展了形式多样的信俗交流。据《泉州天后宫志》记载，1990 年台湾鹿港天后宫信众到泉州天后宫谒祖，从而引发了一阵台湾妈祖信众来泉的寻根热。此后，每年均有台湾信众到泉州天后宫来进香谒祖，其中也有规模和影响力较大的活动。1996 年泉州天后宫举行建宫 800 周年纪念活动，台湾 16 座宫庙负责人及 2,000 多名信众专程前来参加庆典、进香。2002 年泉州天后宫妈祖直航澎湖会香，这也是两岸 50 多年来的首次直航，为两岸妈祖信仰交流史留下了一段佳话。2006 年台湾妈祖联谊会暨大甲镇澜宫谒祖进香团组织台湾 50 多家妈祖庙宇 4,300 多名信众来泉州谒祖进香。2014 年台湾妈祖联谊会与道教协会组织 7,000 信众来谒祖进香，开创了两岸妈祖文化交流盛事参加人数和影响力之最。泉台两地妈祖宫庙交流活动一般有民俗踩街、仿古祭典、进香、召开学术论坛等，为两岸的文化交流搭建起沟通的桥梁。

With the passage of time and the continuous development of Taiwan Island, Mazu temples were also established there one after another. At present, most of the earlier and larger-scale Mazu temples in Taiwan were built or advocated to be built by migrants from Quanzhou, such as Lukang Tianhou Temple (also known as the Old Ancestral Temple or Holy Mother Temple), which was founded in the early Qing Dynasty. In 1725, Shi Shibang offered his land to relocate Lukang Tianhou Temple. In 1814, when the temple collapsed, Lukang *Bajiao* (the eight Chambers of Commerce in Lukang) including *Quanjiao* (a commercial firm consisting of mainly businessmen migrated from Quanzhou), and the local gentry, ship owners and shop owners, responded one after another and donated money for the reconstruction. The reconstruction started in lunar September in the same year, and was completed in lunar March in the following year. In 1816, the local gentry engraved the details of this reconstruction in *Reconstruction Inscription of Luxi Mazu Temple*. It is recorded in the inscription that most of the building materials used to rebuild Lukang Tianhou Temple, including wood, stone, bricks and tiles, were

妈祖信仰增进了泉台两地人们的情谊。（吴松树 摄）
Mazu belief enhanced the friendship between the people in Quanzhou and Taiwan. (Photo by Wu Songshu)

shipped to Taiwan after being processed in Quanzhou. From the middle and the late Qing Dynasty to the period of the Republic of China, a large number of master carpenters and stone carving craftsmen from Chongwu of Quanzhou, were hired to go to Taiwan for repairing or building temples such as Mazu temples, most of which also became important places of interest in Taiwan later.

According to statistics, there are more than 1,000 Mazu temples in Taiwan now, and the devotees account for three quarters of Taiwan's total population. Thus, Taiwan can be called a land of prosperity in Mazu worship. The Mazu worship of Taiwan residents is so pious, and the ceremony of offering sacrifices to Mazu is so grand that the third lunar month which marks Mazu's birthday started to be called "Crazy March of Mazu Worship".

Quanzhou and Taiwan carried out various forms of belief and custom exchanges due to the common Mazu belief. According to *The Records of Quanzhou Tianhou Temple*, in 1990, believers from Lukang Mazu Temple in Taiwan came to Quanzhou Tianhou Temple to pay homage to their ancestors, which triggered a wave of root-seeking in Quanzhou among Taiwan Mazu believers. Since then, there have always been endless streams of pilgrims coming from Taiwan to offer incense and pay homage to their ancestors in Quanzhou Tianhou Temple every year, among which there are some larger-scale and influential activities. In 1996, when Quanzhou Tianhou Temple celebrated its 800th anniversary of its founding, the heads of 16 temples and more than 2,000 believers in Taiwan came to attend the celebration and pilgrimage. In 2002, the direct shipping of Mazu from Quanzhou Tianhou Temple to Penghu for exchanges between temples, was the first direct shipping between the two sides of Taiwan Straits in more than 50 years, which has become a much-told story in the history of Mazu belief exchanges between the Chinese mainland and Taiwan. In 2006, the Taiwan Mazu Fellowship and Dajia Jenn Lann Temple initiated and organized more than 4,300 believers from more than 50 Mazu temples in Taiwan to pay homage to their ancestors in Quanzhou. In 2014, the Taiwan Mazu Fellowship and the Taoist Association of Taiwan organized 7,000 believers to pay homage to Mazu in Quanzhou, creating an unprecedented cross-strait Mazu cultural exchange event with the largest number of participants and the most significant influence. The exchange activities of Mazu temples in Quanzhou and Taiwan generally include folk performance, antique ceremonies, incense offerings, and academic forums, etc., which build a bridge for cultural communication and exchanges between both sides of Taiwan Straits.

闽南人外出到东南亚一带后，把祖籍地的信仰也一起带了出去。这些信仰又影响到了当地人，以至于妈祖到了海外后，就换上了当地人的新面孔，变成“番脸妈祖”。泉州博物馆收藏有一尊清漆线雕番面妈祖坐像，是从马来西亚征集而来。她有一张“番仔脸”，冕冠后缀有一撮玫瑰红发髻，使妈祖“番客”韵味十足，这在妈祖的众多形象中堪称奇葩。

菲律宾不少天主教堂中供奉的妈祖神像全身穿着天主教服饰的神像。1954 年，全世界天主教在菲律宾举行祈祷大会，教皇特封妈祖为天主教七圣母之一，并隆重为妈祖加冠。此后，菲律宾各地又陆续建起不少妈祖庙，其中供奉的妈祖大部分是从华侨祖籍地移驾或分香、分身、分炉的。据统计，至 20 世纪 60 年代，全菲岛华侨奉祀的小规模天上圣母庙或妈祖庙就达 100 多家。

After going out to Southeast Asia, people from Southern Fujian also brought their ancestral beliefs with them which also affected the local people, so after Mazu was introduced overseas, she had a new localized face and was called "Fanlian Mazu". In Quanzhou Museum, there is a varnished thread sculpture depicting a sitting Mazu with a foreigner's face, which was collected from Malaysia. She has a "Fanzai (Foreigner's) face" and a knot of rose-red hair orated on the back of the crown, which makes Mazu full of exotic charm and can be called a wonderful work among all the images of Mazu.

The statue of Mazu enshrined in many Catholic churches in the Philippines is dressed in Catholic clothing. In 1954, Catholics all over the world held a prayer conference in the Philippines, when the Pope specially named Mazu as one of the Seven Holy Mothers of Catholicism and grandly crowned Mazu. From then on, many Mazu temples have been built in various parts of the Philippines, most of which were established by overseas Chinese who moved Mazu or brought the incense, statues, and furnaces of Mazu temples from their ancestral home to the destinations. According to statistics, by the 1960s, there were more than 100 small-scale Holy Mother temples or Mazu temples worshiped by overseas Chinese in the Philippines.

清漆线雕番面妈祖坐像。（泉州市博物馆 供图）
The varnished line-engraving sitting sculpture of Mazu with a foreigner's face. (Courtesy of Quanzhou Museum)

新加坡天福宫建于 1840 年，是新加坡最古老的庙宇之一，其建筑工艺手法和材料均来自泉州，是正统闽南风格的宫观建筑。1973 年，天福宫被列为新加坡国家古迹。1998 年，当地特邀泉州工匠对天福宫进行一次大规模的修复。

随着泉州民众不断的海外移民和海外贸易活动，发祥于泉州的妈祖信仰文化经由泉州港向很多国家和地区广泛传播。泉州天后宫成为妈祖信仰最为重要的传播中心之一，被东南亚地区华侨华人、港澳台同胞尊为“温陵祖庙”。目前，全世界 20 多个国家和地区建有数以千计的天后宫。在全球，妈祖拥有 2 亿多信众，在人类海洋文明发展史上具有重大影响。2009 年 9 月 30 日，联合国教科文组织政府间保护非物质文化遗产委员会第四次会议审议，决定将“妈祖信俗”列入世界非物质文化遗产名录，成为中国首个信俗类世界遗产。

新加坡天福宫。（视觉中国 供图）
Thian Hock Keng Temple in Singapore. (Courtesy of VCG.COM)

Built in 1840, Singapore Thian Hock Keng Temple is one of the oldest temples in Singapore. Both the architectural techniques and materials coming from Quanzhou, it is an orthodox Southern Fujian style temple. In 1973, Thian Hock Keng Temple was listed as one of the national monuments in Singapore. In 1998, the local government specially invited Quanzhou craftsmen to carry out a large-scale restoration project of Thian Hock Keng Temple.

With Quanzhou people's continuous overseas emigration and trade activities, the culture of Mazu belief originating in Quanzhou, has been widely spread to many countries and regions in the world through Quanzhou Port. Quanzhou Tianhou Temple, having become one of the most important centers for the dissemination of Mazu beliefs, is respected as "Wenling (another name of ancient Quanzhou) Ancestral Temple" by overseas Chinese in Southeast Asia and compatriots in Hong Kong, Macao and Taiwan. At present, there are thousands of Tianhou temples in more than 20 countries and regions in the world. There are more than 200 million devotees of Mazu worldwide, indicating Mazu's significant influence in the history of the development of human marine civilization. On September 30, 2009, the fourth meeting of the UNESCO Intergovernmental Committee for the Protection of Intangible Cultural Heritage deliberated and decided to inscribe "Mazu Belief and Customs" on the list of the world's intangible cultural heritages, which makes it China's first world heritage of belief and customs.

参考文献

[1] 傅晶，王敏，梁中荟，任远，王超一 . 泉州：宋元中国的世界海洋商贸中心——系列遗产整体价值及要素构成研究 [J]. 自然与文化遗产研究，2021，6（3）：5-21.

[2] 泉州市城市规划建设专家顾问组，泉州市南建筑博物馆 . 泉州古城踏勘 [M]. 厦门：厦门大学出版社，2007.

[3] 郑振满，丁荷生 . 福建宗教碑铭汇编 [M]. 福州：福建人民出版社，2008.

[4] 北京大学考古文博学院，泉州市文化广电和旅游局，安溪县人民政府，北京大学考古文博学院（安溪）研究中心 . 安溪下草埔遗址 2019-2020 年度发掘报告 [M]. 北京：文物出版社，2021.

[5] 泉州海关 . 泉州海关志 [M]. 厦门：厦门大学出版社，2005.

[6] 陈明，洪美玲 . 法映刺桐——宋元中国的世界海洋商贸中心法制 [M]. 厦门：鹭江出版社，2021.

[7] 郭黛姮 . 南宋建筑史 [M]. 上海：上海古籍出版社，2019：71-79.

[8] 泉州天后宫文物保护管理处 . 泉州天后宫志 [M]. 香港：闽南文化出版社，2016.

[9] 黄仲昭 . 八闽通志 [M]. 福州：福建人民出版社，2017.

[10] 真德秀 . 西山先生真文忠公文集 [M]. 北京：北京大学出版社，2020：卷八，卷四十九，卷五十，卷五十三，卷五十四 .

[11] 宋濂 . 元史 [M]. 北京：中华书局，2016：卷七十六《祭祀五》.

[12] 郭赓武，黄任，淮荫布 . 泉州府志 [M]. 刻本 .1882（清光绪八年）：卷十六 .

[13] 吴之鋘、周学曾、尤逊恭 . 中国地方志集成 . 福建府县志集 .25，道光晋江县志 [M]. 上海：上海书店出版社，2000：卷十五、卷十六 .

[14] 连横 . 台湾通史 [M]. 北京：商务印书馆，1983.

[15] 林再复 . 闽南人 [M]. 台北：三民书局，1985.

[16] 刘枝万 . 台湾中部碑文集成 . 台湾文献史料丛刊，第 151 种 [M]. 北京：人民日报出版社，2012.

[17] 吴幼雄 . 泉州宗教文化 [M]. 厦门：鹭江出版社，1993.

[18] 黄宗羲 . 赐姓始末 [M]. 台北：台湾文献出版社，1995.

[19] 谢肇淛 . 五杂俎 [M]. 北京：中国书店，2019.

[20] 林明太、黄朝晖 . 妈祖文化在海上丝绸之路沿线国家的传播与发展 [J]. 集美大学学报，2015，10.

[21] 泉州市文物局 . 泉州文物（国保篇）[M]. 北京：九州出版社，2021.

[22] 苏镜潭 . 南安县志 [M]. 刻本 .1915. 泉州：泉山书社印，卷 2.

[23] 汪勃，梁源 . 唐宋泉州城空间格局下的泉州南外宗正司、泉州市舶司遗址的考古发掘研究 [J]. 自然与文化遗产研究，2021，6（6）：22-39.

[24] 福建博物院，泉州市文物局 . 泉州德济门遗址发掘报告 [J]. 福建文博，2003，1.

[25] 唐宏杰 . 泉州德济门出土宗教石刻浅析 [J]. 海交史研究，2003，1.

[26] 薛彦乔 . 宋代泉州市舶官员辑补 [J]. 福建文博，2020，4.

[27] 黄柏龄 . 九日山志 [M]. 上海：上海辞书出版社，2006.

[28] 赵惠芳 . 祈风的故事 [J]. 泉州文博，2019，2.

[29] 黄乐德 . 泉州科技史话 [M]. 厦门：厦门大学出版社，1995.

[30] 吕秀家 . 泉州城考古学术研讨会论文集 [C]. 北京：科学出版社，2021.

[31] 泉州历史文化中心 . 杨清江文史类稿 [M]. 香港：闽南文化出版社，2017.

[32] 吴镇国 . 对宋代福建市舶司提举的考察 [J]. 文化学刊，2021，2.

[33] 王晓鹰，眭贞嬿 . 中国海事管理机构的历史演进脉络 [J]. 海事博览，2018，9.

[34] 周海 . 公据——两宋时期的“船舶签证”[J]. 海事博览，2012，9.

图书在版编目（CIP）数据

刺桐花开：宋元泉州的制度保障：汉英对照 / 中共泉州市委宣传部编. --福州：福建人民出版社，2024.6（2025.3重印）
（世遗之城：泉州）
ISBN 978-7-211-09044-0

Ⅰ.①刺… Ⅱ.①中… Ⅲ.①地方政府—行政管理—政治制度史—泉州—宋元时期—汉、英 Ⅳ.①D691.22

中国国家版本馆 CIP 数据核字（2023）第 079090 号

刺桐花开——宋元泉州的制度保障
CITONG HUAKAI——SONGYUAN QUANZHOU DE ZHIDU BAOZHANG

特约撰稿：黄明珍
翻　　译：钱秀金　林　风
责任编辑：周跃进
助理编辑：林冰慧
美术编辑：陈培亮
责任校对：林乔楠
装帧设计：雅昌（上海）设计中心
出版发行：福建人民出版社　　电　　话：0591-87533169（发行部）
网　　址：http://www.fjpph.com　　电子邮箱：fjpph7211@126.com
地　　址：福州市东水路 76 号　　邮政编码：350001
经　　销：福建新华发行（集团）有限责任公司
印　　刷：雅昌文化（集团）有限公司
地　　址：深圳市南山区深云路 19 号
电　　话：0755-86083235
开　　本：787 毫米×1092 毫米　1/16
印　　张：12.75
字　　数：323 千字
版　　次：2024 年 6 月第 1 版
印　　次：2025 年 3 月第 2 次印刷
书　　号：ISBN 978-7-211-09044-0
定　　价：63.00 元